DRUMS IN THE FOREST

Drums in the Forest

DECISION AT THE FORKS
Alfred Procter James

DEFENSE IN THE WILDERNESS
Charles Morse Stotz

THE HISTORICAL SOCIETY OF WESTERN PENNSYLVANIA
UNIVERSITY OF PITTSBURGH PRESS

Library of Congress Catalog Number 58-59529

Copyright © 1958, 2005, Historical Society of Western Pennsylvania

Defense in the Wilderness, copyright © 1958, The Allegheny Conference on Community Development

All rights reserved

Manufactured in the United States of America

ISBN 0-8229-5883-x

FOREWORD TO THE PAPERBACK EDITION

The Historical Society of Western Pennsylvania first published *Drums in the Forest* in 1958, just in time to commemorate the bicentennial of the founding of Pittsburgh during the French and Indian War. The Society commissioned two eminent historians to do the work. Dr. Alfred Procter James, a University of Pittsburgh professor and regular contributor to the Society's *Western Pennsylvania Historical Magazine*, focused his contribution on "Decision at the Forks," an essay on the struggle between the French, British, and Indians to control the Ohio Country and the interior of the continent. Charles Morse Stotz, a longtime Society trustee and the preeminent colonial architectural historian of his time, concentrated his efforts on "Defense in the Wilderness," an examination of forts and fighters of Western Pennsylvania prior to the American Revolution.

Much has changed in the half century since this volume first appeared. The Historical Society now operates as the Senator John Heinz Pittsburgh Regional History Center, the largest history museum in Pennsylvania and an affiliate of the Smithsonian Institution. But some things don't change. *Drums in the Forest* remains good history and still is in demand by history buffs and scholars alike. Now, on the occasion of the 250th anniversary of the French and Indian War, the History Center is pleased to once again make available to the general public this standard source on the seminal events of the French and Indian War.

Today's historians have built on the solid foundation laid down by James and Stotz, paying particular attention to the central role played by American Indians—the Iroquois, Algonquins, Delawares, Shawnees, Ottawas, Hurons, Abenakis, Nipissings, and other peoples of the Ohio River country. These tribes shaped the events we know as the French and Indian War by their alliances—both military and trade—with the European powers. Like the British and French, the Iroquois shared a vision of empire and dominion over western lands and peoples. And like the European invaders, they were politically savvy and militarily strong. In the end, they tipped the balance of power in favor of the British.

The way historians refer to people and events changes with time. James, for example, refers to the "so-called American Indians, or Amerind." Later historians used the term "Native Americans." Canadian scholars use the terms "First Peoples" or "First Nations." Today, most Native people in the United States prefer "Indian," with historians following their lead.

The names of events change over time as well. Americans use the term "French and Indian War," though clearly this is an Anglocentric point of view—the British war against French and Indians. In Canada, where discussion of the war still excites passion and controversy among French- and English-speaking people, the war is known as the "War of the Conquest." In Europe, it is still known as the "Seven Years' War" (1756–1763), though this name does not accurately reflect the North American phase of the conflict, which began in Western Pennsylvania in 1754 at the confluence of the Allegheny, Monongahela, and Ohio rivers at present-day Pittsburgh.

The History Center is pleased to republish *Drums in the Forest* in conjunction with its major international exhibition, *Clash of Empires: The British, French, & Indian War, 1754–1763*. The exhibition brings to Western Pennsylvania for the first time in 250 years artifacts and documents—the very stuff of history—that bring alive the true story of the war that determined the course of North America and the world.

ANDREW E. MASICH, *President and CEO*
DAVID F. HALAAS, *Director, Library & Archives*
Senator John Heinz Pittsburgh Regional History Center

FORT NECESSITY SURRENDER DOCUMENT
July 3, 1754

Young George Washington surrendered his force at Fort Necessity when he signed this rain-spattered paper the night of July 3, 1754. Because the document is written entirely in French, Washington may or may not have realized that with his signature he admitted to the assassination of Ensign Jumonville, the "smoking gun" evidence of a declaration of war (see overleaf).

His Majesty's
DECLARATION
Of WAR against the *French* King.

GEORGE R.

THE unwarrantable Proceedings of the *French* in the *West Indies*, and *North America*, since the Conclusion of the Treaty of *Aix la Chapelle*, and the Usurpations and Encroachments made by them upon Our Territories, and the Settlements of Our Subjects in those Parts, particularly in Our Province of *Nova Scotia*, have been so notorious, and so frequent, that they cannot but be looked upon as a sufficient Evidence of a formed Design and Resolution in that Court, to pursue invariably such Measures, as should most effectually promote their ambitious Views, without any Regard to the most solemn Treaties and Engagements. We have not been wanting on Our Part, to make, from time to time, the most serious Representations to the *French* King, upon these repeated Acts of Violence, and to endeavour to obtain Redress and Satisfaction for the Injuries done to Our Subjects, and to prevent the like Cause of Complaint for the future: But though frequent Assurances have been given, that every thing should be settled agreeable to the Treaties subsisting between the Two Crowns, and particularly that the Evacuation of the Four Neutral Islands in the *West Indies* should be effected (which was expressly promised to Our Ambassador in *France*) the Execution of these Assurances, and of the Treaties on which they were founded, has been evaded under the most frivolous Pretences; and the unjustifiable Practices of the *French* Governors, and of the Officers acting under their Authority, were still carried on, till, at length, in the Month of *April*, One thousand seven hundred and fifty four, they broke out in open Acts of Hostility, when, in Time of profound Peace, without any Declaration of War, and without any previous Notice given, or Application made, a Body of *French* Troops under the Command of an Officer bearing the *French* King's Commission, attacked in a hostile Manner, and possessed themselves of the *English* Fort on the *Ohio* in *North America*.

But notwithstanding that Acts of Hostility, which could not but be looked upon as a Commencement of War, yet, from Our earnest Desire of Peace, and in Hopes the Court of *France* would disavow this Violence and Injustice, We contented Ourselves with sending such a Force to *America*, as was indispensably necessary for the immediate Defence and Protection of Our Subjects against such Attacks and Insults.

In the mean Time great Naval Armaments were preparing in the Ports of *France*, and a considerable Body of *French* Troops embarked for *North America*; and though the *French* Ambassador was sent back to *England* with specious Professions of a Desire to accommodate these Differences, yet it appeared, that their real Design was only to gain Time for the Passage of those Troops to *America*, which they hoped would secure the Superiority of the *French* Forces in those Parts, and enable them to carry their ambitious and oppressive Projects into Execution.

In these Circumstances We could not but think it incumbent upon Us, to endeavour to prevent the Success of so dangerous a Design; and to oppose the Landing of the *French* Troops in *America*; and in Consequence of the just and necessary Measures We had taken for that Purpose, the *French* Ambassador was immediately recalled from Our Court, the Fortifications at *Dunkirk*, which had been repairing for some Time, were enlarged; great Bodies of Troops marched down to the Coast, and Our Kingdom were threatened with an Invasion.

In order to prevent the Execution of these Designs, and to provide for the Security of Our Kingdoms, which were thus threatened, We could no longer forbear giving Orders for the seizing at Sea the Ships of the *French* King, and his Subjects. Notwithstanding which, as We were still unwilling to give up all Hopes that an Accommodation might be effected, We have continued Ourselves hitherto with detaining the said Ships, and preserving them, and (as far as was possible) their Cargoes intire, without proceeding to the Confiscation of them; but it being now evident, by the hostile Invasion actually made by the *French* King of Our Island of *Minorca*, that it is the determined Resolution of that Court to hearken to no Terms of Peace, but to carry on the War, which has been long begun on their Part, with the utmost Violence, We can no longer remain, consistently with what We owe to Our own Honour, and to the Welfare of Our Subjects, within those Bounds, which, from a Desire of Peace, We had hitherto observed.

We have therefore thought proper to declare War, and We do hereby Declare War against the *French* King, who hath so unjustly begun it, relying on the Help of Almighty God, in Our just Undertaking, and being assured of the hearty Concurrence and Assistance of Our Subjects, in Support of so good a Cause; hereby willing and requiring Our Captain General of Our Forces, Our Commissioners for executing the Office of Our High Admiral of *Great Britain*, Our Lieutenants of Our several Counties, Governors of Our Forts and Garrisons, and all other Officers and Soldiers under them, by Sea and Land, to do and execute all Acts of Hostility, in the Prosecution of this War against the *French* King, his Vassals and Subjects, and to oppose their Attempts: Willing and requiring all Our Subjects to take Notice of the same, whom We henceforth strictly forbid to hold any Correspondence or Communication with the said *French* King, or his Subjects: And We do hereby command Our own Subjects, and advertise all other Persons, of what Nation soever, not to transport or carry any Soldiers, Arms, Powder, Ammunition, or other Contraband Goods, to any of the Territories, Lands, Plantations, or Countries of the said *French* King; Declaring, That whatsoever Ship or Vessel shall be met withal, transporting or carrying any Soldiers, Arms, Powder, Ammunition, or any other Contraband Goods, to any of the Territories, Lands, Plantations, or Countries of the said *French* King, the same, being taken, shall be condemned as good and lawful Prize.

And whereas there are remaining in Our Kingdom, divers of the Subjects of the *French* King, We do hereby declare Our Royal Intention to be, That all the *French* Subjects who shall demean themselves dutifully towards Us, shall be safe in their Persons and Effects.

Given at Our Court at *Kensington*, the Seventeenth Day of *May*, 1756, in the Twenty ninth Year of Our Reign.

God save the King.

LONDON:
Printed by *Thomas Baskett*, Printer to the King's most Excellent Majesty; and by the Assigns of *Robert Baskett*. 1756.

FOREWORD

FOR the seventy-six years that followed the cold and misty day in November 1758 when General John Forbes took possession of the abandoned Fort Duquesne with his "little Army," the people of Pittsburgh were too busy making history to worry much about preserving the records of their past.

Not until January of 1834 did there appear, in the *Allegheny Democrat* (one of the eleven newspapers serving the then sizeable Pittsburgh community of over 40,000 persons), the following invitation to "such gentlemen as are friendly to the formation of an Historical Society in this city to attend a meeting to be held at Mr. George Beale's long room, on Saturday, the 11th inst. at 7 o'clock P.M." This was the beginning of an Historical Society for Western Pennsylvania.

After a series of vicissitudes, discouragements, false starts and periods of diminished enthusiasm, the present Historical Society of Western Pennsylvania was organized in 1879.

The Society now has a stable membership, broadly representative of all elements in the community; a beautiful building in Pittsburgh's famed Civic Center; an outstanding early American glass collection; a growing museum and library containing such treasures as original manuscripts, newspapers, family histories and other priceless records of people and events.

Forty-one volumes of Western Pennsylvania history have been published by the Society in the form of articles, documents, and historical news in its quarterly, THE WESTERN PENNSYLVANIA HISTORICAL MAGAZINE. This publication is distributed free to members, reaches a wide circle of readers at home and abroad and is available for study in the Library of Congress and the major historical libraries.

Traditionally, a commemorative issue is an abridged chronological review of all historic events from that day to this. Since the forty-one volumes of THE WESTERN PENNSYLVANIA HISTORICAL MAGAZINE contain a collection of documents, articles, scholarly dissertations, letters, memoirs, journals and historical fact not customarily found in other sources, an abridgement of this cumulative work was obviously impractical. Conversely, a preface to the events celebrated in the Bicentennial of Pittsburgh's founding, would appear to be proper.

This, our Bicentennial number, comprises two separate works on the early days of Pittsburgh and the events leading to its establishment. Each author approaches the subject from a different angle, their complementary efforts making a well rounded treatment unique in this field of historical writing.

Dr. Alfred Procter James, Professor emeritus at the University of Pittsburgh, has been a well known contributor to the pages of this magazine and to regional history for nearly four decades. In *Decision at the Forks* he gives the historical background of the struggle for empire in America between France and England and its local phases up to Forbes' triumph at Fort Duquesne. Dr. James' article, based upon scholarly research in early military affairs, makes a significant contribution.

Charles Morse Stotz, a trustee of the Society and a Fellow of the American Institute of Architects, has long pursued an avocational interest in early local architecture. His article, *Defense in the Wilderness*, is the fruit of over ten years of spare time research in pre-Revolutionary military architecture and related subjects, with emphasis on the five forts built at the Point. This is the first comprehensive treatment of the subject in this country and contains material, drawn and written, never before published.

Friends of the Society have helped to make this project possible; in particular, we owe thanks to the Pittsburgh Foundation and to the Pittsburgh Bicentennial Association for their generous gifts.

The Historical Society of Western Pennsylvania takes pleasure in presenting as its contribution to the Pittsburgh Bicentennial this Preface to the events that built a city.

PRUDENCE TRIMBLE, *Editor*
THE WESTERN PENNSYLVANIA HISTORICAL MAGAZINE

Pittsburgh, Pennsylvania
November 27, 1958

TABLE OF CONTENTS

FOREWORD	1
THE FORBES MEDAL	iv
LIST OF ILLUSTRATIONS	vii
DECISION AT THE FORKS ALFRED PROCTER JAMES	3
DEFENSE IN THE WILDERNESS CHARLES MORSE STOTZ	59
I. SETTING OF THE STAGE	61
II. DEFENSE IN DEPTH	73
III. CHALLENGE OF THE WILDERNESS	88
IV. THE FIVE FORTS AT THE POINT	119
V. EPILOGUE	189
DEFINITIONS OF FORT TERMS	192
BIBLIOGRAPHY	194
FOOTNOTES	198
INDEX	204

THE FORBES MEDAL

The medal proposed by General Forbes on his deathbed, as described in the letter of Lieutenant James Grant to Colonel Henry Bouquet, was rendered for the cover of the original edition by Pittsburgh artist T. Ward Hunter. A facsimile of the original letter, now in the British Museum, is reproduced on the opposite page.

Philadelphia 20.th Feb.y 1759.

Sir,

General Forbes highly sensible of the many fa=
tigues and hardships you and your officers & the Troops in
General under his command have underwent during the course
of the most extraordinary Campaign that has happened in this
or any other Country, and willing at the same time to give some
publick testimony of his approbation to the Gentlemen under
his Command has ordered me to acquaint You and the Com=
=manding Officers of Corps that he has directed a Gold Medal
to be Struck to the following purpose which he hereby
Authorizes the Officers of his Army to wear as an Hono=
=rary reward for their faithfull Services — and as soon as
an Oppertunity offers he intends to inform his Majesty
of it.   In the mean time your Officers and
Colonel Montgomerys may be provided in Town
              The Medal has on one side the representa=
=tion of a road cut thro' an immence Forest over Rocks &
Mountains: The Motto Per tot Discrimina — on the other
side are represented the Confluence of the Ohio and Monon=
=gahela rivers, a Fort in flames in the forks of the Rivers
at the approach of General Forbes carried in a Litter,
followed with the Army marching in Collumns with Cannon
the motto Ohio Britannica Consilio manuque.
              This to be wore round the Neck with a dark blew Ribbon

N.B. General Forbes   By the Generals Command
is of oppinion
that such of your officers   James Grant Lieut. in his Majesty's
as chuse to provide them=   62.d Reg.t or 1.st H.B.
=selves with s above Medal
should have a Copy of this Letter sign'd and attested by you
as a warrant for their wearing it.   J. G.

Colonel Bouquet

LIST OF ILLUSTRATIONS

DECISION AT THE FORKS

THE RIGHT HONORABLE WILLIAM PITT	26
THE MARQUIS DUQUESNE	27
GENERAL GEORGE WASHINGTON	28

From a portrait of General Washington by Charles Willson Peale, the original of which is in the Pennsylvania Academy of Fine Arts.

GENERAL EDWARD BRADDOCK	29

From an etching by H. B. Hall. Courtesy of University of Pittsburgh Press.

GENERAL JOHN FORBES	38
COLONEL HENRY BOUQUET	39
COLONEL JAMES BURD	48
COLONEL HUGH MERCER	49

From Theodore Diller, Pioneer Medicine in Western Pennsylvania. Published by Paul B. Hoeber, Inc., New York.

DEFENSE IN THE WILDERNESS

1. FORTS OF NEW FRANCE IN 1754 — 64
2. FORTS OF THE FRENCH AND INDIAN WAR (Inside back cover)
3. EARLY MAP OF FORBES' AND BRADDOCK'S ROADS (Inside front cover)
4. ENCAMPMENT OF FORBES' ARMY AT RAYSTOWN, JULY 1758 — 70
5. ENCAMPMENT OF FORBES' ARMY AT LIGONIER, NOVEMBER 1758 — 71
6. STOCKADE WALL AND COMMANDANT'S HOUSE, FORT LIGONIER — 72
7. SCALE MODEL OF FORT LIGONIER AT FORT MUSEUM — 73
8. MEDIEVAL FORTRESS WITH BATTLE SCAFFOLDING — 74

9. Medieval Fortress with Supplemental Defense	75
10. The Parts of a Fort	77
11. Typical Walls of the Frontier Fort	81
12. Controversial Fort Site at McKee's Rocks	128
13. Fort Duquesne, Paris Plan	129
14. Aerial View of Fort Duquesne	138-139
15. Fort Duquesne, Plan from the British Museum	140
16. Mercer's Fort, Plan from the British Museum	141
17. Mercer's Fort in 1759 Showing Later Additions	142
18. Mercer's Fort with Fort Duquesne and Its Hornwork	143
19. Composite Plan of Mercer's Fort	145
20. Aerial View of Mercer's Fort	147
21. Plan of Future Fort Pitt Seized with Braddock's Baggage by Dumas	156
22. Plan of Fort Pitt Drawn by Bernard Ratzer in 1761	157
23. Plan of Fort Pitt Prepared by Elias Meyer in 1761	158
24. The Five Forts at the Point	159
25. Survey of Fort Pitt and Environs Made by Elias Meyer in 1762	160
26. Composite Plan of Fort Pitt	163
27. Aerial View of Fort Pitt	170-171
28. Fort Ontario and Fort McHenry	186
29. Fort Fayette	187
30. Bouquet's Redoubt. The "Blockhouse" of Fort Pitt	188
31. The Blockhouse of Fort Pitt. Measured Drawing	189

DECISION AT THE FORKS

Alfred Procter James

DECISION AT THE FORKS

A vital feature of any and all commemoration is respect for its past. In this short treatise, but somewhat long essay, an effort is made to capture some of the logic of long ago events as well as some of the spirit of long ago times. It is assumed that historical perspective is a fundamental background of any satisfactory explanation of things past and present.

In the words of a famous seventeenth century biographer, "Although there may be many sorts of history yet these are the chieftest": "a general history," "a national history," "a particular history."

The category "particular history" may reasonably be held to include all local or regional historiography which, indeed, is, in a way, the biography of a community or limited area though this "particularity" of local history must not be overemphasized, for not infrequently and, to a degree, always, purely local or regional history is a vital part of a larger national general and universal history.

With great validity, this universalism and nationalism of local history may be claimed an aspect of events in Western Pennsylvania which came to a climax we celebrate in 1958.

Thomas Carlyle in his work, *On Heroes, Hero Worship, and the Heroic in History*, mentions, "One life: a little gleam of time between two eternities." From this point of view, the re-occupation of the Forks of the Ohio, by the British-American forces in 1758, was both in time and in space a mere flash of action and existence.

But local history, in fact, is not so momentary and insignificant. With his rather common inconsistency, Carlyle, in the same work made the profound observation that " . . . the whole Past . . . is the possession of the Present," a statement which may be interpreted to claim that the whole past was tied in with the facts and events of late November 1758. That this is so is clearly revealed in consideration of important factors in the background.

It is widely recognized that geology and geography have played a tremendous role in human history.

The greatly remote beginnings of the universe, the solar system and the earth as a planet are part of the picture but cannot here be given more than mere mention. The Appalachian Mountains, however, must be given special consideration. Competent authority claims that they are two hundred and fifty million years old. It is believed that they were at one time four times as high as they were in the eighteenth century A.D. Three-fourths of their height is supposed to have eroded and washed away into plateaus, coastal plains and the Atlantic Ocean. The results are found in the geology and geography of more recent times; and the great influence of these on politics, human settlement and military action is beyond cavil, for documentation of this is both weighty and widespread.

Another significant geographical factor was the series of great advances of ice masses from the north into the northern area of present Pennsylvania. Geologists and other scientists of western Pennsylvania have had much to say about the influence of the ice ages upon the topography, notably the drainage systems and rivers of western Pennsylvania. The earliest ice age was probably more than a hundred thousand years ago. The last, probably the fourth, retired north about twenty-five thousand years before 1758. Western Pennsylvania, as we see and know it, began to assume its present condition in historically dim millenia of the past.

The fundamental result of the combination of Appalachian Mountains and successive ice ages was that the Forks of the Ohio, the later site of Pittsburgh, became topographically the hub of a giant wheel with definite spokes but with an irregular perimeter. These spokes are means of ingress and egress. Already in existence in general outline, they had become, long before 1492, features clearly observable thereafter. Historically, the earliest documented spoke or approach to the Forks of the Ohio seems to have been the route down the Allegheny River. It was used by Hudson River fur traders in the late seventeenth century. It was also used by French-Canadians from the St. Lawrence River in the first half of the eighteenth century. Considered, in clockwise procession, the next spoke or approach was that from the Susquehanna River and its tributaries. The West Branch, the Upper Juniata, and the Lower Juniata made three subdivisions of this general approach. The Potomac River in conjunction with the Youghiogheny and the Monongahela was of great importance. The Ohio River early furnished a relatively easy approach from the Mississippi Valley and the lower southwest. A final spoke or route, in reality a group of routes, came from the upper Great Lakes either by water from Detroit to Sandusky or the Cuyahoga or overland across central Ohio of the present day, and increasingly absorbed traffic. The results of all this on both history and historiography are important.[1] Documentation is widely scattered.

The flora and fauna of the upper Ohio Valley, matters of prime importance, were likewise factors of venerable antiquity. And upon them not only the aborigines, but also the later white explorers, fur traders, settlers, and military forces were greatly dependent. From abundant surviving records, it is apparent that this was true not only at first, but on the part of settlers for several generations.

Amerinds

The so-called American Indian, or Amerind, is a part of the background, remote and contemporary, of the capture of Fort Duquesne and the founding of Pittsburgh in 1758.

That the Amerinds were in the Western Hemisphere in preglacial or glacial times has been claimed though not universally admitted, but that they were here more than ten thousand years ago is now accepted by archaeologists and ethnologists. And through the study of remains, much has been learned of the economic and social life of early Amerinds. South of the Rio Grande some Amerinds had developed various primitive systems of notation or writing. Northward there was less highly developed culture.

Information, recorded in writing, about the American Indian dates from the coming of the European visitors. A small amount of it, based on Scandinavian accounts, is roughly a thousand years old. Most of the material, Spanish, Portuguese, French, English, Dutch, etc., is not yet five hundred years old.

It has long been customary to divide the Amerinds into families, mainly linguistic, numbering three score or more. More than half of these were small groups west of the Sierras. Many of the remaining groups played little role in colonial history east of the Mississippi River. The significant families were, alphabetically, the Algonquian, the Iroquoian, the Muskogean, and the Siouan (Catawba tribe). The famous tribes of Indians whose names are so common in documentary British-American colonial history belonged mainly to one or another of the first three families, Algonquian, Iroquoian or Muskogean.

Though in the early sixteenth century the Indians north of Mexico probably numbered no more than five hundred thousand and those east of the Mississippi less than two hundred thousand and their numbers gradually decreased in the face of the white man's aggression, this relatively small group of aboriginal inhabitants was a big factor in American colonial history. The American Indians, not Europeans, were the first Americans. The continent literally belonged to them politically, legally, and possibly morally. Much acute sophistry has been used in disclaiming this.

The Fur and Skin Trade

The combination of native fur bearing fauna, aboriginal native man, and European visitors and settlers quickly produced trade in furs and skins. Trade with the Amerinds by European fishermen actually antedates English, French, or Dutch settlement along the Atlantic coast of North America.

Active trade with the Indians began soon after settlement by Europeans, whether in Virginia, Maryland, or New England. It was slight in the first years along the Chesapeake, but it was more extensive in New England and along the Hudson. The Pilgrims traded not only around Massachusetts Bay, but up the Connecticut River and as far away as the Kennebec and the Penobscot. This early New England fur trade met with fierce competition from French-Canadian rivals, both along the ocean and overland from the upper waters of the St. Lawrence River.

From the establishment of New Netherland, the Dutch, more interested in commerce than in colonization, carried on a lively trade with the Indians. Albany, near the mouth of the Mohawk River, became the dominant fur exchange center south of Montreal and Quebec. Intense rivalry between the French and the Dutch before 1664, was continued between New France and New York, under the English, for more than a century afterward.[2]

In the meantime Pennsylvania merchants and traders slowly built up a lively trade with Indians south and west of New York colony.[3] This Pennsylvania trade with the Indians of the Ohio Valley likewise met with bitter competition and opposition from New France.

Maryland and Virginia trade with the Indians became a factor in the middle of the eighteenth century and influenced British American policy in Trans-Appalachia. Indian trade in the Carolinas, and, later, Georgia, though regionally significant, affected only slightly events on the Upper Ohio.

Only specialized students of Indian history and of the fur trade are greatly aware of the enormous printed literature and the bulky archival records found to be available for the study of these matters.

Anglo-French Rivalry

Anglo-French rivalry, as a main feature of events of 1758 both as background and as contemporary, is of great importance in medieval as well as in modern European and world history. It arose in the eleventh century and reached an early crisis in 1066. It continued under the Norman and Plantagenet rulers of England and reached another crisis in the Hundred Years War, 1338-1443. And though from time to time in abeyance, the rivalry persisted under other English royal houses, Lancastrian, Yorkist, Tudor, Stuart and Hanoverian, and found manifestation in North America in the seventeenth and eighteenth centuries, not only in economics but also in politics, diplomacy, and military struggle.

Modern Nationalism

Nationalism, as a dominant feature of modern times, arose about four hundred years after the beginning of Anglo-French rivalry. The Age of Discovery and the colonial period of our history were featured by intense struggle for advantage and power on the part of new nationalisms in Portugal, Spain, France, England, Holland, and Sweden. Portuguese power in the New World was largely confined to Brazil and little influenced North America. The once dominant power of Spain in the Western Hemisphere was invaded by rivals, checked navally in the defeat, in 1558, of the Great Armada, and with the exception of Florida, limited to territory beyond the Mississippi. Holland and Sweden planted colonies respectively along the Hudson and the Delaware, but before the end of the seventeenth century had lost political control, though leaving behind in New York and Pennsylvania important cultural deposits.

As early as 1689, it was evident that the final struggle in North America would be between the British and the French.

Rise of the British Empire

The rise and development of the British Empire lies back of the story of the capture of Fort Duquesne in November 1758. What is historically known as modern British imperialism can only with difficulty be traced back beyond the Tudors. British marinism began weakly under Henry VII, 1485-1509, increased under Henry VIII, 1509-1547, and became significant under Elizabeth I, 1558-1603. The British Empire and its North American colonies literally grew up together. The common American idea that the British Empire was an established fixity, pre-existing and antecedent to Virginia, Plymouth, Massachusetts, and Maryland, is erroneous, based on great ignorance of English history and government.

In large degree the North American colonies of the so-called Old British Empire were the veritable empire itself. Without them the remainder was an European national state, not otherwise yet imperial.

Old France in Europe and New France in North America must be depicted in the background of the great decision of November 1758 and they will be given below some consideration as one-half of the major factor of Anglo-French rivalry in the New World. But by reason of the outcome and later developments, greater attention must first be given to the British Isles in Europe and the British-American colonies in North America. In particular the respective contributions, on the one hand, of the British Isles and, on the other hand, of the British-American colonies, to the cause and its eventual outcome demand a large place in any historical treatment.

In the matter of time and possibly in the matter of power and importance British government and policy have, here, priority over American colonial matters.

It has already been noted that the so-called Old British Empire was an evolution, that it literally grew up between 1485 and 1775. Under Elizabeth I, England became maritime and somewhat marinistic. Commercial and naval shipping became significant. The highly romantic age of the Gentleman Adventurers is a part of the background of Fort Pitt and Pittsburgh. Sir Francis Drake, Sir Humphrey Gilbert, Sir Walter Raleigh and others belong in the vista. It is, of course, true that the Elizabethan gentlemen failed to plant permanent settlements in the New World. Figuratively, however, the seed of colonization was planted under Elizabeth. But the first crop of colonies came under the early Stuart kings, James I and Charles I. With opportunistic reason, but without centralized system, colonies of various types were planted in the New World. At first the chartered corporate type, as Virginia, Massachusetts, and later Connecticut and Rhode Island, was predominant, but contemporary were colonies of the proprietary type, as Maryland, Maine, and New Hampshire. And as early as 1624 the oldest chartered corporate colony, Virginia, became the first royal colony.

In this Old British Empire, thus established before the Great Rebellion, the Crown was supposed to be in control of colonization and colonies. The sovereign, however, acted through councils and important ministers. The most important actions were generally taken by the King in Council, that is by the King on the advice and recommendation of the Privy Council, an institution of the dim past. Parliament, while already powerful in the early seventeenth century, had not yet assumed any considerable authority and responsibility in colonial matters across the Atlantic.

The great Puritan military and political figure, Oliver Cromwell, stabilized and perpetuated the then somewhat adult British imperialism, particularly in its economic and maritime features. When on his death most of his other policies were reversed, his economic imperialism was retained under the Restoration of 1660. It was under Cromwell that navigation ordinances began, but they were continued by Charles II and his successors for more than a century. It was under the gay monarch himself that a committee of the Privy Council was given charge of colonial problems. Called, at first, Lords of Trade, this committee in 1696 was reorganized, with the addition of professionals, as the Board of Trade and Plantations, commonly called Lords Commissioners.

Administration of colonial matters was scattered around. Not only the sovereign and his privy council, and the later Board of Trade, but also the War Office, the Admiralty, the Treasury, and the Bishop of London participated in colonial matters. And in the eighteenth century Secretaries of State were added and became important channels of communication between Crown and Colony. This disorganized administration was all the more unsatisfactory by reason of personnel changes, in royal succession, in royal favorites, and by changes in policy and politics within the participating institutions. Efficiency under such circumstances was not likely.

British-American triumph and success in the New World must, however, be greatly attributed to the colonists themselves, whether as individuals, families, or groups, rather than to governmental action and socially organized forces. Yet the contribution of Europe to British America from 1582 to 1758 was vital and calls for analysis and acknowledgment.

Old World Contribution to the New World

With the meager exception of the Pilgrims from Leyden, the

original capital for planting British settlements in the New World came from Great Britain. Later migration furnished a market and payment for colonial property and production in the new settlements. When this continuing importation of surplus men and money from the Old World ceased for a time, as it did in New England 1640-1650, economic collapse and disaster came upon continental British-America. The potential protection and security of the British-American colonies were partly dependent on the strength of the navy and military forces of the mother country. No less an authority than William Pitt, the Elder, in a dramatic statement, said the security and success of the British-American colonies were won on the battlefields of Europe. He had in mind, of course, the Seven Years War in Europe, 1756-1763, but his remark was applicable to King William's War 1690-1691 and to Queen Anne's War 1703-1713. The well-known history of the British debt 1689-1775 throws great light on British financial contribution to colonial welfare.

To political, financial and military contributions by Great Britain to her North American colonies, must be added the somewhat imponderable contribution of the civilization and culture brought across the Atlantic and planted on American soil. The first British-Americans were Elizabethan and brought with them the good as well as some of the evil of Elizabethan culture. Old world skills, arts, sciences, learning, literature, manners, principles, and ideals, as well spiritual as social and material, were imported or brought over. They were not indigenously American. And though planted in North America this culture was continuously fed from Europe throughout the colonial period and well into the national period of the United States of America.

Colonial Development

Some consideration of the establishment of the British-American colonies, with attention to their governments, and emphasis upon their relations to the home government in London, is essential as background to consideration of their contribution to the Anglo-French wars and the events of two centuries ago.

Virginia, founded as a chartered corporate colony in 1607, secured some local autonomy, including a representative legislature, 1619-1624, but became a royal colony in 1624, though without the permanent loss of its legislature. As the prototype of eight later royal colonies, the government of later colonial Virginia consisted of externally appointed functionaries such as governors, lieutenant governors, councillors, judges, attorney-generals, and other officials, but had a house of burgesses elected by the people and representing local wishes and demands. Outweighed in number of offices, the lower house after bitter struggle finally secured domination in local and sometimes in intercolonial and imperial matters.

After an unsuccessful attempt to found a permanent colony, Avalon, on the island Newfoundland, George Calvert, first Lord Baltimore, secured in 1632 a charter for Maryland as a proprietary province or colony. Two years later the first settlement was made. Modeled on the old County Palatines of Norman England, the proprietor owned the land and was nominally supreme in justice, administration, and military matters. His power to make all laws, rules and regulations whatsoever, was limited by the necessity of the assent of the freeman or of their representatives. Occupying a key position along the Potomac and around the upper half of the Chesapeake Bay, Maryland was, though small, populous and rich. It was destined to play an important role in the latter part of the struggle with French and Indians in and beyond the Appalachian ridges, as will be indicated below in some detail.

Within less than one generation, no fewer than six colonies were established in what is known as New England. Ownership of the territory belonged by the Charter of 1606, to the Plymouth Company, later reorganized as the Council for New England. On this territory were planted in turn, the Plymouth Colony, the Massachusetts Bay Colony, Maine, New Hampshire, Connecticut and Rhode Island. Each of these had its own individual features and historical development. But several important features of colonial New England must be given attention.

Massachusetts was in every way the most powerful of the six colonies and was a model to some extent for her sister colonies. The constitutions or governments of New England colonies were largely republican. Miniature republics they have often been called. And New England for its size was relatively populous and wealthy, and thus able to make a heavy contribution to the struggle against France.

Thus with several colonies, distinct and yet much alike, New England in 1689 was prepared to act with some vigor in the conflict and wars leading up to the capture of Fort Duquesne in 1758. The New England forces which fought in Nova Scotia, on Cape Breton

Island, at Quebec, at Ticonderoga, Crown Point, Oswego, and operated against Niagara, while defending mainly their own welfare and interests, played nevertheless a vital role in the establishment of British-American control of the Ohio Valley.

While Oliver Cromwell is given much credit for the establishment of the British Empire, it is clearly observable that Charles II, the gay monarch, did much to round it out in North America. In the language of historians he "filled in the gaps." This action and policy was of vital importance in the final establishment of British-American authority a century later on the Ohio. Little time was wasted in this magnificent imperial expansion under Charles II.

The first gap filled in was that between Virginia and Florida, the latter then Spanish territory. This vast gap was given to favorites as a multiple proprietary and organized as Carolina. Thinly settled and with miserable communications, it eventually split into Northern Carolina and Southern Carolina. In 1729 the Crown bought out most of the proprietary rights and set up two royal colonies, North Carolina and South Carolina. Both democratic North Carolina and aristocratic South Carolina had typical royal colony government. They served as an imperial protection against the Spanish in Florida, the French in Louisiana, and the powerful Indian tribes in the interior with whom they soon built up a profitable trade in furs or skins. They also could and did furnish some troops for action along the upper Potomac and in the Ohio Valley. They played a role, though not a big one, in the Anglo-French conflict.

Two generations after the founding of Carolina, the old gap between Virginia and Florida was further filled in by the establishment of Georgia which for two decades was proprietary, but later was a royal colony whose small population and little wealth prevented much activity in continental struggles.

More important in the background of November 1758, was the work of filling in the gap of territory lying between Maryland on the south and New England in the north. Whatever may have been the motive of Charles II, this particular proceeding began with the royal grant of all this vast territory to James, Duke of York, who, in turn, sent out an expedition, seized the territory then known as New Netherland, and, renaming it New York, established it as a proprietary colony of an illiberal type, ruled by an appointed governor and council. On the accession of James, Duke of York, to the throne as James II in 1686, it became a royal colony. The representative assembly permitted in 1683 and revoked in 1686 was restored under William and Mary in 1691.

New Netherland and New York in 1664 included not only the area of present New York State but also that of present New Jersey, present Pennsylvania and present Delaware. Both defensively and offensively, these vast areas were more important in the struggle with the French, than either Virginia or New England. Geographers, historians, and military authorities have long understood that New York Bay, the Hudson, the Mohawk, Lake George, and Lake Champlain were the solar plexus of American strategical anatomy. The fact could be gleaned from correspondence, and campaigns extending from 1750 to 1815.

Out of the proprietary of James, Duke of York in 1664, were soon carved other new colonies, New Jersey, Pennsylvania, and Delaware. The first of these was transferred to others as early as 1664, and, after numerous changes and confused administrations, and government, finally became a royal colony in 1702. Southern New Jersey was relatively secure from invasion and attack, but northern New Jersey was more exposed. As one of the British-American colonies it supplied men and resources for use on the frontiers of her more exposed sister colonies.

Pennsylvania, the Keystone, was established under Charles II, by a land grant from James, Duke of York, and a charter from King Charles, in 1681. For many reasons it was relatively populous and prosperous from its earliest years. In accordance with its charter and with the liberal ideals of its founder, William Penn, it had a somewhat progressive government including a popularly elected assembly and a liberal code of laws. But conflict between the inhabitants and the proprietors or their representatives as governors was continuous from 1681 to 1776. Theoretically Pennsylvania was in position to furnish great assistance in the Anglo-French conflict. Actually, owing to the disputes with the proprietors and the traditional pacifism of the long dominant Quaker element, her contribution save in dire crises was less than might otherwise have been expected. What she did in the so-called French and Indian War, 1754-1758, is a large part of the immediate background of the capture of Fort Duquesne.

William Penn, not satisfied with the Delaware River water front of Pennsylvania, quickly secured a grant of the territory now known as the State of Delaware, but until 1776 commonly known as the Lower Counties, three in number. These counties were represented in the Pennsylvania Assembly until 1701, but from 1701 to 1776, they had, while under the administration of the proprietary Penns, an assembly of their own. As an almost separate proprietary colony of the Penns, the Lower Counties made their due contribution to the British-American cause, though the contribution was usually indirect through the Pennsylvania administration.

Old France and New France

The counterpart of this British and British-American organization and preparedness for contribution, cannot, as has hitherto above been done, be merely assumed. In some degree it must be outlined and in part delineated. Both old European France and New France in North America were grim realities and their story is an indispensable part of the history of the times.

France, though long politically disorganized and weak, was populous and rich as early as the end of the fifteenth century. French nationalism, old in theory, had become established. French overseas imperialism manifested itself in the sixteenth century. But, owing to dynastic troubles and debilitating religious warfare, little more than exploration was done before the beginning of the seventeenth century.

Imperial Spain remained dominant throughout the sixteenth century. Both British and French inroads on this domination were irritations rather than threats. Fortunately for the later British-Americans, Spanish imperialism rarely operated above the thirty-second degree of latitude.

French imperial incompetence ceased under Henry IV and his successors, Louis XIII and Louis XIV. Initiation of the new French imperialism in the New World began with the organization of French fur trade along the Saint Lawrence and the adjacent Atlantic coasts. The spasmodic trade of several generations under a succession of companies operating under royal grants was replaced by a giant imperial fur monopoly. This monopoly was granted to a group of associates of whom the Sieur de Monts was the most conspicuous. Under this fur company further explorations were made and settlements projected but not accomplished until control of operations came into the hands of Samuel de Champlain in 1608. This indefatigable leader planted settlements not only at Quebec and later

Montreal, but also in Acadia and in what later became Maine. Trouble with the British from Virginia and, later, from New England arose but French progress was only retarded, not stopped. Not only the French fur trade but also the Roman Catholic faith was widely introduced. In 1627, even before the death of Champlain in 1635, a new fur trade monopoly under the Hundred Associates was formed. Exploration and fur trade begun under Champlain were actively prosecuted for half a century.

A new phase came in 1663, when Colbert, the great minister of Louis XIV, secured the surrender of the rights of the fur trade monopoly of 1627 and created a centralized royal system of government in New France. Under final European control, it consisted, in New France, of a governor, a bishop and five councillors, chosen by the governor and the bishop. In the following year the office of intendant, to act as a check on the governor, particularly in the matter of finances, was set up. Another monopoly of the fur trade, under the French West India Company, lasted only for the decade 1664-1674. Royal initiative became supreme. Men, money, supplies, and missionaries were sent in abundance to the reinvigorated Franco-Americans. Agriculture, fishing, and trade were actively supported. Population increased and the explorations and fur trade were expanded. Only the shortcomings and stagnation of centralized autocracy prevented yet further development of strength.

In the political history of New France 1663 to 1689 two great figures stood out, both of them background factors in the eventual overthrow of French power in the upper Ohio Valley. The more powerful of the two, occupying higher office, was the Comte de Frontenac, Governor of Canada or New France, 1672-1681, a worthy successor of the earlier Champlain and predecessor of the later Marquis de Montcalm. It was under him that French-Canadian naval power was established on Lake Ontario with its base at Fort Frontenac or Cataraqui, the site of Kingston, Ontario, of the present day. It was also under him that the Mississippi River was explored and the mouth of the Ohio discovered. What he did for New France was not unlike what William Pitt, the Elder, was to do for the British Empire nearly a century later.

Contemporary of Frontenac was another and more romantic figure, Robert Cavelier Sieur de La Salle who in seeking fame and wealth in the New World made amazing voyages and travels in the Mississippi Valley before his murder in 1687. For these enterprises and for the promotion of the French colony of Louisiana, he is rightly world famous. And while French claims that he explored the Allegheny and Ohio rivers in 1669-1670 are not accepted by the best American scholars, the French claim to the region on this basis of discovery by La Salle lay at the root of the quarrel between French and British authorities in both the Old and the New World from 1713 to 1763. La Salle stands prominently in the historical background of November 1758.

The well-known limitations of eastern Canada in matters of climate, soil, and communication made it impossible that numerically and economically New France could compete successfully with the British-American colonies south of the Saint Lawrence and the Great Lakes. But concentration of power, organization, and action in New France tended to offset the superior but scattered and disorganized strength of British America.

Early Franco-British American Rivalry

The documentary records and the colonial history of New England and of New York, earlier as New Netherland, reveal that French imperialism in the seventeenth century, especially as related to the fur trade, met with insistent and almost continuous resistance from British-Americans.

With the accession of William and Mary in 1689 a crisis in Anglo-French relations immediately arose. William of Orange and Britain proposed to stop the political and territorial advance of France under Louis XIV, the Grand Monarch. This war, begun in Europe in 1690, had repercussions in North America. French and Indians attacked British-American towns as far south as Schenectady, and British-American expeditions were organized in New York and New England to capture Quebec.

Nothing significant occurred and the Treaty of Ryswick, 1697, re-established the status quo ante bellum. This War of the Palatinate in Europe is known as King William's War in America.

The uneasy peace of 1697, really a truce, lasted only four years. French ambitions could be further restrained only by war, and a dreadful struggle which was known in Europe as the War of the Spanish Succession began in 1701 and raged on for twelve years. Known in America as Queen Anne's War, it was featured in Europe by the victories of Marlborough. Fought mainly on the continent of Europe, this long drawn out war saw the gradual establishment of British naval superiority. For eight years the mutual desire of the French and the British for the maintenance of Iroquoian neutrality preserved peace in New York, but border warfare went on in New England, and commerce raiding was common along the Atlantic coast of America. New England reprisal was attempted against Nova Scotia and Quebec but without conspicuous success.

Two important features appeared in the famous Treaty of Utrecht of 1713. One of these shows up in any good series of American historical maps. The retreat of the French Empire in North America was marked by the award to Great Britain of Nova Scotia, Newfoundland, and the Hudson Bay region. The other feature, so far as North America was concerned, was the alleged acknowledgment by France that the Iroquois Indians were English subjects. Since the Iroquois claimed the Great Lakes area and asserted a protectorate over all Indians (and territory) west of the Appalachians and as far as the Mississippi, this meant an enormous extension of British claims in the New World. For a full generation French official documents disputed and denied the real significance of the treaty. For another generation, however, peace, in the real nature of a truce or "cold war," survived. Under the political supremacy of Sir Robert Walpole and his Secretary of State for the southern department, the Duke of Newcastle, a kind of peace was maintained for nearly thirty years. This space of time was well used by British-Americans in building up resources and strength in the various colonies. Such a breathing and growing spell was badly needed.

British-American Frontier Advance

The colonial frontier advance, in the first half of the eighteenth century, is an indispensable feature of the history of the background of the birthday of Pittsburgh.

Settlement along the Atlantic Coast and up the tidal estuaries and navigable rivers was an accomplishment of the seventeenth century. Movement up to the nearest mountains, into the Piedmont area, came at the beginning of the next century and occupied the attention of a full generation. It was in the second quarter of the eighteenth century that another westward spurt carried explorers, fur traders, and pioneer settlers over the eastern ridges of the Appalachian system into its valleys, and even beyond into the valleys of the Ohio and the Mississippi. All the way from Maine to

Georgia, but not always at the same speed, frontier advance took place. It has long been the favorite topic of romantic historians and enthusiastic local antiquarians. The documentary material while incomplete and thereby unsatisfactory, is, in survival, voluminous and highly intriguing.

Frontier expansion in New England was partly westward into the Berkshires and Green Mountains, but it was as much or more northward into Maine, New Hampshire and the region called Vermont. Such advance in the very face of French and Indians was a matter of importance in ensuing conflicts. It both protected older settlements and threatened hostile neighbors.

In New York, settlement pushed north of Albany along the Hudson and west of Albany along the Mohawk, and there was a small post at Oswego on Lake Ontario. But the powerful Iroquois Indians owned the lands which could only be secured from them in friendly agreement or sales.

The Central Frontier

In relation to the occupation of Pittsburgh by the British-American forces in 1758, the most significant frontier advances were made in Pennsylvania, Maryland, and Virginia. While under separate jurisdictions in the colonies and also influenced by overseas control from London, these three advances had the external appearance of one slow but irresistible, somewhat glacier-like, central continental movement. Possibly only serious boundary disputes. which call for some treatment, prevented the unity of this westward movement from being as obvious contemporaneously as it is now historically.

In Pennsylvania the frontier advance moved up the Delaware and its tributaries, the Schuylkill and the Lehigh. But it also moved up to and beyond the Susquehanna. As early as 1725, Philadelphia merchants and Pennsylvania traders entered upon trade with Indians on or beyond the Allegheny River. By the middle of the century fur trade, finance, and economy greatly influenced politics and government. Probably equally important was the westward movement across the Susquehanna and southwestward along the mountain valleys through Pennsylvania, into and through Maryland, into and through Virginia, and sometimes into the Carolinas and as far as Georgia. Very many of these early pioneers were Pennsylvania Germans, but others were of English or Scotch-Irish extraction.

The establishment of Lancaster County in 1729, York County in 1749 and Cumberland County in 1750 were features of this western settlement in Pennsylvania. In military campaigns, 1755-1758, these settlements were of primary importance to British-American success.

This westward moving Pennsylvania stock also made up a good part of the people who moved into western Maryland to places like Frederick and Hagerstown, though they met there another stream of much the same racial stock moving from older Maryland counties such as Baltimore and Prince Georges. As in Pennsylvania, new political and governmental provision was essential and Frederick County, Maryland, was established in 1748. The farthest west Maryland settlement was at Old Town, the home site of Thomas Cresap, or possibly farther west on Wills Creek or on the North Fork of the Potomac. In extreme western Maryland the old eastern Maryland stock seems to have arrived first and dominated local matters. Rock Creek, Frederick, Hagerstown, Old Town, Wills Creek, and, later, Cumberland, were vital places in the campaigns of 1754, 1755, and 1758. And a feathery flying wedge of this Maryland frontier advance pushed across the upper Potomac and up its tributaries, the Great Cacapon, the South Branch, and Patterson Creek as far as Hampshire County, Virginia, of later times.

The trans-Piedmontese Virginia frontier advance was double if not more multiple in type. Its earliest feature seems to have been Pennsylvania German migration from across the Potomac in Maryland, possibly by way of the famous ford at the later site of Williamsport and its ferry and bridges. German names clog the folios of the early archivists of the local counties. But shortly the Fairfax lands drew into the lower Shenandoah Valley representatives of old English families once along the lower Potomac, the Rappahannock, and indeed along the York and the James. And mixed with Germans and English were large numbers of so-called Scotch-Irish.

In keeping with the situation resulting from migration and settlement, the political and governmental situation in the upper Potomac region of Virginia was taken care of by the erection of Frederick County, Virginia, in 1748. But some of the pioneers had arrived in the area more than a decade earlier. Records antedating Frederick County must be consulted in Orange County or in land records in Richmond.

But another stream of westward bound settlers was moving across the Blue Ridge by gaps much farther south. Mainly British, with only a few Germans, this population in fifteen or twenty years spread out in the wider and more fertile valleys of the upper waters of the Shenandoah River. Then with almost unbelievable speed it moved southwest into the upper valleys of the James and the Roanoke. The first political and governmental result of this frontier advance was the establishment of Augusta County, Virginia, in 1748, an arrangement destined to last for another quarter of a century, long after the capture of Fort Duquesne and the establishment of Pittsburgh which, indeed, fell for a season under the political jurisdiction of Augusta County, Virginia.

With the frontier advance in the Carolinas and Georgia it is not essential to deal. Such advance had very little direct influence on the campaigns and battles in Pennsylvania 1754-1758.

French Counter Movement

Neither in Quebec nor in Paris were the French unaware of this British-American activity, development, and increased power. In particular, they knew about and disliked the increased fur trade and contact with the Indians stretching from Albany, Philadelphia, the Chesapeake Bay, and Charleston, South Carolina, across the mountains and almost to the rolling waters of the Mississippi.

In counter measures the French strengthened their footholds on Lake Champlain, at Frontenac, at Niagara, in Illinois, in Missouri and in southern Louisiana. They probably first saw the importance of linking Canada and Louisiana, involving among other things the control of a route from Lake Erie down the Allegheny and Ohio rivers. The first significant official use of this vital link in communications was made by de Longueil in 1739, with a small military force.[4]

In 1739, national and international warfare was renewed in Europe. It began as a naval war, commonly known as the War of Jenkins Ear, between Great Britain and Spain, 1739-41. It was supplemented by the War of the Austrian Succession, 1740, in which are sometimes depicted two Silesian Wars, 1740-1742 and 1744-1745. In these, France, as the ally of Prussia, Spain, Bavaria and Saxony, was heavily engaged. Great Britain eventually became involved as the ally of Austria but more realistically as the opponent of France and Spain. This Anglo-French war, declared in 1744 lasted in Europe for four years, being ended officially by the Peace of Aix-la-Chapelle in 1748. While this war, known in American history as King George's War, began in Europe and was fought mainly on

European soil, the conflict unavoidably spread to the New World, with its most notable event the capture of Louisbourg by a New England expedition in 1745 and its later restoration to France in the Treaty of 1748. Again the peace was in the nature of a truce, with the contest deferred to yet another bout, a feature of which we memorialize in this issue of the local historical magazine.

As already indicated above, the British-American frontier counties of York and Cumberland in Pennsylvania, Frederick in Maryland, and Frederick and Augusta in Virginia were established by 1750. Their inhabitants were affected by affairs and events overseas in Europe, upon the Atlantic Ocean, along the coasts of Canada, on the Saint Lawrence, around the Great Lakes, on the great Mississippi, and around the Gulf of Mexico. But until the outbreak of acknowledged international conflict in 1754 our attention must be given largely to two big items, the central government and politics in London and the affairs and events in Virginia, Maryland, and Pennsylvania. Wider inclusion of factors are necessary on the opening of military campaigns.

Complex Boundary Claims

The regional situation in and beyond the Appalachian ridges was doubly complex. The older but yet enduring complexity was that of international and colonist boundaries and territorial jurisdictional claims. There were in 1748 no less than half a dozen jurisdictional claims to the territory at the Forks of the Ohio. With no consideration here of either priority or validity, the claimants were Great Britain, France, the Iroquois Indians, the Ohio Valley Indians, Virginia, and Pennsylvania. The matter of boundaries was involved in each of the six claims. Archival documentary material on this is both voluminous and accessible. Into the tenuous and vague but somewhat familiar imperial claims of Great Britain and France it is unnecessary to go, for obviously their claims were the cause of hostilities, and the problem was settled by military events. The delicate question of Indian ownership and jurisdiction cannot be fully answered. It involved many matters such as; the relations of Indians and whites, the application of so-called international law to primitive people, the authority of the Iroquois, the local autonomy of the Ohio Valley Indians, and the like, all matters mainly of opinion.

Taken in the order of priority in time, the boundaries of Virginia, Maryland, and Pennsylvania call for general comment. A full and detailed history of Virginia and its historical boundaries would fill a large volume, possibly of a thousand pages. The Virginia claims to the interior of North America started with the second charter of 1609, which granted Virginia boundaries four hundred miles north and south along the Atlantic from sea to sea, "west and northwest." Though her charters were nullified in 1624 and regions sliced off in Maryland in 1632, in Carolina in 1663, in New York 1664, New Jersey 1664 and Pennsylvania and Delaware in 1681 and 1683, Virginia as a colony 1624-1776 and as a state in and after 1776 based her claims on her early charters. That as late as 1783 she was in possession of what is now Virginia, West Virginia, and Kentucky and claimed the entire old Northwest then including present Ohio, Indiana, Illinois, Michigan, Wisconsin, and a part of Minnesota, is well known to students of American history and geography.

As indicated, Maryland was cut away or sliced off from the Virginia territory of 1609. The Potomac River was fixed as its southern boundary west of the Chesapeake Bay and an artificial line drawn across the Eastern Shore. Accepted as a *fait accompli*, this southern boundary of Maryland had one problem only, that of its western limit at the source of the Potomac River. It has been often observed by later historians and geographers that Thomas Cresap as a deputy surveyor for Maryland failed to note that the source of the South Fork of the Potomac was several miles farther west and thus unwittingly left to Virginia and later to West Virginia territory which might rightly have gone to Maryland.

On the famous Maryland-Pennsylvania boundary dispute, elaborate comment is not here called for. It is possible that Maryland's claim to a boundary line north of Philadelphia and Pennsylvania's claim to a boundary south of Baltimore may have injured cooperation between Maryland and Pennsylvania in the Anglo-French wars, but evidence of this is not abundant, nor easily found.

In addition to her trouble with Maryland, Pennsylvania also had problems in regard to her New York boundary, a problem of her southern boundary to the west of Maryland, and the problem of her western boundary. In regard to the last two boundaries the dispute was with Virginia which claimed the territory to the south and west. In regard to the southern boundary, Virginia did not believe that she was bound by any agreement between the Penns and the Calverts and for a full generation claimed the territory lying "under the fortieth degree of northern latitude."

Pennsylvania's western boundary was even more a subject of dispute and difficulty. By the Charter of 1661, the Delaware River was made the eastern boundary from which the province was to extend westward five degrees of longitude. Since the Delaware was highly irregular in outline and flowed somewhat southwest, four possibilities arose: an irregular western boundary parallel to all points of the Delaware, an absurd though ethical adaptation; a line to start from the farthest point east on the Delaware River, a thing not likely to appeal to the Penns; the use of the median line of the Delaware, north-south, which would have been ethical and just; and the use of the farthest west point on the Delaware, which was done by the Penns to the advantage of Pennsylvania, but to the injury of the claims of Virginia.

From whatever angle the boundary may be considered, it seems certain that Pennsylvania got a stretch of land at least ten miles wide, east and west, and 156 miles long, north and south, 1,560 square miles, just short of a million acres, beyond the actual terms of the charter. Not only this million acres but yet another million was claimed by Virginia as not coming to her sister colony by the terms of the charters.

The other big item to be considered and held in mind by celebrators of 1958, is that of land speculation, land titles, purchases, etc., particularly by groups, whether as syndicates, organized companies, or powerful if not always rich individuals. The North American genesis of this is found in the early proprietaries such as Maryland. A slightly different and somewhat new development came with the Northern Neck grant to royal favorites and its acquisition by the Fairfax family. A spasm of such land speculation grew up with and, more so, grew out of the British-American push into the Appalachians 1730-1740. This decade saw the beginning of the occupation of the Shenandoah Valley of Virginia. William Beverley, James Patton, and others began such activities before 1740. They began to put in land grant petitions to the Governor and Council of Virginia. A clause in the Indian Treaty of Lancaster, 1744, doubtless inserted at the request of William Berkeley and Thomas Lee, the Virginia representatives there, quickly stimulated additional and larger schemes. With one of these, the Ohio Company, it is necessary to deal further on, as a specialty, but at least half a dozen other groups in Virginia were influenced and involved 1744-1754.[5]

Land speculation on the upper Potomac in Maryland entered

upon a similar contemporary phase. The parallelism is striking.

Thomas Cresap, the great early western Maryland frontiersman, settled near Hagerstown of later times, in 1739. Two years later he moved to Old Town on the Potomac River a few miles below the mouth of Wills Creek. A local merchant, Indian fur trader, and land speculator, he was a surveyor for a succession of Western Maryland counties. His services were used by prominent eastern Marylanders such as Daniel Dulany and Governor Thomas Bladen. From land warrants for several thousand acres in 1743 and 1745, Bladen had numerous pieces of land[6] surveyed, usually by Thomas Cresap or his deputized assistants. Much of the land was above Old Town, along the banks of the Potomac and of Wills Creek. Owing to geology and geography, this western Maryland area, granted to Thomas Bladen, but later assigned to others, became a vital spot in explorations of 1750-1752, in the Virginia advance over the mountains in 1752-1753 and in Ohio Valley military campaigns of 1754, 1755, and 1758.

In Pennsylvania the fur traders of 1740-1750 became interested as well in land ownership and land speculation. The most prominent of these was George Croghan, but William Trent, John Fraser and others were similarly engaged. Eastern Pennsylvania political and mercantile figures, such as Richard Peters, William Smith, Edward Shippen, and others, invested in frontier lands. Patents, deeds and mortgages fill many pages in the archives of Lancaster, York, and Cumberland, and, later, of Bedford and Westmoreland Counties.

Pennsylvanians as well as Virginians had their attention fixed upon future prospects along the Juniata, the Conemaugh, the Youghiogheny, the Allegheny and the Monongahela.

Land Companies

Of the land companies organized in Virginia in the decade, 1740-1750, two were of greatest historical significance. One of these, the Loyal Land Company, operated with permanent title results in western and southwestern colonial Virginia, which included present day West Virginia. It was of great importance in the later history of southwest Virginia, West Virginia, and Kentucky. Its story is, however, not highly relevant to the early history of Pittsburgh.

On the other hand the story of the Ohio Company[7] 1747-1754 is fundamental in the situation at the Forks of the Ohio, in the period from 1747 to 1758, and beyond. It may almost be claimed that the activities of the Ohio Company precipitated the struggle commonly known in American history as the French and Indian War.

The gradual evolution of the Ohio Company 1745-1747, is not revealed in surviving documentary material. Indirectly it may have been influenced by the Fairfax land possession and policy with which the Lees and Washingtons were greatly familiar. As already indicated it may have been influenced by items in the Indian treaty of 1744. Competition in western enterprise between William Berkeley on one side and the Washingtons and Lees on the other may have been an influence. Some, both contemporaries and writers of later time, have given credit for the idea to Thomas Cresap who actually presented the first petition in 1747.

It is also reasonable to suppose that Lawrence Washington may have first worked upon such a plan. But the best judgment from later records would indicate that the prime mover was Thomas Lee of Stratford, judge and member of the Virginia Council.

Worthy of attention, it would seem, is the fact that from 1745 to 1748, the period of the inception of the Ohio Company, King George's War was in progress in Europe, on the high seas, and along the disputed frontier of New France. No evidence of the earliest conferences and discussions of the Ohio Company seems to have survived. Oblivion, without giving alms, has triumphed forever. But that such conferences and discussions were held is shown by the dual fact that when the first documentation comes, it contains references to both an executive committee and to articles of agreement.

The first land grant petition, of October 24, 1747, made to the Executive Council of Virginia, was deferred in time and referred to the government in London. The eleven gentlemen from the Rappahannock and Potomac valleys were not without opposition in the powerful Virginia Council. And Governor Gooch, old and feeble, thought it might injure the prospects of peace. For more than a year the matter was batted around. Finally, it was decided by the Company to add British residents as members and put in an appeal directly to the King in Council. News about these petitions of the Ohio Company in due time reached both Paris and Quebec. Even before the royal approval in March 1749 and six months before the ordered grant by the Virginia Council, the French had begun countermeasures. Apparently the first and greatly the most important step was the justly famous expedition sent out by the Governor of Canada under Céloron de Blainville, whose trip from Montreal in early 1749, as revealed in journals, is of great historical interest and value. But this countermeasure was far from definitive and effective. It was followed by a policy of infiltration and Indian activity on the part of French trappers, traders, military personnel, and religious agents. Possession of the then potentially richest part of the world was the issue at stake. The regions, hills and valleys, rivers and forests were permeated with propagandistic action, with aggressive use of both strategy and tactics. "Cold" war followed.

In the meantime the Ohio Company of Virginia was not idle nor badly negligent. It ordered large cargoes of European goods for the Indian trade and, in the winter of 1750-1751, had much of a cargo sold along the Ohio and its northwestern tributaries. At the same time it bought property on both sides of the Potomac near Wills Creek. It also sent out Christopher Gist as an explorer and messenger to the Indians in the winters of 1750-1751 and 1751-1752. The complete story of the Ohio Company is much too long for inclusion here. Several books of recent years have greatly enlarged not only the history, but the significance of the Company.

These activities of the Ohio Company did not escape notice. They were commented upon in Annapolis, Philadelphia, New York, Boston, London, and Paris and, of course, in Detroit, Niagara, Frontenac, Montreal, and Quebec. The completion of the Ohio Company Road from Wills Creek to the Monongahela Valley and the coming of the first families west of the mountains may have been well known as far away as Quebec.

The net result of the Ohio Company push across the mountains was another countermeasure, the third important French military expedition in the region.

French Response

The French expedition of 1753, like that of 1749 by Céloron de Blainville, was primarily a continental American affair, though with the centralized control of old and new France, and with French troops along the Saint Lawrence, it was not wholly indigenous nor autonomous. The situation in the British-American colonies was similar. Governors, councils, and assemblies were in control; in South Carolina under Governor James Glen, in North Carolina under Governor Arthur Dobbs, in Maryland under Governor Horatio Sharpe and the proprietary, in Pennsylvania under Governor James Hamilton

and the proprietary, and in Virginia under Governor William Gooch until 1749, under Thomas Lee, President of the Council, acting governor for slightly more than a year, 1749-1750 and after two acting governors, under Governor Robert Dinwiddie from late 1751 to early 1758.

Otherwise than in matters of personnel in command and local problems, the government of New France remained much as it had become organized under Louis XIV. It was under the Comte de Galissoniere that Céloron de Blainville made his trip. French policy 1749-1752 was under the Marquis de la Jonquiere, who was succeeded in 1752 by the Marquis de Duquesne, who sent out the famous expedition of M. Marin in 1753.

On this expedition there has long been in print materials which adequately depict the intrepidity of this French maneuver of 1753. More recently the publication of the long neglected Contrecoeur papers has clarified the details of famous endeavor. Though probably officially intended to establish another *fait accompli* in the "cold" war which had been going on for five years, this expedition was something more. It was a genuine military movement.

Opening Military Actions

Some historians believe hostilities involving warfare, if they did not begin in the west in 1751 or 1752, actually began with the seizure of Venango by the French in the late summer of 1753. The trip to Venango was a difficult one. It involved painful and dangerous movement up the Saint Lawrence from Montreal to Lake Ontario. A feature was the long trip west from Frontenac to Niagara, at which place all personnel and supplies had to be moved up a height of about two hundred and fifty feet to the level of Lake Erie. Great exhaustion, much sickness, and many deaths were the results. But leaders in command such as Marin, Contrecoeur, and others, were determined and heroic.

When the expedition reached a small inlet on Lake Erie where Barcelona, New York, was later located, the old route by Lake Chautauqua and Conewango Creek and thence down the Allegheny, was no longer considered satisfactory. Another harbor and better route was sought and found to the west at Presque Isle, or Erie Bay of later times. A fort was erected, a road laid out to the Riviere aux Boeuf (present day Waterford), a fort built there, and the expedition extended to Venango (Franklin of the present day), where the residence and gunsmith shop of John Fraser, from which he had fled, was taken over and a third fort projected. But the momentum was now gone, supplies were inadequate, water in the inland streams was too low for navigation, winter was approaching, and many went home to Canada for the winter. This expulsion of John Fraser and the seizure of his property has been called the opening of the French and Indian War, but earlier still were seizures of British-American fur traders and attacks upon their Indian friends and allies.

From now available documentary materials, it seems that an Ohio Company settlement was established between the Youghiogheny and the Monongahela in the winter of 1752-1753. And John Fraser, Thomas Cresap, and others were in the region in early 1753. The first English-speaking Transappalachian frontier had been located.[8] A rival land company made surveys in the area in the first quarter of 1753. Information about the French at Niagara, Erie, Fort Le Boeuf, and Venango was brought by friendly Indians who themselves strenuously objected to the French invasion of their lands and home sites. From the Monongahela, information quickly reached Wills Creek, the New Store of the Ohio Company and Old Town, Maryland. With equal speed it reached Williamsburg and possibly Annapolis and Philadelphia.

Particularly distressing, especially to the Ohio Company and Governor Dinwiddie of Virginia, was the problem of the Ohio Valley Indians. A conference with them was called and met at Winchester in the late summer. Presents to them were given, more presents promised, and preparations made to construct posts or forts on the Monongahela and the Ohio.

After preliminary steps in late 1752 and in the early months of 1753, Governor Dinwiddie in mid-June fully reported to the home government, the enlarged operations of the French and asked for instructions. It was probably late in October that he received the well-known instructions drawn up in London and sent him August 28, 1753. He was authorized to send a messenger to the French to demand their withdrawal from the region and in case of their refusal to take the necessary measures to drive them out. In military terminology these measures were an ultimatum. Matters had reached a crisis. The French were preparing to descend the Allegheny in early 1754. Soldiers, Indians, supplies, boats for transportation were projected by them and, as fast as possible, gathered. All this the Ohio Valley Indians, the Ohio Company agents and settlers, and

GENERAL GEORGE WASHINGTON

GENERAL EDWARD BRADDOCK

DECISION AT THE FORKS 29

others, as far as Philadelphia, Annapolis, and Williamsburg, knew.

After some trouble in securing a messenger to deliver in winter the message to the French commanders at the French forts, Governor Dinwiddie hit upon young George Washington, who on a greatly famous trip travelled over the Ohio Company road from the New Store to Gist's place. He may have stopped with John Fraser on Turtle Creek and with George Croghan on Pine Creek. He inspected both the Forks of the Ohio and McKee's Rocks before dropping down to Logstown and going on overland to Venango and Fort Le Boeuf. As might have been anticipated, his message was not accepted by the French commandants. Their answer while guarded and diplomatic was in fact a rejection. The logical result of an ultimatum and its rejection is warfare and this case was not to be an exception.

On his return trip, Washington again passed through Pittsburgh of today, stopped at John Fraser's cabin on Turtle Creek, at Christopher Gist's place along the Youghiogheny, at Wills Creek, and eventually reached Williamsburg in late January. His unfavorable news and report precipitated Virginia war measures and brought on the military campaign of 1754.

William Trent, an old Pennsylvania trader, merchant, and land speculator who had been appointed the successor of Hugh Parker as western agent or factor of the Ohio Company, was in January 1753 at the mouth of Redstone Creek with a small working force constructing a storehouse for the Ohio Company. This post was a base from which Trent proposed to move on to the construction of the long projected fort of the Ohio Company near or on the Forks of the Ohio. Governor Dinwiddie, both a member of the Ohio Company and the political and military head of Virginia, endeavored to speed up military matters. There was absolutely no time to waste, for it was obvious that the French would descend the Allegheny River in early 1754. William Trent was immediately commissioned a captain in the Virginia militia, instructed to raise a company of a hundred men, and ordered to descend the Monongahela and build a fort to be named Fort Prince George, on the triangle between the Monongahela and the Allegheny. On the receipt of orders, Trent began operations at once, arriving at the Forks of the Ohio February 17, 1754, but with less than half of one hundred men. At the same time, George Washington, already a colonel in the Virginia militia, was instructed to raise another company and march to the support of Captain Trent who was at the time on the important spot, one literally destined to be a hot spot for the next five years.

Governor Dinwiddie continued a lively correspondence not only with higher officials in London, but with fellow governors in the American colonies. He saw the conflict as greatly continental and asked for the cooperation of the Carolinas, Maryland, and Pennsylvania, and for the use of the Independent Companies already established in key positions in North America. He seems to have underestimated the difficulties of organization, supplies, and transportation in a world so largely a wilderness.

William Trent found himself in trouble at the Forks of the Ohio. His force was small, only about three dozen men. The Ohio Valley Indians to whom he had brought out presents stayed in the neighborhood and drew heavily upon his meagre supplies. As later depositions of Ensign Ward show, it was vitally necessary for Trent to return to Wills Creek for more supplies. He also hoped to bring back more support in the arrival of Washington's company which reached the Wills Creek neighborhood only in April and was not adequately equipped for service. Affairs at the Forks of the Ohio became ever more desperate.

In mid-April the French and Indians finally came down the Allegheny River. Provided with adequate artillery and outnumbering the garrison thirty to one, the result was inevitable. The British-Americans met with defeat and were compelled to retreat to Wills Creek, where the straggling men arrived before Captain Trent and Colonel Washington had gotten ready to march west from Wills Creek.

After Ensign Ward had carried the bad news to Williamsburg, it was necessary to establish the First Virginia Regiment, ask for the assistance of the Independent Companies, and call further upon adjoining colonies for assistance in men, money, and supplies. The results were very unsatisfactory. Colonel Joshua Fry in command of the regiment, and Washington in command of an advance movement, had less than three hundred men. Another three hundred were on the march to Wills Creek. Circumstances were on the whole highly unsatisfactory.

On or near the site of Captain Trent's crude palisaded enclosure, historically known as Fort Prince George, the French hurriedly constructed a more elaborate work and named it Fort Duquesne. In and around it were gathered several hundred French and Canadian troops and an equally large number of Indians. It was this fort which dominated the Forks for more than four years before it was finally captured in November 1758. Captain Contrecoeur had led the expedition down the river and was destined to retain command during the next two campaigns.

George Washington, in early 1754, though a colonel in the Virginia militia, was only twenty-two years of age and wholly without field experience in war. But he was self-confident, bold to the point of rashness, and highly ambitious. Service under Colonel Fry was distasteful to him, but the early death of Colonel Fry gave Washington final authority over the Virginia militia under him. He decided to cross the mountains and establish himself at a base on or near Redstone Creek, where he could be later joined by others then on the march from New York and the Carolinas. He reached and crossed, in early May, the upper branches of the Youghiogheny. As a mountain base he hit upon Great Meadows. With friendly Ohio Valley Indians he endeavored to co-operate. While in this neighborhood he heard of a small French force advancing and lurking in the forests and glens. An attack on this force involved the famous episode of Jumonville's defeat and death. One great historian considered this small encounter as the beginning of hostilities.

From the Great Meadows Colonel Washington went down the mountain to Gist's place, and sent forces under Captain Andrew Lewis and Captain George Mercer to clear the road to the Monongahela at the mouth of Redstone Creek. This work was not fully completed before the roadbuilders were hurriedly recalled.

The French under Contrecoeur at Fort Duquesne were informed by one of Jumonville's men, who alone had escaped death or capture, about the episode at Jumonville's Glen. Information about Colonel Washington's force at Gist's place was later reported by spies sent out for the purpose.

A relatively large body of French and Indians under DeVilliers, the brother of Jumonville, marched against their rivals for possession of the area. In the oft described maneuvers which followed, Washington capitulated at Fort Necessity on July 4, 1754, exactly twenty-two years before the adoption of the Declaration of Independence. By the terms of the capitulation Washington and his troops retired to Wills Creek, and the Ohio Valley for nearly a year remained uncontestedly in the hands of the French. The British-Americans were actually thrown on the defensive on the frontiers of Virginia, Maryland, and Pennsylvania. The need for more protection from sporadic hostile incursions caused great anxiety along the Potomac and the Susquehanna.

Hitherto military contribution from the home government in London had been indirect and slight. The so-called Independent Companies of New York and of South Carolina were late in reaching the scene of conflict. They seem to have been under the control of the War Department in London, officered by British regulars, and under regular British rules of war, with guaranteed status and pay as British regulars. But these companies were probably composed mainly of enlisted North American colonials. They were literally independent of the colonial militia and strongly inclined to be independent of colonial administration. George Washington repeatedly and greatly objected to the supposed rank of a regular captain over a militia colonel, and when on appeal it was decided to change the militia regiment into independent companies, sent in his resignation and retired to private life. Governor Horatio Sharpe was made the commander-in-chief.

The crisis of the summer of 1754 led to frantic appeal from Governor Dinwiddie for British overseas support. George the Second, his son the Duke of Cumberland, military chief; the Duke of Newcastle, head of the ministry; Henry Fox, Secretary of War; Thomas Robinson, Secretary of State; and others, agreed to send to the harassed colonies heavy military and naval aid, consisting of two regiments of regular troops under Major General Edward Braddock and a large fleet under Admiral Boscawen.

In November 1754, Braddock was given elaborate triple instructions and furnished with copies of earlier documents from the governmental archives. Sailing from Europe in December, with troopships convoyed by Admiral Keppel, he arrived after a bad winter voyage and, landing at Hampton, Virginia, he quickly got into touch with Governor Dinwiddie. After several conferences, Braddock and Dinwiddie wrote to the colonial governors from Nova Scotia to South Carolina and called a conference to meet in Annapolis early in April.

A decision was early made to disembark the two regiments, not at Hampton nor at Yorktown but farther north at Fredericksburg or at Alexandria, Virginia. From northern Virginia the forces were marched to Wills Creek, Maryland, by two different routes, one overland by way of Winchester and Romney, of later times, and the other by way of Frederick, Maryland, and thence to Winchester. The troops reached Wills Creek about May 10, 1755, but much of the month was lost in securing supplies and transportation facilities and in repairing and widening the Old Ohio Company Road to the Monongahela River.

General Braddock's campaign of June and July 1755 has never ceased to be a matter of great historical interest. From more recent studies both of Braddock before 1755 and of the campaign itself, favorable estimation of Braddock has greatly increased. He was a veteran regular, and he understood military organization, order, and management. He was, while not a wilderness tactician, nevertheless an able strategist. His logistics were hampered by geographic, economic, and political difficulties, without which he might easily have succeeded.

For the campaign there were alternative plans available. One was to advance, with power invincible, against any potential enemy. This was the plan actually followed by General John Forbes three years later. There is much evidence that this was the desire and plan of Braddock. The other plan was to advance rapidly with a mobile force and reach Fort Duquesne before men and supplies for the summer had arrived from Quebec. This was the plan which had been followed with none too satisfactory results by Colonel Washington in 1754 and now was ardently promoted by him in the 1755 campaign. Braddock straddled the two conflicting plans and, largely as a result, lost the campaign. He neither moved with irresistible force nor arrived before reinforcements reached the enemy.

On the details of Braddock's last weeks there is much information. He reached the final mountain ridge with an intact force of about 1,400 regulars, 700 provincials, and 50 sailors detached from the navy. But he divided his army, leaving behind on the mountain Colonel Dunbar with about 750 men and much of the army train. Partly a matter of strategical division, this move was as well the outgrowth of inadequate transportation and the resulting scarcity of provisions and military supplies. Whatever the motivation the military maxim of unity in the immediate face of an enemy was violated.

With about 1,400 picked troops he moved on toward Fort Duquesne. To avoid Turtle Creek Valley, considered a dangerous gorge, he crossed from the east bank of the Monongahela to the west bank and then recrossed the Monongahela on the morning of July 9, 1755, destined to be a fatal day for him and his army.

The French at Fort Duquesne had scouted his army and its advance. They now had to fight, or retreat, or surrender. Thanks to the courage and boldness of two French Officers, Captain Daniel Beaujeu and Captain Jean Dumas, they decided to march out and attack before the enemy, with superior numbers and better artillery, reached the vicinity of the fort. About 400 Indians and an even smaller number of French and Canadians engaged in the enterprise.

Much has been made of Braddock's failure to hold Indian allies and use them as scouts. It is true that he did not understand them nor get along amicably with them, but that is not surprising to those familiar with the literature of the war. British-American commanders such as George Washington, William Shirley, John Forbes, Henry Bouquet, William Byrd III and others had similar if not the same trouble and experience with Indian allies. Only William Johnson could and did use them successfully.

On the morning of the battle, Braddock sent forward guides and an advance force under Lieutenant Colonel Thomas Gage. Then he followed with his army and its train of supplies, all in excellent order with flankers and pickets. His great blunder seems to have been that of moving forward in a long drawn out column easily stopped by enemy opposition at front and easily attacked on the sides from woods and ravines.

On the marching column, Captain Beaujeu and his forces advanced in mid-afternoon. At first they were checked by gunfire which scattered them and cost Beaujeu his life, but under Captain Dumas the now scattered French and Indians fell upon the column of the enemy. The British-American guides and pickets fled from the front, throwing Gage's force into disorder. The flankers were likewise driven from the hills and forced back. Eventually Braddock came forward and took command of operations. But he kept the army in column and failed to establish a line of battle to withstand the enemy. Within about two hours the final outcome was fully determined. Wise strategy in earlier weeks was ruined by bad tactics on the battlefield. The heroic and historic role of Washington has long been a matter of public lore.

The list of casualties of the British-Americans included, as killed, wounded, or missing, sixty-three of the eighty-nine officers and one-half of the privates. The military and personal property captured on the battlefield involved heavy loss. But possibly, wild plundering on the part of the Indians saved many of the British regulars and colonial militia who fled the scene and straggled back up to the mountain plateau where Colonel Dunbar, with about one-third of the men of the expedition and guarding wagons and supplies, had been left in reserve.

Although it was soon known that the Indian allies of the French had left the region and that only a few hundred French regulars remained at Fort Duquesne, the British-American forces pulled out of the region. Many of the Virginia militia went back to their homes. Colonel Dunbar, disregarding appeals of Dinwiddie and others, retreated from his encampment to Wills Creek, thence to Philadelphia and eventually to the Hudson River valley, taking along with him some of the Independent Companies sent to Virginia at an earlier time.

The British-American colonial frontier of Pennsylvania, Maryland and Virginia was left, in great danger, wide open to sporadic raids by Indians led by French officers or by some trusted Indian chief.

The disastrous outcome of Braddock's expedition was not completely offset by efforts elsewhere under William Shirley, William Johnson, Admiral Boscawen, and others. But relative failure produced strangely little governmental upheaval. Not for two years was the home government in London to undergo a revolutionary change in leadership and control. No profound changes were made in colonial government. Governors such as Shirley in Massachusetts, Delancey in New York, Robert Hunter Morris in Pennsylvania, Horatio Sharpe in Maryland, Dinwiddie in Virginia, Dobbs in North Carolina, and Glen in South Carolina were not unseated but continued for several years. The most significant change on Braddock's death was that in the position of Commander-in-Chief of His Majesty's Forces in North America, where Shirley, Lord Loudoun, James Abercromby and Jeffery Amherst followed each other in rapid order, 1755-1758.

For three troublesome years Fort Duquesne remained what Colonel Henry Bouquet later called it, "a nest of corsairs." Raid after raid from Fort Duquesne hit pioneer settlements along the Susquehanna and the Potomac. Pennsylvania, Maryland, and Virginia were definitely on the defensive with only a sporadic offensive such as the famous Pennsylvania attack of 1756 upon Kittanning. It was in these years that a series of forts was established in central Pennsylvania, a few in Maryland, and a great number in Virginia. George Washington, for the second time Colonel of the First Virginia Regiment, had a busy life establishing, garrisoning, and inspecting a string of little forts on the Virginia frontier.[9]

In British North America in general, but in Pennsylvania,

Maryland, and Virginia in particular, the years 1756 and 1757 were not merely sorrowful but also, on the surface at least, somewhat drab. Down below, but little above oblivion, there was population increase and social growth. But the economic and financial situation, while not unendurable, was highly distressing. As an illustration or example, the old Ohio Company, so influential in the years immediately preceding, became quiescent.

But these drab years are in the immediate background of the Forbes campaign of 1758, and several significant factors require attention.

As demonstrated by events, earlier and later, much depended on the central government in London. Under George II as king and the Duke of Cumberland as highest military authority, the Duke of Newcastle was prime minister from 1754 until late in 1756. As Secretary of State he had Henry Fox, a statesman of questionable reputation. When public pressure uprooted Fox in late 1756, Newcastle found the responsibility too great and likewise resigned. William Pitt, the Elder, became Secretary of State and introduced some of the ideas about which he had been campaigning for several years. His main proposal was to oppose New France in North America by putting pressure on France in Europe. Aid to Hanover and alliance with Prussia were land measures. Reorganization of the navy, after the loss of Minorca by Admiral Byng, was another expectation. But George II did not like William Pitt, whose emphasis on parliamentary sovereignty was distasteful to royalty as well as to the old Whig aristocracy. And the powerful Duke of Cumberland demanded Pitt's removal. His dismissal came in April 1757. But George II found it impossible to set up another administration and, after three months, Pitt came back into power in June 1757, nominally under the Duke of Newcastle as Prime Minister, but really in control himself of virtually everything except management of Parliament. It was under this regime that Fort Duquesne was captured, and Pitt's "system" of 1757-1758 demands therefore some analysis.

The diplomatic, naval, and military situation in Europe is a part of the historical background of Pittsburgh's Bicentennial. When England lost willingness to fight for the Austrian recovery of Silesia from Prussia, Austria turned to France, and Prussia and Britain became allies. This startling diplomatic reversal antedated Pitt's accession to office, but he accepted it and maintained it for four eventful years, 1757-1761. On sea the loss of Minorca still rankled British pride. William Pitt endeavored to strengthen the navy both to threaten French coasts and to weaken French maritime communications with New France. On land the Duke of Cumberland defending the Electorate of Hanover was badly defeated and abandoned active military life. The land warfare was mainly the brilliant campaign of Frederick the Great in Saxony and Silesia, in 1757.

Commanders-in-Chief in British America

The most powerful figure and position in British North America, from 1755 to 1774, was that of Commander-in-Chief of His Majesty's Forces in North America.

The first of these was Major General Edward Braddock. Popularly known, mainly if not only, for his defeat, his papers clearly reveal his military, political, and financial power in 1755. On Braddock's death, his second in command, Major General William Shirley, took over immediate control of the position, with all its responsibilities.

More politician than military specialist, Shirley had many fine strategic ideas, some of which he passed on to Braddock. Popular for the time in New England, Shirley probably aroused and certainly met considerable antagonism elsewhere. His relations with William Johnson were not altogether friendly nor cordial, save in formalistic statement. The military circumstances were unfavorable in 1755, and his proposed campaign against Niagara hardly got beyond the Hudson River. His policies after Braddock's Defeat antagonized the governors of southern colonies. Possibly not because of such things, but for reasons of military politics, Shirley, March 20, 1756, was superseded by John Campbell, Fourth Earl of Loudoun,[10] already appointed Governor of Virginia, February 17, 1756.

Lord Loudoun arrived in New York, July 23, 1756. He had left affairs in great political, military, and naval confusion in Europe and he found them in similar condition in North America. He hurried to Albany, headquarters of several thousand troops gathered for at least defensive action on the northern frontier of New York and along Lake George and Lake Champlain. But he soon found himself in seemingly unavoidable difficulties with Shirley, with General Webb, and with Winslow and other militia commanders. A shattering result was the capture, by the French, of Oswego. During the next year he was incessantly in trouble with colonial governments about money, supplies, quarters, recruiting, and other matters. His plans for an expedition against Louisbourg and for a movement against Quebec, both by sea and overland, came to naught. Miserable weather delayed matters until it was too late. He did not escape the accusation of wasting time.

General James Abercromby was by appointment from London second in command to Loudoun in the New World. When Loudoun went to New York, then to Boston, and eventually to Halifax, Abercromby remained behind in the Hudson Valley.

Forbes

An old friend of Loudoun, who also was acquainted with the then powerful Duke of Cumberland, was Colonel John Forbes, who had served in different capacities in warfare in Europe. In a reshuffling organization, Forbes in early 1757 was made colonel of the 17th regiment. With a large fleet of war vessels and military transports, Forbes sailed in May for Halifax, Nova Scotia, which was reached in July 1757. Here were soon gathered more than seven regiments, most of them recently from Europe. Lord Loudoun badly needed assistance in his duties and found a most efficient worker in Forbes who quickly became his adjutant general and his friendly but frank adviser and critic. This role Forbes continued to play after the return of Loudoun from Halifax to New York. In this connection he wrote many letters and may have drawn up various plans of instructions and operations for the campaigns of 1758. But a profound change in his status had already been made, though it was late in March 1758 before it was announced and established in North America.[11]

Pitt

Pittsburgh is very properly named. The British imperial successes, 1758 to 1761, were greatly determined by Pitt. Of his somewhat unattractive genius there is no historical doubt. The major facts about his career at this time are fairly clear. He had great popularity with the people of Great Britain, a fact of prime significance in the support of parliamentary government.

While he was disliked by George II and the Duke of Cumberland, this fact probably increased his favor with the common people. The measures of his "system" were many. Possibly the most important of these was to make use of his influence with the people to secure more money through increased taxation, money needed and to be used in enlarging the royal navy, supporting, financially, Eng-

GENERAL JOHN FORBES

Henry Bouquet

land's continental allies, and fitting out additional regiments for defense in Europe and attack in North America. Naval, financial, and military pressure upon France, both in the Old and the New World, soon became incessant rather than sporadic. Pitt's policy of placing younger men in command of important movements produced good results, under men like Amherst, Wolfe, Howe, Forbes, Bradstreet, Bouquet and others. A brilliant stroke of genius was his invitation to Scottish Highlanders to organize British imperial regiments and fight for Great Britain and the empire. The acceptance of this invitation and the honorable reception of such regiments established a veritable bulwark of imperial power. Pitt also agreed to assist the colonies in North America in raising and supporting colonial troops. He and others in England had long heard and known that the debtor type of colonial economic and financial matters made such assistance necessary to success. The financial statistics of such expenditure, while significant and interesting, are best reserved for specialists in imperial economy and finance.

Plans for 1758

After two years of great confusion, Great Britain, under Pitt, in 1758, loosed a hydra headed attack against France. Fleets were sent against the coasts of France, subsidies to Prussia were granted, a Hanoverian army was stationed in western Germany, French possessions in western Africa were seized, French authority and power in India were challenged and put in the way of elimination. But the greatest efforts were made in North America.

In the truly global struggle of 1758, the struggle in North America was continental in objective and semi-continental in scope, the latter extending from Labrador to Louisiana and from the Atlantic to and beyond the Mississippi. Primary British objectives were Louisbourg, Quebec, Montreal, Frontenac, Niagara and Fort Duquesne.

Military Enterprises in North America, 1758

It is commonly asserted that three main military enterprises were projected and attempted in North America in 1758. With them general students of history are familiar but to their story return is here necessary. But there was a fourth enterprise of no little importance in the eventual outcome of affairs, 1758-1760. As early as January 25, 1758 some one in the entourage of Lord Loudoun, probably Captain John Bradstreet himself, put out an admirable plan[12] for the capture of Cataraqui (Fort Frontenac) on the eastern end of Lake Ontario. These instructions to Captain John Bradstreet were not carried out in early spring as planned and the forces expected to be used were not available until later in the summer, but eventually Bradstreet did get sufficient troops, made the expedition planned earlier, captured the fort, storehouses, and shipping there and on Lake Ontario, made greatly easier the work of General Forbes, threatened the eventual French loss of all posts between Montreal and St. Louis, and did irreparable damage to French strength in 1759 and 1760. John Bradstreet, who may never have been at the Forks of the Ohio, might well be historically honored by a municipal statue in Pittsburgh.

The main British attack in 1758 was upon the great Fortress at Louisbourg on Cape Breton Island in lower Saint Lawrence Bay. Its importance was not only that of a military and naval base but also as a protection to Quebec, the capital, and also to Montreal. A magnificent combined naval and military force, the latter under General Jeffery Amherst, with great aid from General James Wolfe, attacked the fort and before the end of July captured the fort and took possession of the island, which thus became an English base for operations later against Quebec and Montreal.

The second largest British enterprise of the British in 1758 was an expedition against the French forts on Lake George and Lake Champlain, especially such strongholds as Ticonderoga and Crown Point. The distant objective was, through control of Lakes George and Champlain, a direct attack on the heart of New France at Montreal and Quebec.

For this enterprise, the British, under General Abercromby, as yet Commander-in-Chief, had large forces along the Hudson and the Mohawk, composed of British regulars, colonial Independent Companies, New England militia regiments, and potential Iroquois Indian allies. With seemingly overwhelming power the outcome looked highly favorable for the British-Americans. But such expectation was doomed to miserable failure. Confusion in organization and delay in operations was followed by rash attack on trenches and earthworks hurriedly prepared by the French some miles south of Fort Ticonderoga. British valor, involving the death of Lord Howe, broke in vain against French defense of the trenches. The defeat was more bloody and disastrous than that of Braddock two years earlier. Not only were the French not expelled from Lake George and Lake Champlain but all hopes of advancing against Montreal and Quebec in 1758 came to an abrupt end. It was after this battle that troops were assigned to Colonel Bradstreet. And not long afterward Abercromby was removed from his high command and replaced by General Jeffery Amherst.

Contributions to Success

A central theme of the history of the background of British-American triumph at the Forks of the Ohio two hundred years ago, is that of the contribution, both of the mother country and of her colonies, to the final and permanent result.

In this regard, it is obvious that the naval and military contribution of Great Britain to the French and Indian War in North America can only with the greatest difficulty be accurately evaluated. Statistics can be compiled about regiments, battalions, companies of British regulars who served in North America, and about warships, transports, and packet boats which sailed in North American waters. But such statistics are somewhat meaningless. They do not take into consideration that in both military and naval service, there was only fractional and temporary operation in America, nor do they weigh the fact that all such service anywhere in the world was a factor in North America.

If the matter of financial contribution is given consideration, the relative hopelessness of any specific and accurate conclusion is plainly evident to anyone at all familiar with extant source material on the subject. The expense of recruiting, training, and keeping in the field large bodies of soldiers was unbelievably heavy for that time. The cost of naval power and operations, while possibly less, was nevertheless enormous. From 1755 to 1763 the expense of Indian affairs was a heavy drain on the British Treasury. And the parliamentary assumption of part of the outlay and expenditure of the colonies ran into high figures.

A short study of such data is beyond treatment in a short article, but it is necessary to hold in mind that the taxpayer in Great Britain paid taxes equivalent to twenty per cent of individual incomes and that the debt of Britain rose to £140,000,000.

The Place of Forbes in History

The military campaign against Fort Duquesne in 1758 is regionally and locally tied in forever with the career of General John Forbes.[13] But for this campaign, his name would be known only in the realm of obscure military annals and personnel. Though he died early in 1759, he might well have said before his death what was actually exclaimed by a sickly stooped historian, editor, and archivist, who, when someone asked if he did not regret his condition, replied, "My life work is done."

Probably because of his intrinsic worth and not solely because he was a friend of Loudoun and Cumberland, Colonel John Forbes was appointed Brigadier General and put in command of the expedition against Fort Duquesne. Information about this reached Forbes in New York on March 4, 1758. It probably took two weeks to get the papers to Abercromby and for Forbes to receive his instructions from his new commander-in-chief. As it turned out, some of the preliminary steps had already been taken, in ordering Lieutenant Colonel Bouquet of the First Battalion of Royal Americans, February 14, 1758, to leave Charleston, South Carolina and embark for New York.

Immediately upon receipt of his instructions, General Forbes, from his headquarters in New York, began active preparation for his campaign. As did Braddock in 1755, he entered quickly upon correspondence with colonial governors. In a letter, March 20, 1758, to Governor William Denny of Pennsylvania, he asked for good soldiers, carpenters, light horsemen, workers on the roads, rangers, spies, and numbers of militia to be expected from Pennsylvania. Another letter, three days later, to Denny inquired about the necessary wagons and carriages.

A similar letter of March 21, 1758, to Governor Arthur Dobbs of North Carolina, mentioned the necessity of good troops but commented more fully on Cherokee Indians expected to be added to his forces. A letter of the same type and purport was sent on the same day to Governor Horatio Sharpe of Maryland whose unfavorable report on Maryland politics and troops was answered from New York, April 4, 1758. His month in New York, March 20 - April 19, was not wasted by General Forbes. He had to wind up his affairs with Lord Loudoun and get his arrangements with Abercromby established. Under the latter's orders he moved to Philadelphia in April.

In Philadelphia, Forbes quickly became involved in difficulty by reason of party strife in Pennsylvania about finance, prerogative, and other matters.

For two months and a half, Forbes was compelled to remain in Philadelphia. His situation was not unlike that of Loudoun in New

York in the late summer of 1756. Like Caesar in Gaul, Forbes had to do all things at one time. Troops, supplies, and money had to be secured and properly organized, not only in Pennsylvania, but also in Maryland, Virginia, and North Carolina. His physical condition was already poor and the enormous difficulties of circumstances of many unfavorable kinds must have further worn him down. It is a wonder that with so many difficulties he eventually "reached the stars."

In a letter to Pitt, May 1, 1758, Forbes outlined his progress and his plans and expectations. Already he had from Pennsylvania prospects of £100,000 and 2,700 provincial troops, with an addition of 300 troops from the three lower counties. From Maryland he had expectations of a few troops and a little money. Virginia had voted to raise its troops to two thousand men and to garrison its own frontier forts. Forbes was wrongly skeptical about Virginia's ability to meet her promises, but Washington's First Virginia Regiment was destined to be augmented by the Second Virginia Regiment, nominally under Colonel William Byrd III, but then being organized by Lieutenant Colonel George Mercer.[14] From North Carolina he expected nothing for his particular campaign but here again he was unduly pessimistic.

Of the "Regular Forces" destined for his use, he mentioned thirteen companies of Montgomery's Highlanders and four companies of the first battalion of the Royal American Regiment, but, at the time, a total of only about 1,600 men. And of seventeen companies, ten companies of the Highlanders had not yet arrived from South Carolina, three had arrived but were sickly, and the four companies of the Royal Americans had just arrived in Philadelphia in very bad health. The situation in regard to artillery, arms, and tents was much worse. They had not yet arrived. Forbes reported 652 southern Indians as already at Winchester whither they had been led by Colonel William Byrd III. Forbes proposed to utilize his time by moving supplies fifty or sixty miles beyond the inhabited parts of Pennsylvania. Possibly in connection with this proposal, he advertised in the newspaper for wagons.

In May, Forbes began to dispatch troops to the frontier, sending forward seven companies of regulars and, though his artillery, arms, and tents had not arrived, by May 19 he had gathered on the "back Frontiers" three months provision for 6,000 men. Already before the campaign was started, he was troubled about Indian policy and critical of the two superintendents, William Johnson and Edmund Atkins, for taking no steps in the matter.

General Forbes soon began to lean heavily upon his second in command, Colonel Henry Bouquet of the First Battalion of the Royal Americans, whom he had sent forward to Lancaster, on the latter's arrival in Philadelphia. The instructions of Forbes, May 20, 1758, to Bouquet at Lancaster, revealed his plan of campaign.

In language indicative not only of geographical information then widespread but of the unusual revelation of the relations of Forbes and Bouquet, Forbes wrote, "As I suppose you will march Col. Armstrong's Regt. to Fort Littleton and Loudoun, upon Mr. Burd's people coming to Carlisle so I fancy you will push both these regts. forward to Raes town, leaving at proper distances, escortes for the provision waggons, and carrying forward the 3 additional Companys of Highlanders to join the 4 American Companys at Carlisle whenever any of the provincialls are able to form a body at Lancaster." To which he added an incomplete sentence, "By which all our route will be in safety for Convoys and the head of one army formed at Raes town."[15] Late in May Forbes and Bouquet had decided to construct at Raystown not only a fort and storehouses but also a "General Hospital."

By the first of June, Forbes had already secured a large number of tents and some arms and next he saw the arrival at Philadelphia of the artillery for his army. And as early as the middle of June[16] he projected a survey of the road from Raystown over the mountains to the west. Only in the second week of June did Forbes see the arrival of Montgomery's Battalion of Highlanders and the store ship with needed supplies of many kinds. Not until this time, according to Forbes, did he have enough regulars to keep his "irregulars in due decency and order."

As indicated above, Forbes stayed in Philadelphia two and a half months. Criticism of him for this delay seems much out of place. Logistics and miracles are rarely bedfellows. It is doubtful that anyone could have done more or better.

Colonel Bouquet, who reached Carlisle May 24, remained there until about June 9. In command at the front, he faced problems almost as numerous and complex as those faced by Forbes in Philadelphia. A list of his problems would include: transportation, with its items of horses, wagons, drivers, and forages; the construction and repair of roads; the convoy and storage of supplies; the organization and equipping of troops; keeping of accounts; and decisions about plans for steady advance of the armed forces, regulars and provincials. An intriguing item of May and June 1758, was the collection of a dozen poor horses which had strayed from Braddock's expedition of 1755.

Bouquet left Carlisle on June 8 for Shippensburg and Fort Loudoun. Meanwhile on examination of routes west, he concluded that the worst of four had been chosen and quickly decided to open up a new one over the mountains. In the light of such unfavorable transportation, Bouquet recommended four future steps: such as, holding back troops until the post at Raystown was established; building up, there, stores for the remainder of the campaign; that Virginia cattle and flour come by a road to be opened up from Fort Cumberland to Raystown; and that hay be harvested at Raystown. Among other problems, Bouquet was bothered by a plague of rats at the posts and sporadic outbreaks of smallpox among the troops.

The situation, in June, of the colonial troops from Maryland, Virginia and North Carolina was as unfavorable as that of British regulars and Pennsylvania colonials along the roads from Philadelphia to Raystown. The Maryland legislature was unwilling to support its small force on the frontier, and Forbes, like his predecessors Braddock and Loudoun, had to assume responsibility for their maintenance with the prospect of using them only for garrisons at Fort Frederick and Fort Cumberland. Of the First Virginia Regiment of Colonel Washington, some companies had not reached Winchester before June, while six companies had been sent to Pennsylvania partly to work on badly needed road construction and repair, but partly because of the necessity of using provisions wanting in Winchester but available in Pennsylvania. Colonel William Byrd III and Lieutenant Colonel George Mercer had not yet fully organized the Second Virginia Regiment at Winchester. And though the Virginians ardently wished to advance by Fort Cumberland and over Braddock's Road it was realized by everyone that provisions were lacking at Fort Cumberland and could not be supplied until satisfactory roads could be constructed, along which Pennsylvania supplies could be forwarded to Fort Cumberland. The few hundred men from North Carolina, sent partly by water and partly overland, were without adequate equipment and supplies and had not arrived by June.

The chronology of June 1758 shows Colonel Bouquet at Fort

Loudoun holding a conference June 14 with Indians, brought north to aid in the campaign but already discontented and deserting though demanding presents before leaving. On the same day colonial Pennsylvania and Virginia companies were started from Fort Loudoun to Fort Littleton and Juniata Crossings. Two days later, June 16, Bouquet himself followed and reached Juniata Crossings before June 22, where under the supervision of Captain Harry Gordon, a fortification was begun. That forward movement was the order of the day is seen in the fact that Colonel Bouquet with Colonel James Burd's battalion of Pennsylvania colonials and some Virginia companies reached Raystown June 24, and immediately began the construction of a fort and storehouses. By the end of the month Washington's First Virginia Regiment was at Fort Cumberland, Byrd's Second Virginia Regiment was en route from Winchester to Fort Cumberland and the remaining Pennsylvania colonials, not essential to the security of forts and convoys, were ordered to Raystown. The last step of the month was to order the building of a road from Fort Cumberland to Raystown with parties working from both ends.

Early in July, General Forbes left Philadelphia, almost, as he had anticipated, the last person to leave, and reached Carlisle July 4. He immediately sent Highlanders and Pennsylvania provincials to Fort Littleton and Juniata Crossings with orders to troops already there to go on to Raystown.

During July, Forbes, frequently dangerously sick, remained at Carlisle and Colonel Bouquet maintained headquarters at Raystown, each with heavy responsibility and almost innumerable problems and difficulties. The intricacies of troop movements, supplies, and transportation were manifold and trouble about them inescapable. Hardly less important was the question of routes and roads. Disagreement and trouble about these appeared as early as June, but came to a head in July. A long article or small pamphlet would be needed for the details.[17]

The Route Dispute

Virginians wished Forbes, while drawing upon Pennsylvania supplies and imperial finances, to march west by way of Shippensburg, Fort Cumberland, and Braddock's Road to the Monongahela and Fort Duquesne. Forbes and Bouquet (and Pennsylvanians), probably not unmindful of Braddock's effort to cut a Pennsylvania road in 1755, finally decided to cross the Pennsylvania mountains to

Loyal Hannon and march directly to the Forks of the Ohio. Largely owing to the later renown of George Washington this dispute has remained, and bids fair to continue, a favorite historical theme. Most certainly the issue at stake was definitely two sided and commonly it is prejudged.

To the great astonishment of Colonel Bouquet and General Forbes, Sir John St. Clair, Quartermaster General recommended, June 11, 1758, the abandonment of the plan to move west from Raystown and proposed to divert the campaign by way of Fort Cumberland and Braddock's old road. On the following day, at Conococheague it was agreed that the Virginia and Maryland forces should march late in June to Fort Cumberland. But no decision was made about the route to be followed by the army from Raystown to Fort Duquesne.

From the standpoint of local history, somewhat antiquarian in outlook, the reports of spies, viewers, surveyors, and others sent out from Raystown and Fort Cumberland in July are of great interest and some historical importance.[18] These reports were not merely statements of Indians or trader scouts, but of army men such as Lieutenant Baker, Captain Clayton, Captain Edward Ward, Major George Armstrong, and Ensign Rhor.

In this same month of July, significant events occurred elsewhere in North America. General Abercromby, as stated above, was badly defeated near Ticonderoga, July 6-8. This was unexpected, for he had a greatly superior force. He was, of course, not without problems of personnel, coordination, organization, supplies, and transportation, but there seem to have been lack of leadership and defective tactics. The proposal made by Colonel John Bradstreet in late January that an attack be made by way of Oswego upon Frontenac was put in action in mid-summer. Troops to the number of 5,600 were sent up the Mohawk under General John Stanwix with 2,000 of whom General Stanwix would occupy Oneida and construct there a large fortress. The remaining 3,600 under Colonel Bradstreet were sent on against Frontenac.

It was late in July, after weeks of maneuvering, that General Amherst with a combined army and navy force captured the Fort at Louisbourg and took possession of Cape Breton Island, thus opening the way to later attacks on Quebec and Montreal.

News of these events did not reach General Forbes for weeks after their occurrence. As he wrestled with almost insuperable problems, he lamented that his expedition would, in attempted attainment of objectives, inevitably be the last of the season.

During early August, General Forbes, still often very ill, made his headquarters at Carlisle from which he kept in touch with his advanced forces, and wrestled with problems of army organization and movement, Indian relations, transportation, and supplies. The matter of forage for horses and cattle was most serious, as was also the matter of prices and payment of contractors. It was the middle of August before Forbes was able to leave Carlisle and then he was compelled to stop at Shippensburg where he was to remain for another month. Under such circumstances, he was very fortunate to have in command of his advanced forces Colonel Henry Bouquet, an officer of great administrative ability, featured by much tact, much resulting popularity, and, above all, unique trustworthiness. Throughout August Bouquet remained in or near Raystown superintending affairs there and along the road to the rear, but also engaged in the tasks of scouting the enemy at Fort Duquesne and starting heavy working parties to construct a military road over the mountain and as far as Laurel Ridge. In the face of discouraging circumstances, Forbes and Bouquet succeeded in getting 1,600 men (regulars, Pennsylvanians and Virginians) beyond the Allegheny Ridge by the middle of August. And they succeeded in getting heavy work from all concerned, save possibly the Indian allies, who seemed to care for neither work nor war, of the type undertaken.

Greatly to his credit, Bouquet was able to claim in late August, "I have established harmony between the different corps."[19]

Progress and change came in the last week of August. Forbes and Bouquet decided to send forward over Laurel Ridge and down to Loyal Hannon, before the road was yet completed, a force of 1,600 men under Colonel James Burd, with Major James Grant as adviser. The troops were composed of five companies of Highlanders, probably five companies of Burd's Battalion, six companies of Virginians under Adam Stephens, and a company or two of Royal Americans. Pack horses and bullocks were taken along. But, on an unfavorable report about the site at Loyal Hannon, the plans were changed and the movement delayed until August 30.

At the end of August it had been decided to have Colonel Washington, with what remained of the two Virginia regiments, advance to the Great Crossing by way of Braddock's Road. A Hobson's Choice was presented to Virginia and her regimental commanders,

COLONEL JAMES BURD

COLONEL HUGH MERCER

George Washington and William Byrd III. Neither at Winchester nor at Fort Cumberland were there adequate military equipment and provisions. There were wanting wagons, horses, salt meats, flour, tents, blankets, tools for road work, barrels, sacks, etc. The proposed movement was in reality a ruse and later was abandoned and the Virginia forces advanced to Raystown, Loyal Hannon, and Fort Duquesne along the new Forbes Road.

Late in August, Forbes himself moved west from Shippensburg, probably intending to join Bouquet at Raystown, but he got only as far as Fort Loudoun on the eastern slope of Tuscarora Mountain. It was also late in August that Colonel Bradstreet captured Frontenac and seized or destroyed an enormous mass of goods, including 60 cannon, 16 mortars, ammunition, furs, skins, 2,000 barrels of provisions, and 9 naval vessels.

Colonel James Burd and his forces crossed Laurel Ridge and by Sunday, September 3, arrived at Loyal Hannon. Work was immediately begun on fortification and storehouses. Colonel Burd seems to have selected the final site for such construction, but as will be brought out more fully below, by Mr. Charles Stotz in Part II, he was advised by the Chief Army Engineer, Ensign Charles Rhor, as well as by Captain Harry Gordon, J. C. Pleydell and Robert Dudgeon.

At this point, Loyal Hannon and beyond, attention will here be directed to matters more directly military and, indeed, almost political. Reports of scouts sent out in July and August seemed to reveal some weakness of the French at Fort Duquesne.

Major James Grant, in particular, advocated a hurried advance against the enemy. Probably he had support from the garrison at Loyal Hannon. On the arrival of Colonel Bouquet on September 7, 1758, his permission to make attack on the enemy was sought. The motives in giving such permission are historically uncertain, a matter of mere speculation, though he claimed it was an offensive defensive movement intended to stop Indian attacks.

Grant marched from Loyal Hannon September 9, 1758, and from the advanced post September 11, 1758, with 37 officers and 805 men. After a two days march he reached the neighborhood of Fort Duquesne.

A day was spent in reconnoitering and maneuvering without detection by the French and Indians. Then early on September 14, 1758 a piecemeal spasmodic attack was begun but quickly frustrated and followed by organized French attack upon the British-American forces with heavy losses to the latter. The exact statistics may never be determined, but probably the casualties exceeded 300, or about one-third of the total forces under Major Grant. Those who escaped from the battlefield straggled slowly back to Loyal Hannon.[20]

The outcome of Major Grant's raid was greatly distressing not only to Grant and his officers but to Burd, Bouquet and Forbes. It probably delayed for a full month the later and final advance. It also probably encouraged the enemy to make a counterattack in an assault upon Fort Loyal Hannon a month later, October 12, 1758. In what seems like apology Bouquet claimed that the victory of the French at Grant's defeat possibly made it difficult for the French to keep their Indians at Fort Duquesne, and Joseph Shippen stated, "The Troops now Breathe nothing but revenge and are in high Spirits." Such after-thoughts were not without logic and validity.[21]

The Battle of Loyalhanna, October 12, 1758, came almost in the middle of the two months stay of Colonel Burd at Loyal Hannon. As just stated, it was in the nature of a revengeful counterattack after Grant's defeat a month earlier. But it was more than that. Fort Frontenac was captured in late August. Future provisions and supplies from Canada could not be expected. The Indians, always restless, had either gone or were getting ready to depart. One final effort to stop the British-American forces was a last resort. It was another offensive defensive, this time by the French.

Since some writers have expressed the judgment that this was the great battle of the campaign, attention to its features must be given, for though somewhat episodical it may have been the straw which broke the camel's back.

According to Burd's report to Bouquet, this attack began with the firing of twelve guns at eleven o'clock in the morning. Underestimating the number of the enemy, Burd sent out two parties to surround them, but on the increase in the gunfire sent out 500 men to support them only to have them driven back into the camp. The ruse of the attackers partly succeeded and they followed up the initial success with a two hour attack. But, greatly outnumbered, the attackers were driven back. The effective use of artillery played a role. The casualties of the British-Americans were small, involving only five officers and sixty-two men. The French losses were likewise small and they remained in the neighborhood during the night, though under artillery fire from the fort.[22]

Accounts of the battle vary greatly. It is certain from the French documents that the commander of the attack was Charles Phillipe Aubry, an officer of troops from the Illinois country, and not "M. de Vetri" as stated in English accounts. It is probable also that the number of the attackers was as stated by de Ligneris, four hundred and forty French and one hundred and fifty Indians, a total of less than half of the number estimated by Burd and others.

In many ways the battle was short of glorious. Forbes was not satisfied. He thought it should have been followed by immediate counterattack. But it is historically undeniable that the outcome dispirited the French and Indians, rendered the camp at Loyal Hannon safe from further assault, and enabled Forbes and his subordinates to make, with little danger, the final march to Fort Duquesne.

September and October 1758 were taken up by Forbes and his subordinates in working on the road and getting forward to Loyal Hannon troops and the necessary equipment and supplies for them. The weather slowly became wintry. Life was disagreeable and discouraging. The clergymen with the Pennsylvania troops, the Reverends Charles Beatty, Andrew Bey, and John Steele, probably found much place for themselves in giving both encouragement and admonition.

It was on November 2, 1758 that General Forbes arrived at Loyal Hannon. Bouquet probably had already written out plans for the immediate future. Two centuries later it seems unbelievable that he should have proposed an approach to Fort Duquesne by water, along the Loyalhanna, the Conemaugh, the Kiskiminetas, and the Allegheny, a scheme which did not meet the approval of George Washington.[23]

At an important council of war, November 11, 1758, the arguments for and against advancing were set forth and the conclusion reached that the risks of advance were greater than the advantages and there was "no doubt as to the sole course that prudence" dictated.[24]

But on the following day the situation was profoundly changed. In repelling a desultory attack upon the post, aimed possibly at horses and cattle, a few prisoners were taken. Under insistent pressure, a prisoner revealed the desperate situation at Fort Duquesne where Indian allies had gone off, provisions were nearly exhausted, and most of the regular troops had been sent away down the Ohio or up the Allegheny. With a slight break in the weather, it was quickly decided to advance against Fort Duquesne. But that pessimism remained as late as the evening of November 16, 1758, was revealed in the answers of two engineers to questions asked by the colonels of Forbes' regiments. The answers indicated the difficulty, if not relative impossibility, of holding Loyal Hannon through the ensuing winter.[25] An attempt to eliminate the French was thus necessitated by circumstances as well as desirable as an accomplishment.

While the correspondence and the field reports of the days of the march are limited both in quantity and definiteness, the surviving orderly books of Forbes, Bouquet, Washington, and Joseph Shippen furnish adequate information.

General Forbes, November 14, 1758, divided the marching forces of his army into three bodies or brigades, commanded by Colonels Bouquet, Montgomery, and Washington. These officers were to act as brigadiers, receiving all reports and giving orders regarding their respective divisions or brigades. This order made Bouquet, Montgomery, and Washington acting brigadier generals for the remainder of the campaign, though at its end they reverted to the rank of colonel.

To Washington was assigned the right wing or northern end of the advancing forces. Under him were placed the First Virginia Regiment, two Companies of Artificers, the North Carolinians, the Marylanders, and the force from the Lower Counties (Delaware).

The center was put under Montgomery who had under him his own Highlanders and the Second Virginia Regiment.

The left or southern wing was put under Bouquet commanding three battalions of Pennsylvanians and the First Battalion of Royal Americans.

A reserve of 200 Highlanders, 200 of the Second Virginia Regiment and 200 Pennsylvanians was left behind under Colonel James Burd.

By these orders Washington was supposed to march on the morning of November 15, 1758, Montgomery at one o'clock and Bouquet's division gotten ready at eight o'clock at farthest. The commanders were ordered to draw provisions for eight days and meat for four days, driving cattle with them to complete the eight days' allowance.[26]

Since no orders dated November 15, 1758 have been found, it is presumed that the day was taken up in getting away from Loyal Hannon and forward to Chestnut Ridge.

From the Camp at Chestnut Ridge, an order was issued to the two companies of Artificers covered by the second division of the First Virginia Regiment to begin opening the road at daybreak, leaving behind their baggage to be brought up by the line marching behind.[27]

The forces reached Bushy Run, November 16, 1758, Bullock Camp November 17, New Camp November 18, Turtle Creek November 19, and Washington's Camp November 20. On the last date, Washington's forces were ordered to march at daybreak, November 21, 1758, and open the road forward to the Old Path, probably a reference to the old Traders Path. On November 20, one hundred North Carolinians and Marylanders were detached and sent toward Fort Duquesne to make discoveries.

By general order the army was marched in three columns at seven o'clock November 22, 1758, the first brigade to cover operations and carry a small proportion of the axes, the second brigade to open the road, and the third brigade to bring on the train of artillery. By general orders from Camp Cross Turtle Creek, November 22, 1758, the same order of march was continued, and the advance seems to have reached Bouquet's Camp at the end of November 23, 1758.

An interesting item of November 24, 1758 pronounced dogs a nuisance and ordered that if not sent to the rear they should be shot. At Bouquet's Camp, November 24, 1758 occurred a reversal of the roles of the first and third divisions. There it was decided that the first brigade (of Washington) was to be on the left and the third brigade (of Bouquet) on the right.

According to a letter of Bouquet to William Allen, November 24, 1758, the army spent the day in camp, not without anxiety. But late in the day an Indian scout reported that from a great distance he had seen much smoke at Fort Duquesne, indicating a great destruction by fire. A fuller report by another scout indicated that the French had abandoned Fort Duquesne and all immediate regional opposition to the rolling advance of the British-American forces. A troop of light horse was sent to the smoldering ruins during the night of November 24, 1758, but the army, held back in reserve, marched down upon the famous point and reached its great objective at six o'clock p.m., November 25, 1758.[28]

For two centuries commentators have remarked that final victory came to General Forbes and to his weary troops by default of the French rather than by the outcome of conflict in one great dramatic battle. This can hardly be denied, but it can be admitted with pride rather than shame. Historically the success of innumerable expeditions, campaigns, and wars has been similarly undramatic. It was undeniable in late 1758 and it is still undeniable two centuries later that unlike the unfortunate expeditions, in the same area, of Washington in 1754 and of Braddock in 1755, the campaign of Forbes in 1758 was in character and in final result a distinct success.

Significances in the account of the campaign were many and varied. One of these was the unusual, though uneasy, co-operation of the colonies with the imperial effort. About four-fifths of the forces were colonial militia. Superb work was necessary to establish and maintain any unity of effort and the regional responsibility fell mainly upon Forbes and Bouquet.

Highly significant was the laying out, establishment, and maintenance of roads. Earlier roads from Philadelphia to Lancaster, and thence to Carlisle or to York and from there to Shippensburg were in existence. And in 1755 a road had been laid out from the east as far west as the Allegheny Ridge; and various Indian trails or traders paths to the Ohio Valley were known and in use. But wagon roads were necessary. They were projected from Shippensburg to Winchester and Fort Cumberland, from Fort Frederick, Maryland to Fort Cumberland, from Shippensburg to Fort Loudoun and Fort Littleton and on to Raystown, or Bedford for later years, from Raystown to Fort Cumberland, and above all from Raystown west over three high mountain ridges, Allegheny, Laurel, and Chestnut. No one who has travelled over the old road from Fort Loudoun, across Tuscarora Mountain, up Sideling Hill, up the Allegheny Ridge and up and down Laurel Mountain can be unaware of the heroic work of getting the troops and supplies of Forbes to and beyond Loyal Hannon. In language applicable to other ridges, Forbes properly called Laurel Hill, "that Bugbear." The importance of this transportation success or, if one prefers, victory, is best stated in the words of Bouquet writing August 20, 1758, to Forbes, saying in regard to roadbuilding workmen, "Everyone is contented, and believes himself immortalized by having worked to open this route,"[29] a statement somewhat weakened by the well-known fact that leaders of some of the Virginia colonies working on the road preferred another route.

As stated above, another significant aspect of the campaign was the relationship of Forbes and Bouquet, a chain of understanding weakened possibly, but not broken by the episode of Grant's expedition and defeat. Without this understanding and the amazing success of Bouquet's operations, final victory by Forbes in 1758 was unlikely.

The significance of the individual importance of General Forbes is easily underestimated. Only his sickness was dramatic, but his efforts and accomplishments, from first to last, were noteworthy. Probably the best testimony is that of Colonel Bouquet, who as early as June, complimented him on his success in getting aid from Pennsylvania. In sundry letters of late November 1758, Bouquet gave credit to Forbes, in such remarks as "The glory of our success must after God be allowed to our General." Particular credit was given by Bouquet to Forbes for his Indian policy consummated in the Treaty of Easton and featured by the trips to the Ohio Valley made by Christian Frederick Post. Historically sound in later centuries is the remark of Bouquet, "His prudence in all his measures, in numberless difficulties he had to surmount, deserves the highest praise."[30]

The final, great significance of the campaign was what Bouquet called "the immense advantage of this important acquisition." The control of the gateway to the middle west was attained and destined to remain relatively secure for all later time.

Pittsburgh occupies one of the most beautiful spots in the world. Bouquet saw this, saying November 25, 1758, that when he reached Philadelphia he wished to talk "chiefly about the beauty of this situation which appears to me beyond my description,"[31] a statement which can be accepted by others who like Bouquet have known the Alps and the Rhine.

Results of the Decision

The aftermath of final decision at the Forks in late November, 1758 was anticipated by many in high and low status. Old World British commanders, British-American colonials, and native Indians, alike, foresaw probable developments in the years immediately following. General Forbes, Colonel Bouquet and others recognized quickly that establishments made in the upper Ohio valley would likely be permanent. Such recognition was in the face of temporarily bad conditions.

Though he called it small, the relatively large army of Forbes could not be retained on the Ohio, but short of provisions and shelter, had to be marched back to the east, leaving a weak force at the Point. Most of the provincials in the army returned quietly but quickly to civilian life. The Highlanders and Royal Americans were marched and counter marched along the road to Carlisle and Philadelphia.

As is more fully brought out in the following material, only a few hundred provincials were left at the Point under Colonel Hugh Mercer of the Pennsylvania Regiment. Shelter and supplies, even for so small a force, were matters of difficulty. Shelter was eventually provided, largely in the construction of a new fort, the third of five, in turn, at the place.

It was realized that French forces with Indian allies, were still located at Venango, Le Boeuf, Presque Isle, Niagara and elsewhere. The attempt to recapture the Point was greatly feared by Colonel Mercer and his small garrison. As is brought out by Mr. Stotz the risk was eliminated by events at Quebec and Niagara in 1759.

The problem of ownership of the Point was not settled in 1758 nor for almost a generation. The Indians wanted and expected the departure of French and British alike. When disillusioned, they resorted to warfare under the able leadership of Pontiac with no little early success, but with eventual and probably inevitable failure.

Possibly the most lasting effect of the decision at the Forks of the Ohio, was the breach in the dam against settlement, a final result of which was the eager and later quick occupation of the entire Ohio Valley.

DEFENSE
IN THE WILDERNESS

CHARLES MORSE STOTZ

DEFENSE IN THE WILDERNESS

Two hundred years ago this November twenty-fifth a travel-worn English army occupied the Forks of the Ohio. Their ailing commander, General John Forbes, viewed from his litter the smoldering ruins of Fort Duquesne. The monumental landscape of hill, forest and water may not have moved him, but the acrid smoke from the fallen French stronghold must have been perfume to his nose. Braddock's defeat that had so shaken England had been avenged. Before him the Ohio's waters streamed westward to the vast inland basin; England now controlled them. Whatever solace this may have been to a weary and sick man, his first concern had to be with the perils and labors that lay immediately ahead. To a practical Scot and a soldier, first things must come first.

He named the place Pittsburgh as a gesture of recognition for that ungainly master strategist who from his desk in London had ordered the seizure of this vital little triangle. Next, he must get the bulk of his more than 6,000 ragged weary men back over the mountains before they starved to death. And, finally, he must make secure his triumph for his King by building a stronghold at the Point. He ordered 250 men to remain at the Forks for this purpose, this number being all he could "possibly maintain during the Winter, considering 400 miles of land carriage thro an immense Wilderness, and the worst roads in the world."[1]

This was not to be the usual frontier fort of earthwork and timbers but a solid, massive construction worthy of its need. Such a fort he knew would require yet another conquest of the mountains to bring the supplies and materials to the remote wilderness site and would require at least a year or two to build. In the meantime a temporary fort must be built without delay, taking advantage of the winter season, to prepare for the inevitable attack by the French whose forces lay but a few days journey up the Allegheny. Having thus well served his King, Iron Head, as Forbes was known to the Indians, returned with his troops over the mountains. He must then have known he was a doomed man, for he died three months later from the illness which he had endured with such fortitude.

In the four years before this event two forts had been built at the Point and each in turn had been taken and destroyed. These were the English Fort Prince George and the French Fort Duquesne. Within the three years which followed this event, two more forts were to be built at the Point by the English, neither of which was destined to be taken in battle or siege. These were the temporary Mercer's Fort and Fort Pitt, the most elaborate work of the English military engineers in America to that time. A fifth fort, Fort Fayette, of less consequence to history or the art of fortification, was built a full generation later, by the forces of the young United States, a short distance from the Point on the Allegheny River.

This article is largely concerned with the first four of these forts. To understand fully the reason for their creation and their physical character, a consideration of the background against which they were built is presented in the following three sections. Part One, *Setting of the Stage,* deals with the disposition of the French and English in North America in the mid-eighteenth century, the influence of geographic conditions on the natural routes of travel and a brief mention of the principal forts in the country. Part Two, *Defense in Depth,* tells of the evolution of the frontier fort and gives a working knowledge of fort design and construction. Part Three, *Challenge of the Wilderness,* based chiefly on the Forbes campaign, describes how the forts were serviced and includes road construction, problems of transportation, the soldier and his equipment and the nature of life in the outpost garrisons. Part Four continues with the establishment of the five forts at the Point, their design and construction, the purposes they served and something of the life in and about them.

There will frequently appear in these pages the names of military engineers and their assistants who worked in western Pennsylvania. While the records provide scant information about most of them, one, Captain Harry Gordon, engineer and builder of Fort Pitt, stands out as a figure to rank with General John Forbes and Colonel Henry Bouquet. He served and fought with Braddock and Forbes and looms large in local affairs until he succeeded Colonel Eyre in 1764 as chief engineer in America, and was raised from the rank of captain to lieutenant colonel. He often risked his life in battle. He earned the affection and praise of his officers and his men for his conduct and dedicated effort. It would therefore seem fitting to dedicate to Captain Harry Gordon this brief account of the forts he served so faithfully.

I. SETTING OF THE STAGE

ON a May morning in 1754, a group of French soldiers who had spent the night in a glen on Chestnut Ridge were preparing to break camp. They were suddenly surprised by an outburst of gunfire from the rocky ledges above them. The leader, Joseph Coulon de Jumonville, and a number of his companions were killed. The twenty-two year old Virginia colonel, George Washington, had won his first battle and the first blood had been shed in the French and Indian War. The more than two hundred years that have passed since this event is a short time in the total span of history but a long time when measured by the brief span of a man's life. Voltaire, in 1754, was a man of 60, Samuel Johnson in England was 45 years old and Goethe was but five. Bach had died only four years before and Mozart was to be born two years later.

Eastern North America in the mid-eighteenth century was the stage upon which England and France appeared as actors in this drama of conflict. Viewed in retrospect, the French and Indian War seems a picturesque episode in history. The contemporary records show it to have been a grim succession of fortuitous successes and blunders. Armies trained in Europe and accustomed to fighting in familiar open country were combined with provincial troops whose greater familiarity with wilderness conditions was offset by lack of discipline and co-ordination. To the herculean labors of organizing, supplying and moving troops through little known country was added the hazard of successful dealing with the Indians, whether as enemies or allies. Another actor in this drama, the trader, had preceded the soldier into the remote Indian lands and had made the Indian dependent on the white man's weapons and trade goods. With the trader went the French priest and, to a lesser extent, the English missionary. These vanguards of the white invaders very much complicated relations between white man and Indian, though they carried valuable information to the military leaders. In spite of the endless pow-wows, treaties and giving of presents, the rights of the native owners were largely ignored. As another people centuries before had been dispossessed by seekers after a promised land, so the Indians succumbed to a race that considered America its birthright.

The Character Behind the Scenes

Still another character, the settler, must be considered. In fact, he was the primary instigator of the piece and, after all the other actors had gone, remained to occupy the center of the stage. At first he lingered behind the scenes while his fellow countrymen, wittingly or not, made a place for him. The enemies of the French were the English, but the Indians, from the first, recognized the settlers as the villains to be dealt with. The Frenchman was their friend. For almost a century the Indians had permitted the French to establish their far-flung missions and trading posts throughout the vast inland country. The French understood the Indians' traits, plied them with the King's presents, learned their language, baptized and even intermarried with them. If the trade goods of the French were more costly than those of the English and even inferior in variety and quality, the French gave no material signs of intending to occupy the Indian lands by settlement. "They excited no jealousy and gained the affections of an ignorant, credulous but brave people, whose ruling passions are independence, gratitude, and revenge."[2] The French could readily cement the allegiance of the Indians by pointing to the English interlopers who had entered the forbidden area and the many more poised on the eastern slopes of the Appalachians, biding their time until they could occupy the rich Ohio country. These people who were to establish the civilization of our district are thus described by the author in his *The Early Architecture of Western Pennsylvania*: "Throughout the whole turbulent period, in spite of wars and governmental decrees against settlement, the [English] settler was stubbornly taking personal and permanent possession of the land, blazing his property without authority, and establishing a 'tomahawk claim' when he could get no better title. The Indians, who viewed the trader with suspicion and frequently regarded the soldier and government agent with distrust, heard with consternation the sound of the frontiersman's axe and rifle echoing through their forests. Here were the actual destroyers and usurpers of the Indian's shelter and game. Here were men, and women, too, schooled to hardship and suffering, who knew the ways of the forest and forest warfare and who, in their deep-rooted desire for permanent home sites, could not understand the Indian's right to land that he did nothing to develop. In successive waves they advanced the frontier and entrenched themselves upon the land. Making fortresses of their homes and putting little faith in poorly trained frontier armies, they relied on their own vigilance and marksmanship for protection. As Theodore Roosevelt graphically described them, they were 'a grim, stern people . . . swayed by gusts of stormy passion, the love of freedom rooted in their very hearts' core'."[3]

Goaded on by the French, the Indians harassed the communications to the forts and the frontier settlements of the English in a war which, if not involving large numbers, was of harrowing character. The Indian allies were of vital importance to the French in all of their military engagements, including those against Washington at Fort Necessity, Braddock on the Monongahela, Grant at the Point and the Forbes army at Ligonier. For this aid, the Indians received little reward beyond the pillage of the defeated troops and the satisfaction of venting their racial frustration on the miserable ones who fell into their hands.

Nevertheless, the English built their frontier forts primarily as defense of the territory against the French, not against the Indians. True, these forts were useful as places of refuge in time of Indian raids, but the decisive actions against the Indians were won on the Indian's terms. Bushy Run, Fallen Timbers and other such engagements were fought in the open where each tree was a fort and each fallen log a shelter. Commandants were ordered not to waste the cannon fire of their forts on the Indians. In Pontiac's War many forts were taken by the Indians by trickery or force of numbers or fire arrows, but the simplest palisade, if well garrisoned and supplied, was adequate protection. The rude earth and log fortifications of Fort Ligonier and Fort Detroit sustained the attacks of the Indians in 1763 with little more difficulty than formidable Fort Pitt. As a matter of fact Ecuyer complained that the "extensive and Open works" of Fort Pitt required "more Men than would otherwise be necessary against an Enemy [the Indian] who has no Chance but by Surprise."[4]

Natural and Human Barriers

Illustration 1 is an outline drawing of eastern North America with the salient geographic features that determined the routes of travel and consequently the location of the French and English forts. The most significant feature is the densely forested Appalachian system reaching southwesterly from Canada almost to the Gulf of Mexico. This range is composed of a series of parallel ridges, seen from a plane as furrows in a plowed field, with the highest moun-

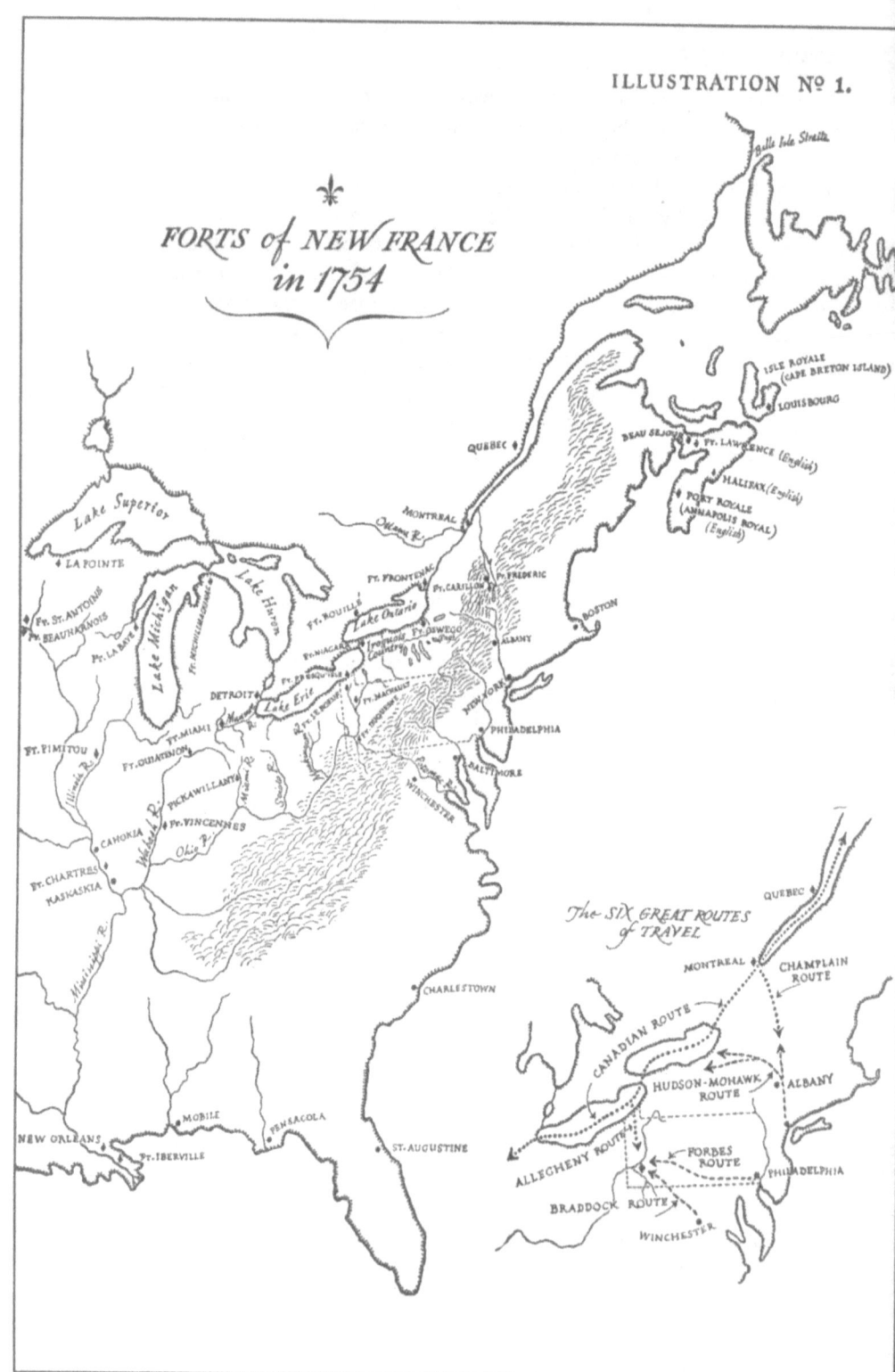

DEFENSE IN THE WILDERNESS 65

tains in its northern and southern extremities. These mountains were a formidable barrier to travel not because of their height but by reason of their great extent from east to west. From the first to the last ridge in Pennsylvania is a distance of sixty miles.

It is important to note that there were only two navigable water routes which passed through this great mass of mountains. The first was the Hudson River Valley and its northern extension through Lake George, Lake Champlain and the Richelieu River to the St. Lawrence River. The Indians had long recognized the strategic value of this route; in fact, the Indian name for Lake Champlain meant "gateway to the country." The second water route was the Mohawk River, a westerly tributary of the Hudson. This strategic route of travel, joining the lakes to the ocean, was used by the natives from prehistoric times. It was only natural, therefore, that the dominant Indians, the Six Nations or Iroquois, should have occupied the Mohawk valley and the country south of Lake Ontario. Their influence reached well beyond this area; the Indians in the Ohio country were their vassals. These able warriors, who controlled the natural access to the interior country, constituted a barrier as difficult to surmount as the mountains themselves. French and English alike sought their allegiance. Traditionally hostile to the French and their Canadian Indian allies since the days of Champlain, the Iroquois were not always on the side of the English, but their presence as a buffer force was a serious deterrent to the French.

The English and French Lands

Between the Appalachian Range and the Atlantic Ocean lay a strip of relatively level seaboard land, fertile, of good climate and well supplied with harbors and navigable streams. This area was occupied by some 1,250,000 English inhabitants, many of whom had settled on the eastern slopes of the mountains. They were divided into thirteen colonies, disunited and dissentious, lacking a trained army and strangely slow to grasp the realities of the problems which arose beyond the mountains. They were contemptuous of the French to the north, west, and south whom they outnumbered almost 15 to 1. The agriculture, industry and general prosperity of the English far exceeded anything in New France.

In contrast to the narrow string of English settlement by the sea, the French possessions north and west of the Appalachian Range swung in a great arc from the Gulf of St. Lawrence through the

St. Lawrence River, the Great Lakes, the Illinois country and the Mississippi River to the Gulf of Mexico, an almost continuous water route three thousand leagues in length. The colonies of Canada and Louisiana were not self-supporting and constituted a serious yearly drain on the resources of France. The severe Canadian climate afforded only a brief growing season and agriculture in Louisiana was poorly developed. To remedy this condition, it was planned to make the fertile farm and grazing lands of the centrally located Illinois country the "bread basket" of New France. But the exhortations and threats of the government failed to persuade the people of France to settle the Illinois lands or elsewhere in the new world in adequate numbers to provide any semblance of competition with the English colonies.

However, France was the leading naval and land power of the world and maintained in Canada a seasoned fighting force of great mobility and singleness of direction, well beyond anything the English colonies could muster. Though the leaders of the French in America were dependent on court favor and were riddled with graft and corruption, they dreamed fondly of a great New France and laid their plans to overcome the many obstacles to its accomplishment. France viewed her possessions in the new world as a potential, if not proven, asset of great value in the race with England for a world empire. Thus these European rivals, who were almost continuously at war on the continent, shared the ownership of eastern North America. Each recognized the land rights of the other until certain areas of friction developed in the early eighteenth century, among which was control of the vital entry to the Gulf of St. Lawrence, the northern extremity of the Canadian Route.

The Canadian Route

Illustration 1 shows the vast lands of New France in relation to the seaboard possessions of England. This map shows the important French forts existing in 1754 but only those English forts in Nova Scotia. When Acadia was ceded by France in 1713, English troops occupied Port Royale and renamed it Annapolis Royal and the land Nova Scotia. Halifax was not founded until 1749. Acadia was one of the few flourishing agricultural communities of New France and its people unwilling subjects of the British king. After years of passive resistance, the French built Fort Beau Sejour in 1750 on the disputed land at the head of the Bay of Fundy. At the same time the British erected Fort Lawrence a short distance away from the French fort. Beau Sejour was taken in 1755 and renamed Fort Cumberland.

The fortified city and harbor of Louisbourg on Isle Royale (Cape Breton Island) was the base for French naval power in America and guarded the entrance to the Gulf of St. Lawrence. Built in 1720, Louisbourg was in British hands from 1745 to 1748. The English, well aware that Canada depended upon supplies brought from France, made this a prime objective and retook Louisbourg in 1758. The loss of this key stronghold, together with the fall of French Fort Frontenac in the same year, had a profound bearing on subsequent events at the Forks of the Ohio.

The first fort was built at Quebec, the capital of New France, in 1541. The fortifications of this beautiful city of large buildings and churches were greatly strengthened in 1749. It fell in 1759. Montreal, an island city encircled by bastioned ramparts with a powerful battery mounted on a hill in the center, was taken in 1760.

Proceeding up the St. Lawrence River past minor posts such as La Galette we come to Fort Cataraqui or Frontenac (the site of modern Kingston), the shipbuilding and supply base for navigation on the Great Lakes. Valuable supplies destined for Fort Duquesne, together with nine ships, were seized here when it was captured by the British in late August of 1758. Of equal importance was Fort Niagara, blocking entrance to Lake Erie. La Salle built a trading post and mission here in 1679 which was replaced with a small stone fort in 1726. The siege of Niagara in 1759 brought about the recall of a large French army assembled at Venango (modern Franklin) and poised to strike the temporary Mercer's Fort at Pittsburgh. This army was ambushed and destroyed on their return and Niagara fell to the English. A smaller fort, Little Niagara, defended the portage road around the falls, and in the river above the falls there were boatyards and wharves.

There was a small post on Lake Erie at the mouth of the Sandusky River. Fort Detroit, founded by Cadillac in 1701, served as a trading post and guardian of the routes to the Illinois country as well as the western lakes. It was taken by Rogers' Rangers in 1760. The western post of Michilimackinac and the forts of the Illinois country and the Mississippi are shown on the map but are not discussed as they are not relevant to this article. Except for Fort Chartres on the Mississippi and Fort Vincennes on the Wabash, these were trading centers and missions, largely established in the seventeenth century.

The Champlain Route

This route may be considered as a southerly branch of the Canadian Route with forts guarding the natural British approach. (See Illustration 2, inside back cover.) The route from the St. Lawrence River to Lake Champlain led up the Richelieu River, past Fort Chambly, to Fort St. Jean at the northern end of Lake Champlain. The southern end of the lake was protected by Fort Frederic, a trim stone structure built in 1731, rebuilt in 1734 and enlarged in 1742. Upon its evacuation in 1759, the English destroyed it and built Fort Crown Point on adjacent land. A short distance to the south, the French built Fort Carillon to guard the entrance to Lake Sacrament (George). First built of horizontal log walls in 1756, it was rebuilt in stone the next year. The first English attack in 1758 was disastrously repulsed but in July of 1759 the English took the fort, renaming it Ticonderoga.

The Hudson-Mohawk Route

This route constituted the defense against penetration from Canada. Raiding parties of the French and Indians had at one time reached down to the well fortified city of Albany, which, like Schenectady, was established in 1695. As shown inside back cover, Half Moon was built on the Hudson River at its junction with the Mohawk, and Saratoga just above this point. In 1756 Fort Edward was built near the headwaters of the Hudson and Fort William Henry at the southern end of Lake George. The latter fort was captured and destroyed by Montcalm in 1757. Fort George was constructed by the English in 1759 near the same site.

There were a number of minor posts on the Mohawk River, as well as Fort Herkimer, built in 1756, Fort Stanwix, built in 1758, and a fort at Oneida Lake. More important than any of these, however, was Fort Oswego built in 1722 on Lake Ontario, at the mouth of the Oswego River. This post, viewed by the French as a threat to their lake navigation, was an important trading center which enjoyed a degree of protection by its location in the Iroquois country. While at first the French gained access to the western lakes by the Ottawa River and Georgian Bay, the focus of interest turned on the Ohio country in the forties, when Canada realized this post was a threat to their life line. Montcalm was determined to destroy Oswego, which he did in 1756 and carried away the garrison as prisoners. A new fort was built there in 1759 by the English. Fort Ontario, on the opposite bank of the Oswego River, was built in 1763.

The war for ownership of America developed from conflicting claims to ownership of the lands at the headwaters of the Ohio. This area, which had been largely ignored by both French and English during the preceding half century, came into abrupt and sharp focus in the 1730's. Furthermore, the ownership of these lands was vital to France to protect her Canadian life line and to control the inland basin to which the broad, placid Ohio provided a great natural highway unequaled in America. From the head waters of the Ohio, the Allegheny River reached northward almost to Lake Erie which lay on the long established lake route of the French to the Illinois country. The French were thus provided with an additional access to the interior by the Allegheny Route, a southerly branch of the Canadian Route discussed above.

The Allegheny Route

The exploratory expedition of Longueuil in 1739 and that of Céloron in 1749 to formally claim the land, had proceeded by way of the portage from Lake Erie to Chautauqua Lake, thence by way of Conewango Creek to the Allegheny. In these trips no forts had been built, but the French had learned that no time was to be lost in ousting the English traders and in circumventing the plans of the Ohio Company to build a fort at the Forks of the Ohio. One might liken these Forks to an arrow pointing at the heart of the French country, a dramatic accident of geography.

In 1753 a large force under Marin discovered a better route, landing at Presqu'Isle (modern Erie) where they built a fort and developed a portage road to Lake Le Boeuf (modern Waterford) where another fort was built in the same year. The following year Fort Machault was built at Venango (modern Franklin) and following the capture of Fort Prince George, the French built Fort Duquesne at the Forks of the Ohio. Thus for the first four years, the civilization on the site of Pittsburgh was French. However apparent it now may be to us that the scales of destiny were balanced against her, France then had little doubt of her ability eventually to consolidate this new settlement with other possessions of her embryo inland empire. This hope ended when Duquesne fell in 1758.

Machault, Le Boeuf and Presqu'Isle were abandoned in 1759, following the disasters at Niagara and Quebec.

The Braddock Route

Although the Monongahela River reached southwards into Virginia and its tributary, the Youghiogheny River, lay just over the mountain from Will's Creek, these streams provided no aid to Braddock. The Youghiogheny was not navigable. The alternate route from Laurel Hill to Redstone Creek and thence down the Monongahela was not considered. To the English settlers in Virginia this was the natural route of expansion into the western country. While New France lacked settlers to occupy the country, many hardy, adventurous pioneer families of the American colonies had already entered the promised land of the west and continued to do so even after having been warned by military edict against settlement in the Indian country.

The Braddock Route began at Fort Cumberland, the outpost on the juncture of Will's Creek and the Potomac, and struck across the mountains over terrain even worse than that later encountered by Forbes. Braddock built no forts en route, as did Forbes, and failed in his attempt to take Duquesne in 1755. However, Fort Necessity, a crude circular stockade about a log house, east of modern Uniontown, had been built by Washington in 1754. Fort Burd (modern Brownsville), a fortified depot for goods en route from Virginia to the Forks of the Ohio, was built in 1759.

The Forbes Route

Beginning with the occupation of the Forks by the French in 1754 the English suffered a series of humiliating defeats, losing Oswego and Fort William Henry to the French and failing in their drives against Forts Carillon and Niagara. The only bright spot was the conquest of Fort Beau Sejour. War was formally declared in 1756. Gathering their forces in 1758, under the shrewd leadership of William Pitt, the British established four objectives. Abercromby was sent against Forts Carillon and Frederic, Amherst organized an army and navy to retake Louisbourg, Bradstreet laid plans to seize strategic Fort Frontenac, and Forbes was assigned the formidable task of organizing an overland campaign against Fort Duquesne. Forbes entrusted the direction of his campaign to one of the most conscientious and efficient officers of the day, Colonel Henry Bouquet, a Swiss soldier of fortune.

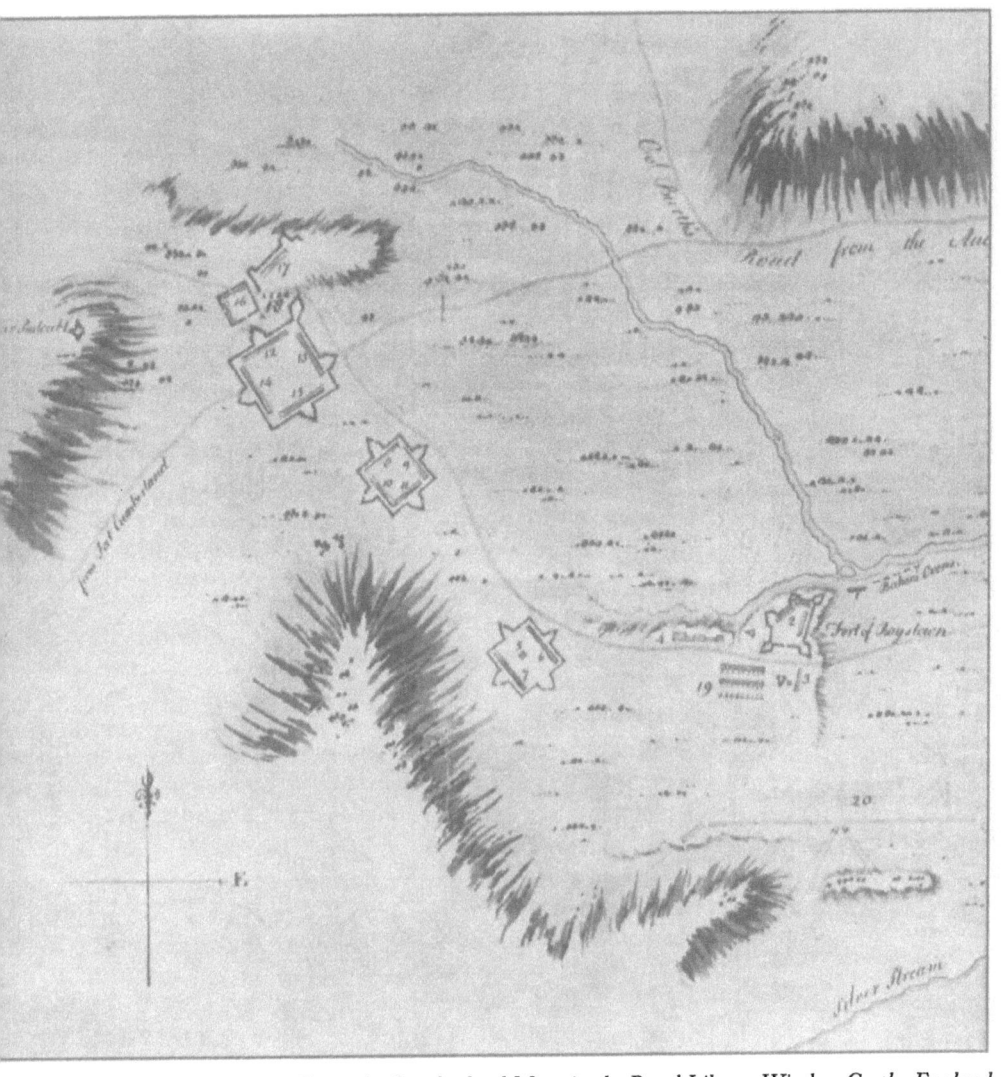

From the Cumberland Maps in the Royal Libary, Windsor Castle, England

PLAN OF THE ENVIRONS, FORT, AND ENCAMPMENTS OF RAYSTOWN

1. *Penderoastist Settler*
2. *Store Houses*
3. *Hospital*
4. *Settlers*
5. *Generall's House*
6)
7) *Col. Montgomery's Regt.*
8. *Marylanders*
9. *North Carolina Troops*
10)
11) *Pensylvania 3d. Battn.*
12. *Col. Washington's*
13. *Field Artillery*
14. *Pensylvania 2d. Battn.*
15. *Pensylvania 1st. Battn.*
16. *Royl. Americans*
17. *Provincial Train*
18. *Indian Camp*
19. *Part of ye Train of Artillery*
20. *Spot where Col. Bouquet Exercises the Troops. Marching in Columns, & forming ye Line of Battle*

This is a portion of a drawing made in 1758 to show the encampment of Forbes' Army in July at Raystown (Bedford).

Illustration 4

The Forbes Route led almost due west from Philadelphia to the Forks of the Ohio. Reasonably good roads already existed as far as Harris' Ferry (modern Harrisburg) on the Susquehanna and beyond to Carlisle. Fortified posts had been built at Carlisle (Fort Lowther), Fort Loudon and Fort Lyttleton. The portion of the campaign treated in this article begins at Fort Bedford. The map comprising the end papers in the front of the book shows the Braddock and Forbes roads. This drawing is from the Crown Collection of American Maps in the British Museum.

The base for the Forbes Expedition was built in the summer of 1758 at Rays Town, officially named Fort Bedford by Forbes on December 1, 1758. The writer found a drawing of Fort Bedford in the Windsor Castle, entitled "Plan of the Environs, Fort and Encampments of Raystown" which shows the disposition of the troops in their picketed enclosures, before the army set out for the Forks of the Ohio. See Illustration 4 which reproduces the area in the immediate vicinity of the fort. Here the troops were assembled and trained. The indication, 20, is the "Spott, where Col. Bouquet Exercises the Troops, Marching in Columns, & forming ye Line of Battle." The fort proper was of the simplest palisade and ditch construction with five bastions. There are two picketed redoubts, serving as ravelins, and an outlying star redoubt. The buildings within the fort were used chiefly for the storage of food and military supplies. Near the fort are a number of buildings used by settlers, or contractors who supplied the army. Around the fort were fields for cultivation and pastures for the horses and cattle. This post, like Fort Ligonier, was a "post of passage," serving General Forbes' policy of making a slow advance secured by fortified stations as the army moved along.

Another main way station begun in September, was established at Fort Ligonier, fifty miles west and halfway to the Forks of the Ohio. Braddock's experience had demonstrated that the lack of a fortified post to fall back on after a reversal meant complete defeat. The plan of Fort Ligonier (Illustration 5) from Windsor Castle, made by J. C. Pleydell, shows the encampment of Forbes' troops at that post. The army remained a much shorter period at Ligonier and was protected only by the outworks of the fort. However, Ligonier, unlike Bedford, was surrounded by a retrenchment of considerable extent, and the face of the fort was constructed of horizontal log ramparts. A portion of this fort as reconstructed by the

ENCAMPMENT OF FORBES' ARMY AT LIGONIER, NOVEMBER 1758
From the Cumberland Maps in the Royal Library at Windsor Castle, England
Illustration 5

author in 1954 is shown in Illustration 6. The model of the complete fort is shown in Illustration 7.

There were also a few fortified posts on the route of much lesser extent. The first of these was at the crossing of the Juniata River. This small stockaded fort is shown in a sketch preserved in the Bouquet Papers. Here extensive stockaded enclosures provided shelter for troops en route. There were four storehouses as well as barracks for a small permanent garrison. "Flatts" or rafts were used to ferry the army across the river. Another post, of which we have no description, was at Stoney Creek. Small garrisons were maintained at these places throughout the period. The forts at the Point, the primary subject of this work, are described in detail in Part Four.

STOCKADE WALL AND COMMANDANT'S HOUSE, FORT LIGONIER
RECONSTRUCTED IN 1954
Illustration 6

II. DEFENSE IN DEPTH

THE fortified castles and towns of medieval Europe appear to the traveler as the ultimate of impregnability. And indeed they were in their time. But their time ended with the perfection of the cannon. Massive and elaborate fortresses such as Carcassone in southern France became museum pieces for other generations to ponder. Illustration 8 from Viollet-le-Duc's *Dictionnaire Raisonné de l'Architecture* shows the elaborate engines of war utilized in the reduction of these fortresses. The first cannon, using balls of stone, was fired about 1340. By 1425 artillery had become sufficiently effective to breach the stone wall; the fortified places were no longer secure in defense. Illustration 9, also from Viollet-le-Duc, shows the utilization of new outer defenses against cannon fire, as the high stone walls became untenable. After a long process of experimentation, trial and error, there evolved a completely new system, defense in depth rather than height. By mid-eighteenth century a highly formulated alphabet of fort terms had been adopted by all the European countries. In this development France took the initiative, giving the science a terminology which passed unchanged into other tongues. A brief review of this revolution in military fortification design will serve to explain and give meaning to the forms of the forts built by the French and English in America.

At first the characteristic high towers of the early forts were lowered and increased in diameter with vaults to contain the guns. Battlements were replaced with breaches for the cannon. Walls were strengthened by lowering them and backing them with earth. These measures improved resistance to enemy fire and increased the effectiveness of their own offensive fire, but one serious defect remained; the round tower did not afford a protective flanking fire. That is, the guns of the besieged could not command the space immediately before the walls. This eventually led to the creation of a radically new form to be seen in almost every fort built in the eighteenth century in America, the bastion, which was first used about 1500. (See Illustration 10.) The plan (known as the trace) eliminated any "dead" space not commanded by the fire from the fort, at any point on its perimeter. The bastion, being completely open to the

SCALE MODEL OF FORT LIGONIER AT FORT MUSEUM
Courtesy of Fort Ligonier Memorial Foundation
Illustration 7

From E. Viollet-le-Duc's Dictionnaire Raisonné de l'Architecture Francais
MEDIEVAL FORTRESS WITH BATTLE SCAFFOLDING. BESIEGERS ARE USING ENGINES OF WAR ANTEDATING USE OF CANNON.
Illustration 8

From E. Viollet-le-Duc's Dictionnaire Raisonne de l'Architecture Francais

MEDIEVAL FORTRESS WITH SUPPLEMENTAL DEFENSE OF EARTHWORK
AND TIMBER SHOWING TRANSITION TO DEFENSE IN DEPTH.

Illustration 9

sky, permitted the free escape of gun smoke which had previously been a hazard of suffocation for the gun crews in the confined towers. In addition to the bastion, there were many other minor variations, all based on the principle of completely commanding the area occupied by the attackers.

The most celebrated practitioner of this new system was the Frenchman, Sebastien le Prestre de Vauban (1633-1707). Combining the already well developed forms and theories, Vauban applied them in masterly style to the more than one hundred forts and harbor installations he designed under Louis XIV. He conducted over fifty sieges with such outstanding success that his influence was felt until the time of Napoleon. Another name well-known to the soldier and engineers of the armies in America was that of Menno Coehorn (1641-1704), a Dutchman who invented the mortar which bore his name. This field piece was designed to lob a shell in high trajectory over ramparts which could not be pierced by horizontal fire. One of its principal targets was the enemy's powder magazine. In the council of war held at Fort Ligonier in November 1758 Harry Gordon advised Forbes that "One Coehorn Mortar would be Sufficient to Destroy the Place by Blowing up the Magazine."[5]

British Fort Designers and Their Drawings

The military engineers who accompanied the armies in America knew Vauban and Coehorn as legendary geniuses who had established the principles of their science. But for the practical everyday application of these principles in the field they depended upon the handbooks of the time. Among the many which may be examined in the libraries today is the *Elements of Field Fortification,* by Lewis Lochee, Master of the R. M. [Royal Military] Academy. This pocket sized primer provides in simple language and diagrams the elements of the bastioned fort. Another standard authority of the day was *A Treatise Containing the Practical Part of Fortifications,* by John Muller, published in London in 1755. These books, or others like them, undoubtedly were carried by the French and English military engineers in America. An examination of the forts of both countries reveals little or no basic variance in design and construction. Likewise each exhibited ingenuity in adapting the European fort designs to the new conditions of the American wilderness.

The exigencies of warfare in the 1750's left no time for refinement or elaboration in fort design. As in the instance of Fort

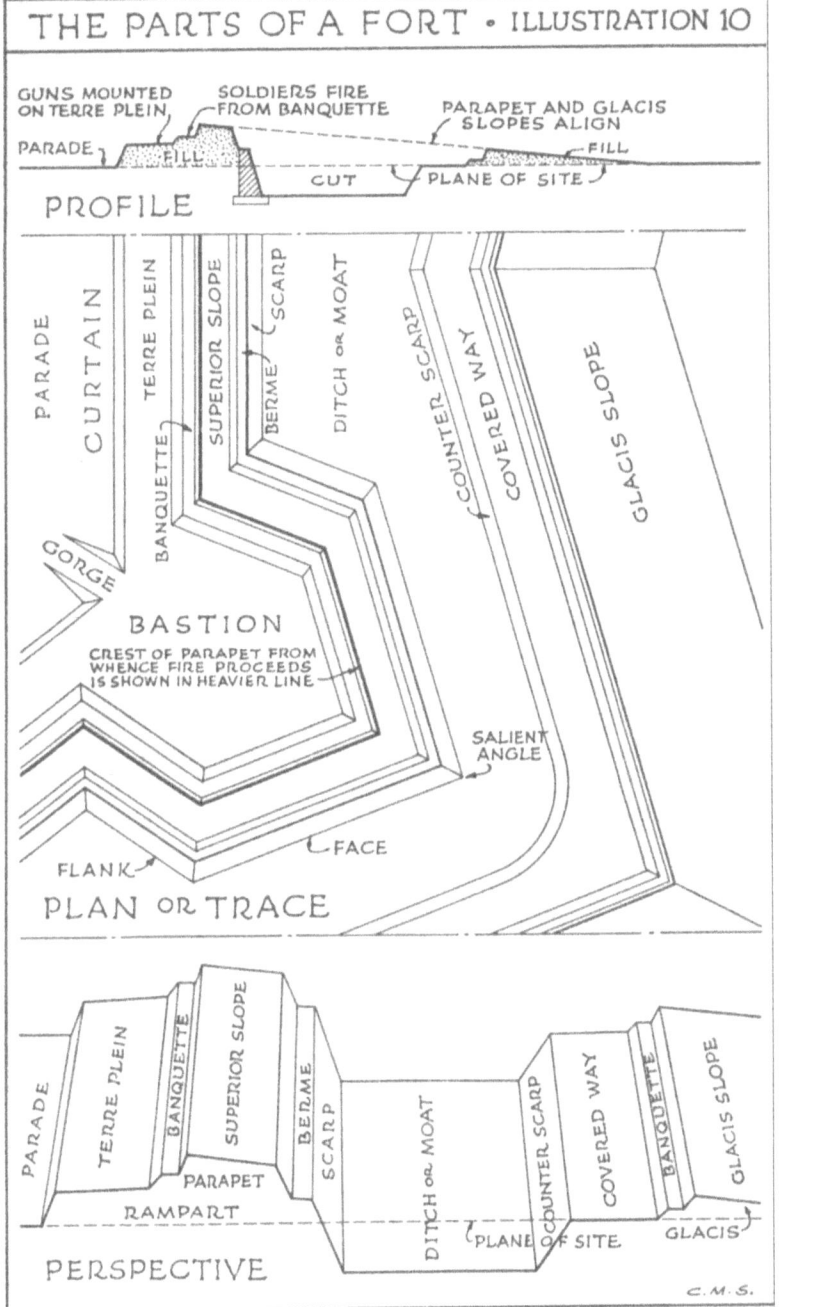

Ligonier, pre-determined sites were changed at the last moment. Severe limitations in transport forced the engineer to use building methods suitable to the timber, earth, stone and other materials that lay about the site. Lack of time demanded action and prompt decision in providing cover for live stock, precious food and war material, and lastly for the troops who used tents until their quarters were ready. If the work was of great moment and time was not a critical factor, masonry construction could be utilized as in the fortifications of Louisbourg, Quebec, Albany and other well secured centers. Fort Pitt was partly built of masonry, an exception among frontier posts.

The British government established the policy in 1754 that "considerable forts, cased with stone," should not be built in America "till the plans and estimates thereof have been sent to England and approved by the Government here." So Major General Edward Braddock was advised, before he left England, by the Duke of Cumberland, captain general of the British army. Cumberland also warned against building too many forts "of which they are perhaps too fond in that country." [America] He also added that "His Royal Highness thinks that stockaded forts, with pallisadoes and a good ditch, capable of containing 200 men or 400 upon an emergency, will be sufficient for the present."[6] The same policy of caution was reflected in the King's reluctance to send British regulars to Virginia to settle the dispute over the Ohio country as he had no desire to break the uneasy peace then existing between France and England. These instructions, and others like them, account for the comparatively small and weak fortifications built in the coming contest. No wonder that a later critic wrote, "These American forts are in general no such formidable things; they are for the most part no more than a fort of retrenchment of Trees and Earth & even when they have a facing of stone they are generally too small to sustain a regular siege and may be reduced by simple bombardments."[7]

From the beginning, however, the fort to be built at the Forks of the Ohio was considered an exception to the royal policy of building small, extemporized frontier posts. Assuming he would readily drive the French from the Forks, Braddock was instructed then to build "a good and sufficient Fort, on the most convenient pass upon the said River."[8] The writer believes that we have conclusive proof that Braddock was prepared to do just that, for he carried with him

DEFENSE IN THE WILDERNESS 79

on his expedition sketch plans for the elaborate fortification of the Point. These plans, as will be discussed later, agree in every important detail with the "good and sufficient" fort built there some years later, Fort Pitt.

With few exceptions the frontier forts were built in haste with the enemy near at hand; many were never completed. Made of the timbers and earth which surrounded them, they were truly ephemeral creations. The effects of rain and frost, rot and rust were devastating. When their urgent need had been served, they were neglected, as the complaints of the commandants in their correspondence so eloquently attested. In his research leading to the reconstruction of Fort Ligonier, the writer was led to visualize these wilderness strongholds in new and more realistic terms.

"The reconstructed frontier fort holds for us moderns a romantic appeal that was probably not shared by the soldier of the time as he viewed the original. Poorly fed, clothed and paid, and usually without adequate protection from the elements, he was surrounded by a vast, gloomy forest that harbored an invisible, cruel enemy whom he feared desperately. The fort was usually crowded with men and animals that churned the ground into mud or raised clouds of dust. It was filled with odors, vermin, and confusion and, except in the heat of campaign, its garrison was often insubordinate."[9]

There is a large library of military maps and contemporary fort drawings extant in European Archives such as the Bibliotheque Nationale in Paris, the Public Record Office and British Museum in London, and Windsor Castle. Libraries in the United States and Canada have some drawings, but the most convenient and complete single source of information is the *Crown Collection of American Maps,* assembled by Archer Butler Hulbert, which contains reproductions of drawings in the English archives. Plans of almost all of the forts mentioned in Part One may be seen in this remarkable collection. The typical walls of the frontier forts may be divided into the palisade or picket wall, the horizontal log wall, and sodded earthworks. These are shown in Illustration 11, and described in some detail below.

Frontier Fort Details

The commonest and readiest form of defense was the picketed wall. This could be made only where the earth could be worked easily. A ditch was dug about four feet deep to receive the pickets.

Trees were felled and cut into sections twelve to sixteen feet in length and averaging a foot in diameter. The upper end was sharpened with an axe and the bark was usually removed. The stakes were hauled by wagon or on the wagon trucks which were disassembled from the wagon bed. The stakes were then stood in the ditch tightly together, after which the earth was replaced and packed about them. Sometimes halved stakes of smaller diameter were placed between them on the inside to cover the interstices caused by irregularities in the pickets. Usually the pickets were bound together on the inside with small halved saplings in a single line near the top of the pickets and bound to the pickets with vines or, more rarely, secured with heavy nails. On the inside of the palisade, a firing step was constructed of earth or a halved log with flat side upward, or a platform of planks. Port holes with beveled sides were cut at convenient height for the men to fire through. In the picketed bastions larger ports were constructed for the cannons. This type of wall was good enough defense against the Indians but was worthless against cannon fire. Stockades were therefore used only on the protected side where direct attack by the enemy was unlikely. A typical palisade wall may be seen in the reconstructed Fort Ligonier. (See Illustration 5.) Most of the early forts such as Fort Ligonier and Fort Duquesne were built in this manner, half of stockade and half of horizontal logs as described below.

The horizontal log wall, shown in Illustration 11, was universally used in timber forts where protection was needed against cannon fire. Two walls of squared logs laid tightly one upon the other were built about ten or twelve feet apart. The two walls were held in position by bonding logs which joined them at intervals and were secured by dovetail connections. This basket work of logs was then filled with earth. None of the portable cannon of the period could pierce this wall. This type of construction may be seen in restored Fort William Henry, Lake George, New York. One of the bastions formed of horizontal logs was reserved for the powder magazine, a structure with walls and roof of logs, partially sunk in the ground and covered with about four feet of earth. This formed a raised platform on which cannon could be mounted.

Fascine earthworks were mounds of earth containing fascines, or bundles of broom, brushwood or small branches bound together with vines. Fascines were two to eighteen feet in length and six to eighteen inches in diameter. When over seven feet in length they

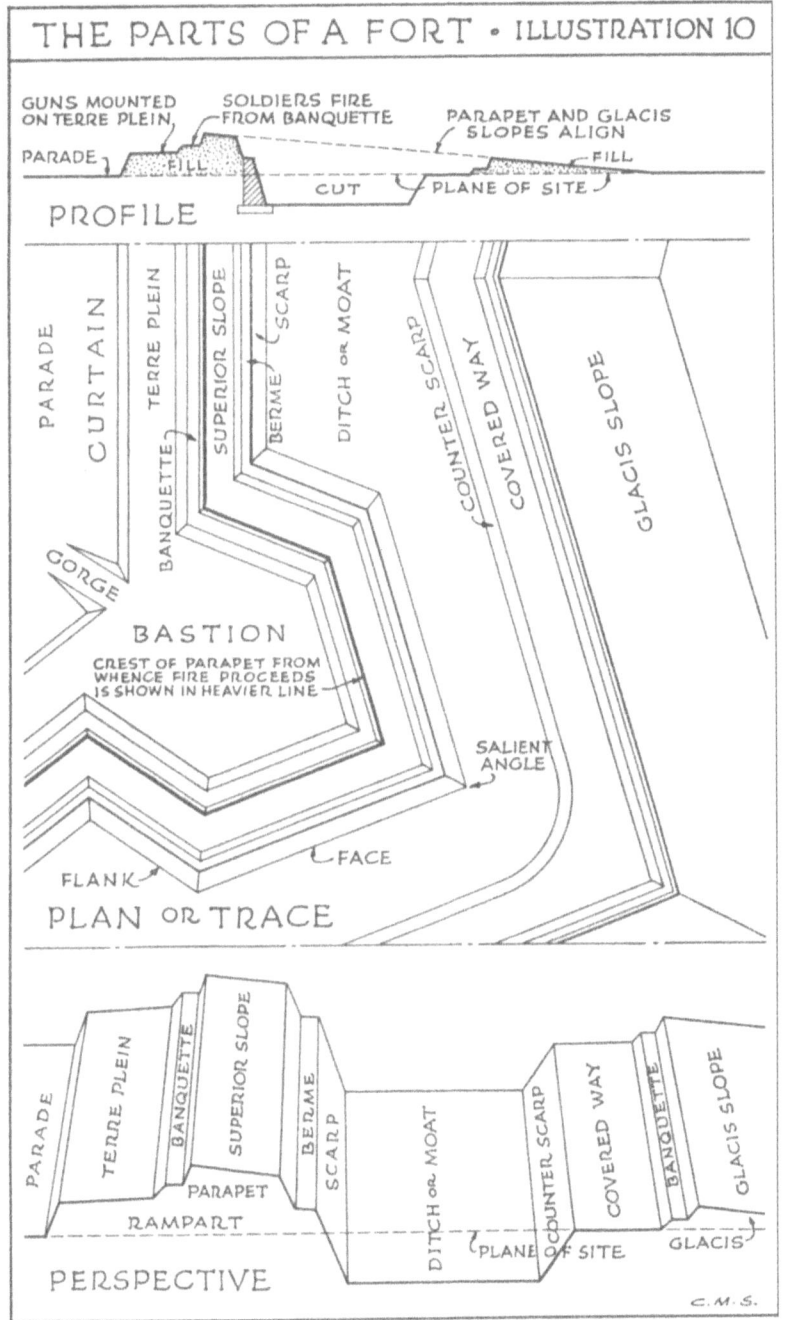

were called saucissons. The purpose of the fascines was to provide a degree of stability in the mound of earth and reduce erosion by rain. These continuous mounds were broken at intervals to provide embrasures for the cannon. The upper and lower batteries of Fort Ligonier, as yet unrestored, were of this construction. This type of wall may be seen in restored form at the entrance to Fort Niagara.

All of these types of structures were subject to rapid deterioration from the elements. None of these primitive fortifications could remain usable for more than a few years without continual repair or replacement.

The steep sloping walls of earthworks such as used on three sides of Fort Pitt could be held in place for a much longer period by "sodding." This was accomplished by cutting large blocks of sod, about twelve by eighteen inches and three inches thick. As the earth was piled up, the bank was faced with these sods, bonded like bricks with alternate headers and stretchers as shown in Illustration 11. The green side was laid downward. To further secure them in place small wooden pickets were driven through them at intervals. The omission of these pickets in the sod work at Fort Pitt was later much regretted. The sods were not laid horizontally but at right angles to the slope of the bank. The grass on the edges of the sod grew out to provide some protection against erosion and was thus also more resistant to shot. The grass growing on these banks required cutting at least twice a year. Banquettes were commonly lined with sods or fascines exposed on the face and secured with wooden stakes driven through them vertically into the earth bank. Better than sods or fascines for the interior slopes of the parapets were pickets driven into the ground to a depth of about three feet to form an exposed solid facing for the sloping bank. These were kept in line by being interwoven with twigs of willows or osiers.

The dimensions and proportions of earth ramparts followed set rules. The profile through the wall of Fort Pitt shown in Illustration 10 is similar to that of smaller forts. The natural level of the ground, known as the "plane of site," was maintained as the parade ground level inside the fort. The earth taken from the ditch was used to form the rampart and glacis, the extent of which was necessarily determined by the depth and width of the ditch. The banquette was the platform on which the soldiers stood, usually two deep. The height of the parapet was determined by the comfortable clearance needed by a soldier in firing. The width of the parapet varied with the degree of protection desired from the enemy's cannon fire. Embrasures were made in the parapet for cannon which rode on platforms of thick plank. The top of the parapet sloped forward at an angle usually equal to that of the glacis, or the gently sloping land in front of the ditch. The glacis diminished shelter for the enemy against direct fire.

It was customary to provide a berme to keep the parapet from falling into the ditch. The dimensions of the ditch were determined by the size of the parapet but were generally at least 15 feet wide and 10 feet deep. The angle of the scarp walls depended on the kind of soil encountered. If the berme was omitted the scarp was made with a correspondingly greater slope. In forts of any degree of permanence, such as Fort Pitt, the scarp wall was revetted with brick or, as in the case of Fort Ticonderoga, with stone. The crest of parapet was to have at least 5 foot command over crest of counterscarp. Parapets ranged from 6 to 10 feet in thickness. The unusually large parapet of Fort Pitt measured 18 feet.

The wood and brush were cleared around the fort as far as cannon range, about 1,000 to 1,200 yards, to deprive the attacking enemy of cover. The clearing thus made provided timber for most of the needs of the builders. Wells were usually dug where water could be reached easily. There were three wells within Fort Pitt. In smaller or temporary posts the fort site was usually located to take advantage of springs or streams. Where springs could not be included within the walls, access to water was protected by outworks.

Tools and Supplies

Certain materials and implements indispensable to fort construction had to be transported by the army. Of first importance were the "intrenching tools." These included spades, shovels, pick axes, felling axes, hand bills, hand hatchets, wheelbarrows and handbarrows. Grindstones were an absolute necessity without which the axes and other cutting tools would soon be useless. The cutters axes were re-ground each night while on the march. Although some nails, spikes, hinges, pintels and other hardware needed to hinge doors, fasten shingles and the like were transported, these articles were also fabricated at the site by the blacksmith, whose forge was also needed for making wagon parts and many other articles. Thus a stock of iron and steel had to be conveyed for his use. Lead was carried in bulk for molding into bullets. Because of difficulty in carriage, glass was sparingly used, if at all, in the simpler forts. Glass was not made in the district until some years after the period under discussion.

There was no necessity for transporting brick which could readily be made from the clays and shales of the district, pressed by hand into wooden molds and burned in improvised kilns. All brick was "hand-made" until comparatively modern times. Where out crops of limestone could be found, lime was likewise produced in local kilns. There were plentiful outcrops of coal in western Pennsylvania to provide fuel and tar needed in boat building. Pitch, another necessity for boat making, was obtained from the pine trees which at that time grew plentifully on the mountain slopes, though there was no adequate supply near Fort Pitt. Oakum had to be carried in.

Tools for carpenters and armourers must be brought. These included hammers, hatchets, augers, chisels, drawing knives, frows (for riving shingles) and saws of several types. Many of the orders for tools and implements were filled in England. It is amusing to find a note of perplexity from the British War Office, dated April of 1759, "The Inclosed Warrant came to my hand yesterday in which I observe we are ordered to supply Pioneer Axes 11, Pioneer Saws 1. These are Stores that never have hitherto been supplied by the Officer to any Regiment . . ."[10] Facilities for sawing planks and boards for the construction of barracks, boats, cannon platforms and many other uses was of immediate concern at the site. This could be done with a long two-handed saw, one man standing above and the other working in a shallow pit beneath. For quantity production, however, a sawmill was needed. Such mills were operated by water power. This required damming some stream near the fort. The Loyalhanna was dammed just below Fort Ligonier for that purpose and our present-day Saw Mill Run behind Mount Washington got its name from its use for this purpose for Fort Pitt. For such sawmills, the machinery, largely made of wood, had to be transported by wagon from the east.

Among the other artisans or "artificers," as they were known, who accompanied the armies, were the cooper and the boat builder. Kegs and barrels were indispensable for transport of many kind of supplies, chiefly powder, flour and salt meat. The repair and replacement of barrels was a never ending activity, as bags were at that time much less used as containers. Special tradesmen constructed ovens, usually in the open, for baking. Outdoor ovens are shown in Illustration 4 of Fort Bedford.

While artificers trained in the various building trades were employed by term contracts to construct the forts, it was expected that the vast demands for common labor would be supplied by the militia soldiers. Bouquet wrote Forbes when Fort Bedford was being started in June of 1758: "the Virginia troops do not wish to work without being paid. The Pennsylvanians have all offered voluntarily to work for a gill of rum a day. While awaiting your orders, I shall have the former mount guard, and employ the latter on the works." As might be imagined this unequal condition led to trouble. He adds, "If one wished to put it on the basis of paying the troops in America when they must work, the army would cost nearly four times as much, because no step can be taken without axe or spade in hand."[11]

The English Military Engineer

In 1758, Bouquet ordered that "All the Artificers belonging to the Works are under the Direction of the Chief Engineer. All other Artificers, employ'd for the Service of the Army, such as Sadlers, Wheel-Rights, Black-Smiths, Gun Smiths, Oven-Makers, &ca. are under the Direction of the Quarter-Master-General . . . ."[12]

The quartermaster's activities will be discussed under the next section. It is here pertinent to consider the then young profession of military engineering and the military engineers who were primarily responsible for the design and construction of the forts of the mid-eighteenth century in America. With the tremendous expansion and great diversity of the profession of engineering, as we know it, to serve modern science, we are apt to forget that the appellation, engineer, was first applied to the man who designed and constructed "engines of war." Vauban was the first to recognize the importance to the army of men trained in military engineering. In 1690 he founded the "Corps de Genie" which achieved international renown as the leading school of fortification and siege-craft. The English, who were indebted to the French for much of their knowledge of the subject, were somewhat slower in raising the status of their engineers who held no military rank until 1757, after which time every engineer officer received a signed commission from the King. It was another thirty years before they were united in a corps known as the "Royal Engineers," a name by which they are still known today.

The construction of the simplest forts or even stockades required competent direction. Bouquet complained of the scarcity of engineers in a letter of July 1757. "Two or three could direct the Fortifications of all the Colonies, & save large Sums that the people are laying out in slight Works, which soon fall and Decay , . . and after all, are generally useless, by their bad Construction."[13] The few available competent engineers were overworked during the decade of fort building between 1753 and 1763. In addition to the design, construction and maintenance of forts, these men were needed in the surveying and construction of roads and bridges through the wilderness, the selection of sites to be fortified, the requisition of materials to be carried from the east and the preparation of periodical returns of inventory. The adaptation of the fort to the site was the real test of the engineer. The commander not only leaned heavily on the engineer in these activities but also in battle and in the final act of war, the defense of the post itself. Harry Gordon, the leading engineer in the west, left an account of his experiences in Braddock's tragic engagement which is one of the most thrilling first-hand descriptions of wilderness warfare.

Bouquet appears to have thought highly of Harry Gordon both as a companion, as a faithful officer and expert engineer and spoke of his "indefatigable Activity." Colonel Burd wrote Bouquet, "his [Gordon's] Extraordinary Zeal & activity does not Surprise me, I am glad to hear every officer praise him."[14] A note from Bouquet to Gordon in 1765 shows the mutual regard between these men. " . . . Your very kind sentiments for me, and the great honor you have always done me in publishing them, are obligations that I know how to value . . . I have no Claim to the praises you give me, but I lay a great one to the Friendship that dictates them . . . "[15] Isolated in a wilderness, overburdened with duties and surrounded by an unregenerate host of soldiers, civilians and begging Indians, men of this caliber must have greatly prized such friendships.

Among other forts Harry Gordon built or designed Fort Edward, Fort Augusta, Mercer's Fort and Fort Pitt. As chief engineer in the central department, he was advanced sums of money to pay the artificers, rendered account for it to the Board of Ordinance and receipted for the money to his commanding general. Gordon's career in the army is outlined in the title of his declared accounts which are preserved in the Public Record Office in London.

"Declaration of the Account of Lieutenant Colonel Harry Gordon as Engineer employed in Building & Repairing several forts and places in North America from 18th August 1756 to 26th November 1761 and as Chief Engineer from 16th September 1764 to 25th November 1767." The accounts show his presence and direction, after his advancement as chief engineer, at practically all the forts in America from Florida to Quebec and as far west as Fort Chartres. It is interesting to read: "In all the money paid by this Accountant & the Engineers employed under him to the several persons for the respective Time of Service within the Time of this Account amounting in New York Currency to £ 28,321/0/4." Although he was thus charged with great responsibilities he appears to have received scant reward, as may be seen in his statement of further claims for extra services: "More for the Extraordinary Expenses & fatigue he was at in his Extensive Voyages & Journeys in the years, 1765, 1766 and 1767 in penetrating as far Westward to view the forts on Lake Huron from whence he returned to New York and the next season visiting the forts on the Ohio, making a Survey of the Course of this River, ascending the Mississippi to the uppermost settlement thereon, exploring the Lake and Coasts of West Florida in an open Boat to Mobile & Pensacola and along the Coast to Charles Town from then by land to New York. The next year reporting the Communication between Hudson River and the Lakes on the Frontiers of Canada, the River St. Lawrence and the Garrisons there and for several other Services for which he never has received any Gratuity."

Chief Engineer Colonel Eyre, whom Gordon succeeded in November of 1764, came to America in 1755 with the 44th Regiment under General Braddock. He constructed Fort William Henry of which he was later commandant. He fought at Ticonderoga with Abercromby and later built a new fort there. Eyre visited Fort Pitt to appraise the flood damage in 1762 and recommended steps for its repair. He was lost at sea in 1765 while returning to England.

In the glimpses that we have of the various assistant engineers, draftsmen and surveyors in the military correspondence, we can piece together little of their careers, abilities and personalities. Among these men was a favorite of Bouquet's named Du Plessis who supervised road construction. He was killed by the Indians at Venango in 1760.

Lieutenant Hutchins prepared a drawing of Fort Pitt and later measured and drew up the French Fort Machault at Venango. He made the illustrations for *An Historical Account of the Expedition Against the Ohio Indians in* 1764, including a map of the route followed by Bouquet's army, and a drawing of the field of battle of Bushy Run. Ensign Charles Rhor, another engineer of prominence, reported to Bouquet at Carlisle in May of 1758. He was assigned to direct Burd in the construction of Fort Ligonier. Captain Robertson, upon Gordon's recommendation, served at Bedford and Ligonier and assisted in the search for a new site for Fort Pitt. The engineer Thomas Basset appears first in the accounts when he arrived at Fort Loudoun in June of 1758. In May of 1762 he was engaged in the rehabilitation of Fort Pitt. Lieutenant Elias Meyer surveyed and established data for the layout of Fort Pitt, as well as a survey of the environs of the fort in 1762.

Some of the engineers were employed as draftsmen. Many of the drawings were unsigned so the record is not complete. Captain Robert Dudgeon made one of the best drawings of Fort Ligonier, executed in ink and water color and preserved at Windsor Castle, and another of Fort Duquesne after its capture. The drawings made by J. C. Pleydell of Fort Ligonier, Fort Bedford and Fort Duquesne are illustrated in this article. William Twiss prepared the excellent Meyer drawing of Fort Pitt and George Wright another drawing of the same fort. One of the two best plans of Fort Pitt was signed by B. Ratzer who also surveyed and drew a plan of New York. He became a captain in 1773 and a major in 1782.

III. CHALLENGE OF THE WILDERNESS

THE challenge of the wilderness is nowhere more authentically and colorfully described than in that remarkable collection of military correspondence, the Bouquet Papers, which deals partly with the Forbes Campaign. Here in plain terms, we learn first-hand of the problems and frustrations of campaigning in the virgin forest. One of the most effective of these is a letter, written by Colonel Henry Bouquet to the Duke of Portland in December of 1758, shortly after the capture of Fort Duquesne. The army was "reduced to a sad state of affairs, . . . with neither tents nor baggage, and in need of clothing, with the weather bitter cold, . . . but the troops are suffering without a murmur, delighted that they have destroyed this nest of pirates, who have cost so much blood."

Bouquet sums up the campaign. " . . . The obstacles which we had to surmount were immense, 200 miles of wild and unknown country to cross; obliged to open a road through woods, mountains, and swamps; to build forts along our lines of march for the security of our convoys; with an active and enterprising enemy in front of us, elated by his previous successes, and superior in this type of war. It was only with infinite trouble that we were able to transport provisions, artillery, and munitions. Our little army was composed of new recruits and provincials, most of them engaged in the month of June for the campaign, and a great number of whom had never seen a musket . . . ."[16] This is a translation from French, the native Swiss language in which Bouquet usually wrote. The records contain a number of good-humored complaints from his correspondents in the east about his undecipherable English. Bouquet replied to them, " . . . . you must be so good as to make some allowance for my writing in a language I am so little master of, or give me leave to express myself in French."[17]

The French had supplied Fort Duquesne by two water routes, one from Quebec by way of the Lakes and the Allegheny River, the other from the Illinois country up the Ohio River. Although these communications were long and travel was slow, they had many advantages over the land routes established by the English to reclaim the lands seized by the French. The Braddock and Forbes Routes gained no advantage from the streams they paralleled or crossed but rather found them obstacles to be forded or bridged. The establishment and maintenance of these lines of communication over the mountains were to tax the fortitude and resources of the English. Military action could not be swift and decisive and a great deal of time, money and patience were required.

In the summer of 1758 General John Forbes assembled in eastern Pennsylvania his "small army" of about 6,000 men. These included provincials from Pennsylvania, Virginia, Maryland, North Carolina, Delaware, as well as Scotch Highlanders and Royal Americans. The quartermaster general, Sir John St. Clair, was a vacillating incompetent who sorely tried the patience of Forbes. The second in command, Colonel Henry Bouquet, was a tower of strength to the sick general who at times lacked the strength even to write a letter. There was a mutual regard between these men. On Forbes' death, Bouquet wrote Amherst, "He had honored me with his Confidence as my General, and with a tender affection as a friend."[18]

An appraisal of General John Forbes' accomplishment is rendered more impressive by taking a candid view of the adverse conditions with which he contended. The records contain little of the romantic view generally associated with frontier warfare. The magnificent primeval forests and the picturesque roads and forts constructed in them are treated with brutal realism in the eighteenth century records. The writer hopes to convey this quality to the following narration of the physical and human aspects of Forbes' great achievement. Liberal quotations from contemporary accounts are deemed necessary to convey this color of reality.

Choice of Route

One of the first fundamental decisions Forbes had to make was the choice of a route. In this matter he was most deliberate, maintaining an impartial attitude in the face of conflicting advice from proponents of the Virginia and Pennsylvania interests. To each he said, "—that the good of the service was the only view we had at heart, not valuing the provincial interest, jealousys, or suspicions, one single two pence."[19] The routing of Braddock by way of Fort Cumberland had been a fundamental mistake, largely resulting from Dinwiddie's partisanship for Virginia's interests and his ignorance of the enormous task required in surmounting the forests and mountains of the route. Lord Halifax alone in England had insisted that

Braddock proceed through New York toward the much more accessible and strategic Fort Niagara. Braddock had been expected, after he had taken Fort Duquesne, to continue northward by the French route to Niagara, a completely unrealistic understanding of geography, supply problems, and human endurance.

The Virginians expected Forbes to establish a route from Fort Bedford to Fort Cumberland so that supplies and men could join with their forces at the latter post and proceed thence by Braddock's Route to the Ohio. Colonel Burd, who had worked on Braddock's road and had also cut a road in 1755 from Bedford to the Allegheny Ridge, worked closely with Bouquet and apparently convinced him that the Pennsylvania route was preferable. According to Burd: "... Mr Breddock was in a hurry to gett along and would not allow time to make the road as it ought, or easily could, be made, it is not more than 10 foot wide and carried right up every Hill almost without a turn and the Hills almost perpendicular, . . . " although he said that a good engineer could still make a good road of it.[20]

It would seem that Bouquet passed along Burd's suggestion, for on July 25 Forbes wrote Abercromby that the Pennsylvania route would: "facilitate our matters much by shortening the march at least 70 miles—besides the advantage of having no rivers to pass, as we will keep the Yeogheny upon our left." On August 11 Forbes also pointed out that the enemy was not expecting them the new way while every pass and defile of Braddock's route was watched.[21] The Pennsylvania route proceeded from the granary of America, abounding in horses and wagons. Braddock had the poorest horses and wagons and these were assembled at Winchester only after threats and long delays.

Road Construction

The records do not reveal any precise description of the character of the "road" followed by Forbes from Bedford to the Forks. The route is almost invariably referred to as "the communication." There can be no doubt that the maximum width of the road, seldom over twelve feet wide, was determined by providing adequate clearance for the army wagons. The width of the road may be gauged by the statement of Colonel John Reid that he found it "impracticable to march the Pack Horses more than two a breast . . . " The cutting of trees in a virgin forest was a challenging task for, after the labor of felling, their enormous bulk must be fully removed from the path. After the great trees were cut, it was another matter to disentangle them from their neighbors and bring them to the ground. To do this the trees had often to be trimmed first at their tops. It was obviously impossible to root out all the stumps which must have remained serious obstacles for the wagons. There were also dead fallen trees to contend with.

The route was chosen with care to avoid large rock outcrops, swamps, and steep grades, but, as the records testify, this was not always possible. The route from Bedford to Ligonier was the most difficult stretch because of the bad grades, dense undergrowth and lack of forage for the animals. We learn from Hulbert that "The road makers followed implicitly the Indian path where it was possible; when on the high ground the road was so rugged that many waggons were entirely demolished and more temporarily disabled; when off this track in the ravines they were buried axle deep in the bogs." By August 16, 1758, there were 1,400 men cutting and clearing this route, with as many soldiers deployed in the woods to protect them.

Near Stoney Creek a bad swamp was encountered. Armstrong, in charge of this section, was ordered to set about "bridging the Swamp." This does not literally mean the construction of a bridge but "corduroy" surfacing with logs laid closely together. This method was used by the French on the marshy portage from Presqui'Isle to Le Boeuf. Bouquet wrote about the same time that the 500 men working on the road from Bedford to Cumberland were making little headway "because of the swamps which they must bridge with causeways, . . ." Adam Stephen decided to go himself and reconnoitre "the Shades of Death," as this swamp was called. He proclaimed it "a dismal Place! and wants only a Cerberus to represent Virgil's gloomy description of Aeneas's entering the Infernal Regions." He continues: "I attempted them on horse back, but found Admittance so difficult that I was Obligd to part with horse, Sword & Coat, and make my way good with the Tomhawk. Near thirty of Us Spread, & wanderd through those Shades, perplexd with Lawrels, Logs & Rocks; coverd with weeds, or Brambles interwoven with Young Locust; and were so lucky in our researches, that had it not been for this days Rain, before night a Coach & Six might have easily past through the place." At this time there were no Indians in sight. Stephen believed the Indians had no knowledge of this roadwork and said "what a glorious thing it would be, to have a

Lodgement on the Loyal-Hannon [Ligonier] before they ever suspected your Intentions."²²

The corduroy roads required continual replacement. After heavy rains the greatest difficulty was experienced in moving the wagons at all. Callendar advised Bouquet: "Hemp Ropes with Strong Iron Hooks fix'd to them will be necessary to assist the waggons where they may Stall, as in miery places the wheels dirty and abuses the Mens Cloaths." Bouquet said: "Each wagon should have two ropes with two strong iron hooks at the ends, so that the soldiers can pull them out of the mudholes, and help them climb the mountains."²³

Stephen wrote from Stoney Creek "that altho' the Road is Opend and made as well as could be expected considering all Circumstances" it would require a large force "to improve & repair bad places; as horse tracts, & Using of the Road discover Several things that did not appear so bad at first. Monsieur Rhor & I, have been very busy these two days in chusing the best, & bad it is, but depend on it, we will make the best of it." Stephen's most picturesque description deals with the construction of the road beyond the "Shades." ". . . we Intend a Straight Course towards the Top of the mountain, without regarding the Path, if Rocks will permit. There is nothing would have a greater Effect upon these Rocks, than the Essence of Fat Beef gradually mixt with a Puncheon of Rum, This would add weight to every stroke given them. Please send us three or four Cross Cut saws to Seperate the numberless, damnd, petryfyd old Logs hard as Iron, & Breaks our Axes to pieces. There is not a Dear in this neighbourhood, & the Salt pork, has very near dryd up your Spring, at this Encampment."²⁴

Captain Gavin Cochrane wrote Major John Tulleken in 1759, commenting on the conditions in this area: "we had most terrible rocky & Steep roads & where we were not troubled with stones, the roads were most intolerably slippery, . . . " Where roads bordered the steep sides of the mountains, such as Sideling Hill, the inner side was reduced by slides of earth and rock, and the outer side, hanging over steep slopes, was rutted by the rain with dangerous gullies. He adds on the 21st that he was obliged to leave the wagons at Stoney Creek though he had only "eight hundred weight in a waggon." Tulleken estimated in July 1759 that it would require eight days to travel with wagons from Bedford to Ligonier.²⁵

It was a difficult problem to get the wagons over the mountains.

Armstrong wrote Bouquet in September 1759: "Thru the Poverty & weakness of our horses Our utmost invention has been put to the Rack, to surmount the Aerial Heights of Allegheny [Ridge] . . ." Forbes observed to Abercromby that he ". . . found the Waggons in place of carrying 200 w^t were only abl^e to carry 12 to 1400 w^t . . ."[26]

As Forbes said, in making his decision, this route required no major bridge construction. At the Susquehanna River crossing there were "only two Flatts [flatboats] on Each Side to ferry over the Waggons." This shallow river could easily be forded by men and animals in most seasons. The Juniata River crossing, where a small post was built, was made by raft or, when practicable, by fording. A bridge was built over the Loyalhanna at Ligonier and is shown on the contemporary fort drawings. Some notion of the seriousness of building a bridge of any size in those days and conditions may be gained by a report made by Captain Richard Pearis on "Dimensions of Bridge" to be made over Will's Creek near Fort Cumberland. This bridge was required because the frequent high water and swift current held up passage of wagons and animals for days at a time. Also the timber supply for Fort Cumberland was on the opposite shore. The bridge was to be 270 feet long and 20 feet high, supported by six "pillers" (piers), filled with stone, and able to "stand any Flood."[27]

Bridges furthermore required almost constant maintenance. Pearis was ordered by Bouquet in November of 1759 to repair the bridge over the Little Crossing of the Youghiogheny . . . . "youll cutt new Loggs and make it Sufficient . . . . you are to pin down every Logg upon the Bridge (but you need not) Cover them with Fasheens [fascines or bundles of brush] & Earth as formerly directed."[28] This method of surfacing was used by Xerxes centuries before on the boat bridge his army used in crossing the Hellespont.

The roads were necessarily surfaced only to the extent of rough grading to eliminate holes and hummocks so as to permit passage of supply wagons. The effect of rain and frost on the roads was disastrous. Maintenance and re-building were a constant challenge. Colonel Eyre, on his visit to inspect Fort Pitt, criticized the road builders for not having more carefully selected routes on mountain grades to prevent the water from running on the roads as in a stream bed. Eyre urged the installation of diagonal logs in the road at intervals, to divert the water to the sides.

Wagons and Horses

The following "Advertisement for Wagons, Horses, Drivers, Etc." appeared in the *Pennsylvania Gazette* on May 11, 1758. "Each wagon four good strong Horses, drag chain 11 ft long with hook at each end, knife for cutting grass, falling-axe, shovel, 2 sets clouts, 5 sets nails, iron hoop at end of every axle-tree, linen mangoe, 2 gallon keg of tar and oil mixed together, a slip, bell, hobbles, 2 sets shoes, 4 sets shoe nails for each horse, 2 sets spare hames, 5 sets hame-strings, bag for provisions, spare set of linch pins, hand screw for every 6 wagons. Drivers to be provided also. Owners to receive for service of above 15 shillings per day until return home. For 4 horses with driver for artillery without harness or any other thing, 10 shillings, 6 pence per day. Every horse to be provided with 6 gallons oats per day or Indian corn in proportion. Each wagoner to bring gun for protection of horse when grazing. Wagonners to have charge and driving horses. Wagons wanted at Carlisle to be obtained in 'back counties'." The response to such appeals was most discouraging.

The difficulty of getting an adequate number of horses and wagons led Burd to suggest the expedient of getting the Assembly to pass a law "to oblige every Person without exception who has a Waggon to make one Trip with Provisions to the Army Penalty of 30 pounds —they to provide Forage and to be paid as the law directs."[29] This recommendation, as far as we know, was not considered by the Assembly.

Burd said in the spring of 1759 that if another escort was lost the posts would have to be abandoned. It was difficult enough to raise the quota of horses for Forbes' campaign, but after the incursion of the Indians on the frontier in the spring and summer of 1759, the farmers were more reluctant than ever before to trust their horses and wagons to the army. It was difficult to collect their money from the army and the pay was not commensurate with the value of this equipment on their farms, especially at harvest time.

Bouquet learned that horses "bought on the Frontiers of Virginia where they are commonly bred in the Woods" were better suited to work on the communications. The relatively cumbersome wagon was a necessary nuisance and hazard. As wagons could not readily be maneuvered around the obstacles on the narrow roads, it is likely that nothing was carried by wagon which could be loaded on pack horses. A pack horse, as we read in a Memorandum of January 1759, "cant Carry More than One Hundred Fifty Pounds, of goods and Fifty pound of Corn . . ." We read in another place where "200 Pack Horses . . . will carry 1200 Bush.ls of Oates, . . ." The relative number of wagons and pack horses varied, but in Bouquet's forces sent to relieve the siege of Fort Pitt in 1763 there was a convoy of 23 wagons, 285 pack horses and 160 bullocks.

This Memorandum continues with a graphic account of the difficulties encountered in land carriage with horses: ". . . one Third above the number of Horses to Carry goods, Must Carry Forrage, that is Indian Corn or Oats as there is no food upon The Road of any Kind. As soon as the Horse Load of Forrage is Eate the Horse must be sent or left at the first Post, Consequently Forrage must be Bought and Bags to Carry it in, and a Couple of Oil Cloths for the Drivers to Lay under, as there is no Shelter for them the whole Road. Every Bundle of goods that will take Hurt by Rain or Snow Must be Cover'd with a piece of Oil Cloth." To add to the load, "Spare Horse Shoes, Nails, Hammer, and spare Ropes Must be Taken along with them, The Horses all to be Ruff Shod as The Roads is full of Ice. Hopples and Bitts for the Horses, and Likewise a Kettle to dress the Drivers Meat, & one Falling Ax, to Cut Wood on the Road." He adds, "But it would be perhaps Cheapest to Contract with some Able Man to deliver the Goods at Pittsburgh, at so Much P Hundred, . . . "[30] The quartermaster was occasionally plagued with delivery of decrepit nags that obviously had been substituted for those originally contracted for. Seven hundred pack saddles were examined upon delivery, found defective and required complete re-stuffing. Making agreements with contractors in the east to deliver materials and food as well as cattle on the hoof to the western forts for a stipulated sum, relieved the army officers of a great responsibility and a serious drain on their manpower. The use of contractors could, of course, be practical only after forts had been established and roads completed to them.

The conveyance of food and supplies was subsequently done by contract. The principal contractor was Adam Hoops. When difficulty was experienced in securing regular supplies from eastern Pennsylvania, the route from Virginia was used. Thus in the summer of 1759, Bouquet arranged with Hoops to deliver 100 head of cattle each week, proceeding from Winchester by way of Braddock's route to Pittsburgh. By that time, on Burd's suggestion, the road had been reopened to the Monongahela and Burd had built a fortified store at that point, the present site of Brownsville. Fort Burd, as it was called, stood near the site of Trent's storehouse (described above), which had been destroyed by the French. From here boats could carry goods on to Pittsburgh. Hoops was engaged in September 1759 to supply meat to July 1, 1760 for 1300 men at Pittsburgh, 250 at Ligonier, 100 at Cumberland and Bedford and 25 at Redstone Creek (Fort Burd). Vats and barrels had been built at these posts to store the salt meat. The contracting agents were authorized in June of 1764 to deliver to Fort Loudoun by the first of October "the quantity of Flour, and of Large, & Fat Cattle, necessary to victual for Twelve Months" for the entire year of 1765 for 300 persons at Fort Pitt, 60 at Ligonier, 60 at Fort Bedford and 30 at Fort Cumberland.

The correspondence reveals the painful demand made on Adam Hoops to write in English and the equally excruciating problem imposed on his good friend, Bouquet, in deciphering them. Bouquet, who wrote normally in French and with difficulty in English, was thus required to read a German's version of the language. In this picturesque sample of their correspondence, Hoops in December of 1761 offers Bouquet the hospitality of his home: "I flater my Self to hauf ye plisher of Seeon you hear this Wonter Shud you pay thas Sety aviset I hauef a Logden prepered for you att my houes wich ples to Excpt of and you will obedg, Sir, your obdent Humbel Servent, ADm HOOPS."[31]

Whether supplies were carried by the army's horses or those of the contractors, these animals were the most vulnerable of living things on the march. The Indians had learned to use and depend on the white man's horse. In their frequent attacks on supply trains, they killed the horses they could not capture. This mortality was greatly increased in 1759, when the French, after their defeat, set the Indians on the communication with great effectiveness. Captain Bullit, bringing a convoy from Virginia, was attacked on May 23 about four miles from Ligonier. Of 100 men, 36 were killed or missing, all of the 50 wagon horses were killed or taken and most of the provisions were carried off on the same horses to the French forts. Captain Morgan, bringing desperately needed supplies to Fort Pitt, was attacked at Turtle Creek, lost five men and brought in the wounded and the supplies with great difficulty. The Indians became such a serious menace that even the hard-bitten Croghan was compelled to venture on the communication with the greatest caution.

Mortality among the horses was not confined to death by the Indian bullets and arrows, as we learn by reading the account of two contractors for pack horses, Robert Callender and Barnabas Hughes. This account gives "A List of the Different Bregads [brigades] of horses Killed & taken by the Enemy."[32] This claim, made at the rate of £7 for each horse lost, tells the story better than any narrative. We select a few entries at random.

	horses
Give out at Quamahone by Reason of ye Officer making me Drive to hard	2
Lost at Sney [Stoney Creek] by ye Enemy Philip McGowen Driver killed	29
Give out nigh Pittsburgh	1
Taken @ Differant Times by the Officers	4
Lost at Stoney Creek by Not Being allowed time by the Officer to hunt them	2
Give out by being Keep within ye Guard Six Days at fort Ligonier where there was no Pasture, & then Comm^d to drive off too fast	10

It should be mentioned that the officers, finding their forces in a desperate situation, often had no choice but to order the men to drive the horses to their death; the lives of the convoy and the garrison they were going to relieve were at stake.

Water Carriage

Travel by water, though less difficult than by land, presented serious problems, as witnessed by Marin's frustration when he was unable, because of low water in French Creek, to move his army in the fall of 1753 and occupy the Forks of the Ohio as ordered by Duquesne. Had the English taken full advantage of this delay, caused by a whim of the weather, to adequately fortify the Point, the course of history might have been greatly altered. The French were again deprived of the advantages of water carriage in the following winter when it was decided that they could not wait for the opening of the rivers and lakes because of the urgency of getting to the Forks of the Ohio before the English were established there. Deprived of the use of their canoes and batteaus they dragged their equipment and supplies by sled over the ice and snow. At certain seasons water was too low, even in the Allegheny and the Ohio, for the larger craft. Bouquet, on his first trip to Fort Burd up the Monongahela, stated that " . . . our Empty Battoes run aground twenty times, ... " On the other hand, travel by land was never impossible, even in the worst weather conditions.

Transport of troops was largely by Indian bark canoes or by pirogues, formed by hollowing out trees. Most of the freight was carried in batteaus, flat-bottomed boats with tapered ends, built of planks and operated with poles or oars. Flat-boats, barges and keel boats of larger capacity, were built somewhat later than the period under discussion. Harry Gordon stated that a batteau (battoe he spells it) 24 feet long could be made in two days by six men, one man to flitch knees, one sawyer for making plank. One barrel of pitch and one hundred pounds of oakum could caulk thirteen batteaus.

Wilderness Strategy

The arduous and perilous penetration of the mountain forests by military forces in America was a far cry from the progress of great armies in Europe over established roads, through populous areas and lands abounding in cattle and crops. Here there was no living off the land by pillage or purchase of food and supplies; the dense and gloomy woodlands contained little food for man and almost none for the animals. In Europe the location and nature of the enemy was generally known and even the field of battle usually could be anticipated, but in America, knowledge of the movements and striking force of the enemy was difficult to obtain. Moreover the Indian that lurked in the forests constituted a new and sinister hazard. Always a potential enemy, the Indian was suspicious and resentful of French and English alike. At unpredictable moments the Indian could harass the thin lines on the communication and at times utterly annihilate the invading white man's forces.

The army was thus required to live off itself, and solve the problems of self protection as it went along, leaving to the uncertain and distant future the successful engagement of the white enemy. The resourceful Bouquet developed a technique for movement and defense of troops and supply trains in the forests which is lucidly described in the published account of his expedition against the Ohio Indians in 1764. The success of this campaign stands out brilliantly against the frightful record of disasters both before and after this event. This account is quoted liberally because it remains the best statement of the problem faced by the English armies in the wilderness.

"An European, to be a proper judge of this kind of war, must have lived some time in the vast forests of America; otherwise he will hardly be able to conceive a continuity of woods without end. In spite of his endeavors, his imagination will betray him into an expectation of open and clear grounds, and he will be apt to calculate his manoeuvers accordingly, too much upon the principles of war in Europe.

"Let us suppose a person, who is entirely unacquainted with the nature of this service, to be put at the head of an expedition in America. We will further suppose that he has made the dispositions usual in Europe for a march, or to receive an enemy; and that he is then attacked by the savages. He cannot discover them, tho' from every tree, log or bush, he received an incessant fire, and observes that few of their shot are lost. He will not hesitate to charge those invisible enemies, but he will charge in vain. For they are as cautious to avoid a close engagement, as indefatigable in harassing his troops; and notwithstanding all his endeavours, he will still find himself surrounded by a circle of fire, which, like an artificial horizon, follows him everywhere.

"Unable to rid himself of an enemy who never stands his attacks, and flies when pressed, only to return upon him again with equal agility and vigour; he will see the courage of his heavy troops droop, and their strength at last fail them by repeated and ineffectual efforts.

"He must therefore think of a retreat, unless he can force his way thro' the enemy. But how is this to be effected? His baggage and provisions are unloaded and scattered, part of his horses and drivers killed, other dispersed by fear, and his wounded to be carried by soldiers already fainting under the fatigue of a long action. The enemy, encouraged by his distress, will not fail to encrease the disorder, by pressing upon him on every side, with redoubled fury and savage howlings.

"This is a problem which I do not pretend to resolve. But as every man would, in similar circumstances, determine himself some way or other, I will propose my own sentiments, founded upon some observations which I believe invariable in all engagements with savages.

"The first, that their general maxim is to surround their enemy.

The second, that they fight scattered, and never in a compact body. The third, that they never stand their ground when attacked, but immediately give way, to return to the charge.

"These principles being admitted, it follows 1st. That the troops destined to engage Indians, must be lightly cloathed, armed, and accoutred. 2d. That having no resistance to encounter in the attack or defence, they are not to be drawn up in close order, which would only expose them without necessity to a greater loss. And, lastly, that all their evolutions must be performed with great rapidity; and the men enabled by exercise to pursue the enemy closely, when put to flight, and not give them time to rally."[33]

This account is illustrated by diagrams showing the deployment of the army on the march, its baggage train and lateral scouting troops as well as the formation of an improvised fortified camp when under attack. These observations were the fruit of Bouquet's bitter experience in some ten years of wilderness warfare. They reflect the keen judgment of the incomparable Bouquet who learned the Indian's ways and successfully adapted his strategy to meet them.

It was the strict obedience to Bouquet's orders for "Disposition in case of an Attack on the March" that saved his forces in the engagement at Bushy Run. "The Troops are to halt, and form immediately the Square, The Soldiers being at least one Yard distance from one another. The Cattle & light Horse are to come in to the Square in the center. The Powder in the Center. Four Brigades of Bat Horses are to unload when they receive orders, along the Rear of Each Face of the Square and crowd their Horses behind their loads that the whole may come in. This must be done without Hurry, or Noise to avoid Confusion. The soldiers are to have one knee on the ground, resting upon their Arms, and not fire a Shot till they are ordered."

The unfamiliarity of the continental troops with forest conditions put them to some disadvantage. Bouquet wrote Amherst in July of 1763: "Having observed on our March that the Highlanders lose themselves in the Woods as soon as they go out of the Road, & cannot, on that Acct. be employed as Flankers; I have commissioned a Person here to procure me about thirty Woodsmen to march with us." He does not mean to disparage the Scots for he later wrote: ". . . the Highlanders are the bravest Men I ever Saw, and their behavior in that obstinat affair [Bushy Run] does them the highest honor."[34] Following Grant's defeat in 1758, Bouquet reported that "The Provincials appear to have done well and their good men are better in this war than regular troops." Bouquet, after lifting the siege of Fort Pitt, did not think it wise to proceed then against the Indians "as I cannot think of employing Regular Troops alone, who are totally unacquainted with the Woods, and unable to Flank and Reconnoitre without the Assistance of Woodsmen to procure Intelligence; . . ."[35]

Recruitment

The problems and exasperations of recruiting provincials for service on the frontier appear throughout the records of military correspondence and orders. Recruiting officers were instructed by Bouquet at Charlestown in 1757 to select men who fulfilled the following requirements: "You are not to enlist any Man under five feet four Inches high, or above the Age of thirty five years, or a Papist or a French Deserter. Your Recruits must be broad shoulder'd, well limb'd, and without Infirmities, Ruptures, Scal'd heads or sore legs, but every Way fit for Service."[36] The same standards were likely used in seeking soldiers for Forbes Army in 1758. However, Bouquet refused to admit French deserters from Canada in his ranks as "they always have a fleur de lis in their heart or on their shoulder." He advertised for volunteers to serve in his Indian campaign of 1764 in these words: ". . . This is to give Notice to all Voluntiers who are disposed to Serve their Country in joining the Expedition under my Command, That they will receive Provisions from Fort Loudon and back again to that Post with Ammunition, and whatever occasional Assistance they might Stand in Need of in Case of Accidents during the Campaign." As a special inducement he added, "All those who Shall take Prisoners or Scalps of Enemy Indians during the Course of the Expedition may depend upon proper Certificates and Recommendations to enable them to obtain the Reward by this Government." He adds a "P.S." which was not calculated to cause a stampede of volunteers: "I hope the volunteers understand that it is not in my Power to allow them Pay."[37]

In 1758 the response from Pennsylvania was disheartening. After having raised a part of the quota it was next to impossible to outfit the men. George Stevenson wrote to Colonel Henry Bouquet in May of 1758: "I can't conceive what this province means, by raising Men, and suffering them to spend so much Time, without Cloaths and Accoutraments, when his Majesty's Service so much wants them . . . they have neither sent the Money, nor the Arms."[38]

The public response became progressively worse. When Bouquet asked for volunteers for his Ohio campaign in 1764 to subdue the Indians who had been continually on the warpath since the Pontiac uprising, "The People being upon the Point to abandon their frontier . . . unless I can take the bloody Savages off their back," he finally expostulated, "For my own Part I am So much disgusted at the Backwardness of the Frontier People in assisting us in taking Revenge of the Savages who murder them daily with Impunity, that I hope this will be the Last Time I shall Venture my Reputation and Life for their Sake."[39]

Arms

Building the roads and obtaining means of conveyance were no less challenging than the problem of recruiting and securing military equipment for the men. Bouquet wrote to Forbes from Carlisle in May of 1758: "I find their Battalions in the most frightful disorder. Their guns are entirely unfit for use, more than three fourths unfit to fire, the wood in pieces, and the screw-plates attached to the guns with string. They have no tents, neither the officers nor the soldiers. Not a single kettle, axe, or tomahawk. No ammunition or provisions, and no one to furnish them. Mr. Hoops [the agent] is obliged to feed them, and keeps a separate account of his distributions." The commissioners of Pennsylvania offered no substantial aid. At another time Bouquet wrote: "The sabers, or rather hangers, which were given to the light cavalry, are a joke. It is their principal weapon, and they could not kill a chicken with this tiny knife." It scarcely seems credible as we think of the triumph at Fort Duquesne five months later, that Bouquet could have written Forbes in June of 1758: "You are not to overlook the fact that no one in this country can be relied on. At all times, private interests outweigh the general welfare."[40]

Bouquet wrote from Carlisle in May that "The new guns that Bird has received, burst; and not a soldier dares to fire them. The rest are old rusty muskets as heavy as two of our guns. If guns fit for service are not provided without delay, we shall certainly receive a setback." Another drawback was that "The difference in caliber of the provincials' guns is a great inconvenience, since they have no molds, and our bullets cannot be used in them." It is interesting to note that "A large part of the provincials are armed with grooved rifles, and have their molds. Lead in bars will suit them better than bullets—likewise the Indians—, but they also need fine powder FF."[41] The records contain a detailed set of instructions for casting shot in the field. Bouquet's "Detail for a March,"[42] 1758 (from Ligonier) gives reliable information of his army's needs: "Proportion of Artillery, Ammunition, Tools, Provisions, Rum, and forrage for a Detachment of 3000 Men including officers, &c or 2500 R.F.

4	Six Pounders	Horses	16
40	Rounds Each, Powder &ca	1 Waggon	
6	Cohorns & Amm: Buck Shott.	2 do	
24	Barrills of Cartridges or the quantity of Powder & Balls for 12 Spare Rounds pr Man	4 do	
200	falling Axes & two Grind Stones	1	
	Intrenching Tools	1	
	Rum & forrage	6	
		15 at 6-	90
	A forge Cart	Draught H.	106
	Flying Hospital	6 Pack horses	
3000#	of flour 1/2 allowance for five days to Col. Armst: detach:	25 at 120#	
15000#	do 1/2 allowance for ten days for 3000 Men	125 at do	
7200#	do for 8 days for 1800 Men to be carried by themselves.		
9,000#	Meat for five days for 1200 Men at 1 1/2# pr Man	30	
18,000#	do for 10 days for do	60	
48,600#	do for 18 days for 1800 Men:	162	
75,600#		252 Bullocks	

Clothing and Equipment

However badly the men were clothed, serviceable shoes were an obvious necessity. Bouquet mentions that "Experience makes me feel the necessity of having a good supply of shoes, .. besides the 3 pairs which each soldier ought to carry including the ones on his feet. The dew in the woods make the leather as supple as old linen, and as the roads are stony, a pair of shoes is in pieces in a week." Moccasins were fashioned from cured deer skin. Burd, in a "Proposal for Protection," recommended the use of green uniforms for purposes of camouflage, as most of the action was in the summer. This may have been the reason that Forbes ordered that the new Pennsylvania levies have "all short green Coats, lapell'd with the same . . ."[43]

DEFENSE IN THE WILDERNESS

Lieutenant Alexander Baillie in a letter to Bouquet of August 28, 1762, made a "Return of the Weight for the Cloathing, Arms, Accoutrements, Ammunition, Provision, Necessary's &C^a of a Grenadier, upon a March."[44] This came to a total of 63¾ pounds and consisted of the following:

Item	Weight Lbs.	Q^{rs}	Item	Weight Lbs.	Q^{rs}
A Regimental Coat, with Hooks, Eyes, &c^a	5.	2.	A Knapsa(ck) with Strap, and Buckles	1.	2.
Waistcoat	2.	1.	Containing 2 Shirts, 2 Socks, 2 Pair Stockings	2.	3.
Pair of Breeches	1.	2.			
Hat with cocade, Button, Loop, & Hair String	1.	--			
			A Pair Summer Breeches	1.	1.
A Shirt with Sleeve Buttons	1.	--			
			A Pair Shoes	1.	1.
A Stock with a Buckle					
A Pair Knee Buckles.	--	3.	A Clothes Brush, pair Shoe Brushes, & Black Ball	1.	--
A Pair Stocking & Garters					
A Pair Shoes with Buckles	1.	2.			
A Regimental Firelock, with a Sling & Buckle Hammer Cap & Stopper	11.	1.	A Pair Leggins & Garters A Handkerchief	1.	1.
			2 Combs, a Knife, & Spoon	--	2.
A Waist Belt with a Buckle	--	2.			
			A Haversack, with a Strap Containing Six Days Provision	--	3.
A Hanger, Sword Knot, and Scabbord	2.	3.		10.	1.
A Bayonet and Scabbord	1.	1.			
			A Blanket with Strap & Garters	3.	2.
A Tomahawk, and Cover	1.	3.			
A Cartridge Pouch with Belt, Buckles, & Match Case Containing 24 Cartridges	3. 2.	-- 1.	A Canteen with a String, & Stopper, full of Water	3.	1.
Brush & Wire, Worm, & Turnkey Oyl Bottle & Rag. 2 Flints & a Steel	--	1.		63.	3.

We are able to visualize the every-day articles required by a soldier in a memorandum from Bouquet to the Governor of South Carolina, in March of 1758: "The Soldiers who were not Billeted on Public-Houses, were Lodged in Convenient Houses hired for that purpose, & properly furnished with Necessarys and Utensils as follows: To each Room: 1 Pot, 1 Frying Pan, 1 Ladle; 1 Flesh Fork, 1 Trivet or Pot Hook; 1 pair Dog Irons, I Shovel, 1 pair Tongs; 1 Broom, 1 Tub or Box to carry out the Dirt; 1 Long Table & 2 Forms; 2 Platters, 2 Bowls, & 12 Trenchers; 2 Pitchers & 2 Mugs, 1 Hatchet; I Candlestick, 2 Chamber Pots; A Rack for the Men's Arms & wooden Peggs to hang their Knapsacks; Haversacks Cloaths &ca. For every 2 Men One Bedstead; 1 Bed; 1 Bolster; 3 Blankets. And a reasonable Proportion of Wood, Candles, Small Beer, Pepper Salt & Vinegar."[45]

In contrast to this list it is revealing to read of actual conditions in the field. Blane complained to Bouquet about conditions at Fort Ligonier: "I must als [also] beg leave to ask what you intend to do with the poor starved Militia who have neither Shirts, Shoes or any thing else nor are they to be got here." And even at Fort Pitt things were no better as we see in a letter from Captain James Robertson to General Stanwix of August of 1759: "The Condition The Detachment of Highlanders, I have the honour to command here is in, oblige me to lay the Case before you. The men have scarcely a Stitch of Cloathes, their Coats were all in Raggs before the End of last Campaign; they had few or no hose then; their Plaids were Extremely bad, and now numbers of them have none at all; so that they are oblige to sleep at Night in the Raggs they ware all day whether wet or dry. to this, Sir, I may add that I have no mony to given them, nor no Credit left; so far as I know, to get any."[46]

Sickness

Added to these deplorable conditions was the problem of sickness from exhaustion, exposure, unsanitary conditions and both insufficient and bad food. Most pernicious was the ever present scurvy which persisted even though its causes were generally understood.

Colonel Armstrong, in a reminder to General Stanwix in May of 1759, mentions: "I hope you have not lost Sight of the great necessity of fresh Provisions for those poor fellows along this Communication who are living all Winter & Spring upon Salt Pork without Vegetables." J. C. B., an unidentified French soldier and storekeeper at Presqu'Isle, suspected that scurvy was a diet problem. He was forbidden to give bread, wine or brandy to anyone but the officers and the surgeon. "The commissary gave me the same orders. I saw with reluctance, however, that we were reduced to letting the sick suffer and die with nothing but medicine to help them." He broke the rules and secretly gave a selected 22 of the men in the hospital small portions of bread, wine, brandy and fresh game in place of the salt meat diet. "I had the satisfaction of seeing my patients improve daily, and at the end of a fortnight they were quite convalescent. Four or five of the others were buried each day." On the other hand the doctor at Fort Niagara, James Stevenson, offered this terrifying prescription: " . . . we have very little Rum in the Garrison & a proper quantity is necessary to prevent the Scurvy, especially if the Spruce Beer is not made with the due proportion of Spruce & Molasses." The officers were also instructed that "constant & even Severe Exercise is the most Efficacious Antiscorbutick, . . ."[47]

Colonel Burd was deeply distressed about the scurvy victims: "their teeth ready to drop out of their mouths and their flesh as black as coal." We know that scurvy is a "deficiency" disease caused by lack of Vitamin C and characterized by failure of strength and by mental depression and resulting in shallow complexion, sunken eyes, tender gums and muscular pain. The men recovered rapidly and completely with a diet of fresh vegetables. It was not until 1795 that the British navy finally discovered a practical antidote for this common scourge, began regular rations of lime juice, and eliminated scurvy completely.

Insubordination and Unrest

Considering the hard conditions and perils of service in the wilderness it is small wonder that desertion and insubordination were common problems. Bouquet dealt tolerantly with those called up for misdemeanors, observing that "being Set down in a wilderness Detached from the world it will make great alterations in peoples tempers." Defections were a serious matter to officers even in remote posts such as Venango where, in 1760, many deserted. Bouquet, in desperation, wrote Forbes: "If you cannot come soon, I beg you to send me a warrant for general courts martial. An example must be made to stop desertion. We have a man here [Bedford], who has offered his services to do the hanging."[48]

By late 1763 insubordination had become a very serious problem. Captain Stewart in leading a convoy from Bedford to Ligonier lost eleven men by desertion in the first two days. He said, "We have had nothing since we Came to bedford but the Greatest Mutiny and Disobedience of Orders. some of the R. Americans threatned to Shute their officers . . ." Ecuyer puts it a little stronger in writing from Bedford at the same time. " . . . I have served over 22 years, but have never seen such a tribe of rebels, bandits, and hamstringers, especially the grenadiers. I have been obliged, after all imaginable patience, to have two of them horsewhipped on the spot and without court-martial. One wanted to kill the sergeant and the other wanted to kill me . . . In the name of God let me retire into private life. It is in your power, Sir, to let me go, and I shall have eternal gratitude. I was on the point of blowing his brains out, but fear of killing or wounding several of those around us stopped me. What a disagreeable thing!"[49]

The tedium of service in the constricted quarters of the garrison during the occasional periods of inactivity proved to be almost intolerable, even for men with the patience of Bouquet. Ecuyer wrote in April of 1763: "Lieutenant Donnellan and Surgeon Boyd have been fighting with fists and cudgels without decisive results for three days. However, after several such useless encounters, I was forced to put them under arrest in order to prevent further disorders." It is beyond the scope of this article to present the many entries in the records of unrest and discord in the garrisons and the slovenly communities that grew up about them. The case is well stated by Dr. Stevenson writing from Fort Niagara in 1761: "The want of Society, & being obliged to pass our time, so miserably uniform, hurts us every way, but we hope for better days . . . . . our people are in Shocking Condition without any thing regular, about them, having been so long labourers that the soldier is buried under the Clown."[50]

The "expresses" or the men who carried the letters that remain today our library of knowledge of those times were dispatched almost daily by officers from all parts of the communication. No matter what the circumstances or risk to the bearer, this service had to be maintained. Ecuyer sent and received letters while Fort Pitt was under siege. Bouquet wrote a dispatch at nightfall describing the first day's action at Bushy Run. This message had to be carried through the lines of the Indians who lay all about them in the forests, waiting to renew the fight at break of day. Yet there is no word of praise or even mention in the records of these indomitable expresses beyond a passing reference in a letter from Colonel Reid to Bouquet in September of 1764: ". . . that Brown, one of the former Expresses, has been murder'd by the Savages, and his head Stuck upon a Pole in the Midle of the Road, . . ."

Low and High Society at the Forts

The commandants at Fort Pitt were unanimous in their complaints about the white hangers-on who largely occupied the Lower Town. Ecuyer, concerned about loss of stores by theft, said, "I shall be obliged, therefore, to take more and more measures considering that everyone here, except the garrison, is the scum of nature." The social life in Fort Pitt was, from all accounts, not of a high level. Bouquet in December of 1760 issued an order forbidding sale of strong liquor: "The Commanding Officer is informed that several Women belonging to this garrison keep dram Shops, That practice being contrary to order & good dicipline, and evidently productive of very bad Consequences: . . . ." After the first of the year "none but licenced suttlers are to sell, give, or any other way dispose of strong liquor Whatever." Bouquet, after sending away a woman for an infraction of post regulations, said: "She is not better than the Rest of her kind that are here who Seem a Colony sprung from Hell for the Scourge of this Place."[51]

Lieutenant William Potts in a letter of January 1763, kept Bouquet informed on the more elegant aspects of social life at Fort Pitt: "We are all in High spirits here, And as we have News so seldom from the Busy world, we Amuse ourselves weekly not only with a Club But a Grand Assembly. The Last Night we Musterd 12 or 13 Couples Old, and Young, for you must know the Mothers and Grandmothers, Attend to vouch for the Chastity of their Daughters, as well as be their Guardians for the Night as we have none but those of the Strictest Virtue." George Croghan, the veteran trader, seemed to be everywhere. "But Croghan Generally pushes Aboute the Glass so Copiously and briskly amongst the Old Women that before half the Night's over they forget their Errand as well as their Charge, and what then follows is easily guest at." Ecuyer, the commandant, supplemented this social note by another written the same day: "I forgot, Sir, to tell you that we have a club every Monday and a ball every Saturday evening, made up of the prettiest ladies of the garrison. We regale them with punch, and if it is not strong enough, the whiskey is at their disposal. You may be sure that we shall not be completely cheated."[52]

Liquor was considered a necessity on the frontier. Colonel John Reid, on his arrival at Fort Pitt in August 1764 with a new supply, wrote Bouquet: "Even the Commanding officer at this place was reduced to the necessity of drinking Water for Six Weeks past, you may Therefor imagine we were welcome Guests." As Bouquet said: "A soldier will work cheerfully to earn his rum, . . ."

The Lost Village of Pittsburgh

A relatively peaceful condition prevailed at the Forks of the Ohio between 1758 and 1763. With the building of Mercer's Fort in 1758 and 1759 and the construction of Fort Pitt between 1759 and 1761 there was a gradual increase in population both of the garrison and in the motley colony that sprang up around the fort. Included were "suttlers" or tradesmen, "artificers" or workmen, contractor's agents, Indian agents and traders and others difficult to classify. No one was permitted to own buildings or property but this did not prevent the construction of a great variety of small log houses, bark-roofed huts, plank warehouses and many other haphazardly built shelters. Our only knowledge of these buildings is through reference in the written record which contains several census counts, descriptions of flood damage, removal of houses upon threat of attack and other occasional entries.

Colonel Burd made a count[53] in June of 1760 of the number of houses and inhabitants that "do not belong to the Army" at Fort Pitt. He found 146 houses, 19 unfinished houses and 36 huts. These were occupied by 88 men, 29 women, 14 boys and 18 girls. The following year he built a house for himself on the hill outside the fort. This building was subsequently used as a school until its demolition in 1763.

A return was made April 15, 1761, which listed every house with the owner's name and, in some instances, his occupation. The number of men, women and children in each house is also noted. The list is divided into four sections, denoting separate building groups, The Lower Town, The Upper Town, The Artillery and an Officers' Area. The Lower Town, which stood within the Epaulement on the Allegheny River side, was sheltered by the fort. Everyone who could not be accommodated in the fort proper was brought into this area during the siege of 1763 and it is presumed that these dwellings were not destroyed at that time. In 1761 the Lower Town had 58 houses containing 104 men, 19 women and 10 children. Fourteen of these were soldiers including three "battoe men," one baker, nine artificers and three ship's carpenters. The houses of George Croghan and William Trent were in the Lower Town, which was well named judging by its low moral tone as reflected in the records. Ecuyer, after the flood of 1763, said: ", . . . I could wish that not one house had escaped, so as to force them to build elsewhere."[54]

The Upper Town contained 87 houses, in which lived 93 men, 43 women and 23 children. Two of these buildings were hospitals, then accommodating seven soldiers. It was the invariable practice, except in time of attack, to keep all sick men outside the fort to isolate small pox and other contagious diseases. Captain Bassett, the engineer, as well as a number of soldiers lived in this the Upper Town. There were seven "emty" houses.

A third area known as the "Artilery," and containing eight houses lay just outside the Epaulement on the Monongahela shore. Here lived nine artillerymen, six women and five children. The fourth area is not identified by name or location but it likely lay on the Monongahela shore also. It contained two houses marked "The Mess House & the Generals House" for which no occupants are listed. Captain William Clapham and Captain Barnsley set a high tone for the community, as each had a house with three servants. There were two other officers' houses, making in all eight houses with a total population of thirteen men, seven women and no children.

As mentioned elsewhere, those who could afford to do so, apparently moved out of the confining, unsanitary quarters of the fort when the Indians were not actively hostile. Captain John Schlosser wrote from Fort Niagara in July of 1760 that: "Our men are still camping in the ravelin and covered road [way] because the 44th regiment left the barracks so dirty and odorous that it is unconceivable that they did not all die from filth and stench . . . "

Of the 332 persons living outside the fort in April of 1761 (ignoring minor errors in arithmetic) there were, exclusive of the fourth area, 233 "Inhabitants" and 79 soldiers. There were, all told, 75 women and 38 children.

The contemporary drawings show the fort layout in plan and the gardens on the Allegheny but none of the outlying structures mentioned above. To visualize the appearance of the Point in this period before the Indian uprising we must imagine, in addition to the fort itself, helter-skelter arrangements of crude dwellings of log, plank and bark, one in the area north of the fort but enclosed by its outworks, another group along the bank of the Monongahela about where the Diamond Market stands today, and the small group of buildings for the artillery adjacent to the fort on the Monongahela Bank. The officers' houses probably abutted these and there was a scattering of houses on the slopes of Grant's Hill.

The area lying on the bank of the Allegheny River and reaching up toward present day Tenth Street and southward into the center of the triangle, was occupied by The King's Garden for the garrison. Adjacent to it were smaller garden plots, grazing land for the cattle and horses and a large field of corn and other grains. There were also small private garden plots next to some of the houses in both the Upper and Lower Towns. The gardens are more fully described elsewhere.

By 1763 Pittsburgh had become a sizable, though highly improvised frontier village. However picturesque it may seem to us today, it was by all accounts a very undesirable place to live except for the hardened traders and backwoodsmen. The officers and soldiers longed to return to the safety and comfort of the East.

Indians at the Forts

The free enterprise system of the English in Indian trading was sharply contrasted with the state action and private monopoly of the French, as pointed out by Lawrence Henry Gipson. The looms and forges of England, and also, unfortunately, the distilleries of America, supplied the Indians with better goods at lower prices than could the French. Thus was created a vast credit structure beginning in the manufacturing centers of England, and reaching, through the American traders and Indian agents, to the remote Indian settlements of the western plains. The Canadian beaver and other northern animals with their heavier fur brought the highest prices. Eager to obtain the better trade goods of the English, the Indians of New France smuggled their hides through the French lines to trade at Oswego and Albany.

One of the most important functions of the frontier fort was to provide facilities for trading and conferences with the Indians. They must have clothing, food, powder, and shot and their horses must be shod. Supposedly they would offer in trade their furs and hides, venison, corn and other commodities. But often the Indians had nothing to offer and the garrison frequently ran low in trade goods. The French had built a number of cabins for the Indians at Logstown and quarters for their chiefs at Fort Duquesne. The English Indian Commissioners constructed a storehouse for Indian goods at Mercer's Fort in December of 1759 and an Indian conference house at Fort Pitt in the summer of 1762. Additional facilities were required for storage of hides and furs and the trade goods for which they were exchanged.

From the records of various invoices of Indian goods, we find a bewildering variety, including such items as vermilion, kettles, broaches, mirrors, ribbons, penknives, coat buttons, trinkets, calico, crosses, hair and arm ornaments, garterings and brass jew's-harps. The jew's-harp, the only musical instrument mentioned in the records, apparently fascinated the Indians. Wampum was necessary in all formal Indian dealings. The commercial wampum from England was made of small beads strung in the approved lengths and forms required by the Indians to reinforce each principal point in their address. This manufactured wampum largely replaced the relatively scarce and costly Indians' wampum of shells. In February of 1760, 25,000 black wampum was delivered to Fort Pitt at a price of forty-five and a half pounds sterling.

The standard of currency in Indian trading was the fall buck skin. From this came the slang expression of a "buck" as the equivalent for a dollar. The equivalents of a buck skin were listed by George Croghan as follows:[55]

1 Fall Buck a Buck
2 Does a Buck
2 Spr(ing) Bucks a Buck
1 large Buck Beaver a Buck
2 Doe Beavers a Buck
6 Raccoons a Buck

4 Foxes a Buck
2 Fishers a Buck
2 Otters a Buck
3 Summer Bucks for 2 Bucks
3 Summer Does for a Buck

Parchment & Drest Leather to be taken as Summer skins.

Having established the above table of equivalent values for the Indians' skins, Croghan fixed the following prices for trade goods stocked in trading centers at the various frontier forts. This list, made in Detroit in February of 1761, is endorsed in Colonel Bouquet's handwriting. These prices applied uniformly throughout the British area.

Strouds	4 Bucks	6 Fathom Gartering	1 ditto
Match Coats	3 Bucks	2 Fathom Ribbon	1 ditto
Blanketts	4 ditto	1" Vermillion	6 ditto
1 Pint Powder	1 ditto	4 small Knives	1 ditto
4 Bars Lead	1 ditto	1 Fathom Callicoe	3 ditto
1 plain Shirt	2 ditto	1 large flag Handkerchief	1 buck 1 doe
1 Rufled ditto	4 ditto	1 Fathom Callemanco	2 bucks
1 pair Stockings	1 ditto	Kittles (Brass)	1 to 10 Bucks
100 Wampum	1 ditto	Tin Kittles	1 Doe to 3 Bucks
2 (Cutteaus)	1 ditto		

Arm Bands   Ear bobs
Wrist Bands   Crosses
hair Plates   Half Moons   } These with all other kind of Silver Ware according to Weight & fashion.
Broaches   Gorgets
Hair Bobs   Trinkets

1 Worsted Cap single............1 Doe
1 double ditto............1 Buck
Embossed flannel............2 Bucks a fathom
Looking Glasses }
Flowred Ribbon } according to their size
Trunks } and goodness
Threads............according to their finess

The storage and care of the skins and their transportation to the East was the source of considerable activity at the garrison and on the communication. Likewise the importation of the goods from Europe, their carriage westward and storage and sale at the posts was a considerable industry. The diary of James Kenny, who kept store at Fort Pitt, is mentioned elsewhere. This colorful account of first-hand contact between Quaker and Indian provides one of the few reliable and extended descriptions of life in the village of Pittsburgh.

The flourishing Indian trade established by George Croghan and his fellow traders as representatives of the contractors in the east was interrupted by the entrance of the French into the Ohio valley in 1753. After the expulsion of the French in 1758 from the upper Ohio, normal trade was never completely re-established because of the intermittent warfare with the Indians. Eager to regain the allegiance of the natives, the Indian Commissioners in Philadelphia established trading stores at the forts. The construction of such buildings at Mercer's Fort and Fort Pitt are described elsewhere. In establishing acceptable terms of trade, the experience of the veteran Croghan was invaluable as he understood the Indians and, though known as a sharp dealer, was respected by them.

The Indian village on the north bank of the Allegheny occupied an area that was almost entirely cut off from the land by a channel of water so that it became an island in higher stages of the river. This is recognized on Meyer's drawing, Illustration 24. Great numbers of Indians came to trade and to beg food, until the open hostilities following the uprising of 1763. These Indians presented a grievous problem to the commandants, even more serious than the unruly white inhabitants.

The Indians could not be ignored nor wished away. As established in treaties the fort was tolerated by the Indians only as a temporary device to drive the French from the district and firmly to establish English trade supremacy, not ownership of the land. The settlement of houses about the fort was tolerated as a necessity in housing those employed in the fort construction and Indian trade. But, once the fort had achieved its ends, Indians expected it to be removed and, more important, that everything resembling white settlement be abandoned.

English relations with the Indians suffered from the confused and disunited policies of the colonies. Though Bouquet felt he should not "interfere in Indian Politics" he could not stand idly by. He recommended to General Jeffery Amherst in April of 1760 the following terms for inclusion in his agreement with the Indians: "As the necessity of H.M. Service obliges him to take Post & build Forts in some Parts of their Country to protect our trade with them, to prevent the Enemy from taking Possession of the Same & hurt both the Indians & us. In that Case he assures them that no Part whatever of their Land joining the Said Forts shall be taken from them, nor any of his People permitted to hunt upon the Same, but that they shall inviolably be theirs, & that even he promises that they shall Receive some Presents as a Consideration for the small Spots upon which the Forts shall or do stand." Bouquet also foresaw the serious problem of supply. "And as it is very expensif & difficult to carry Provisions for the use of the Garrisons of said Forts, & also to supply our brethren the Indians when they come to see us, If they will allow us a spott of ground adjoining every Fort to be used to raise Corn for the said Purpose In that Case they will themselves settle the Limits of that Part of their Land so appropriated, & receive a Consideration for the same as will be agreed between us & them." These terms were substantially incorporated in the subsequent treaty. The British government, as an act of good faith, in 1762 issued an edict "to prevent People hunting or Settling to the Westward of the Allegheny Hills."[56]

Bouquet, desperately trying in 1762 to reconcile Indian relations with white encroachment, viewed the settlers as "a number of Vagabonds, who under the pretence of hunting were making Settlements . . . " and after his successful Indian campaign in Ohio in 1764 advised Gage that "The Licenciousness of the Frontier Inhabitants in general is carried to a high degree of Insolence . . . " and that it would be impossible to preserve peace with the Indians unless "Severe Measures" were taken to restrain them.[57]

Needless to say, the commandants at Fort Pitt and especially those of the smaller western forts had their hands full in dealing with the Indians who came there from western Pennsylvania, Ohio, and as far away as the Great Lakes, seldom less than two hundred at a time. In his quandary, the commandant recognized that many of the Indians were allies or spies of the French and that the powder and shot doled out to them in exchange for furs and food would likely as not be used on his own men or frontier settlers. To refuse the Indians was equally risky, even when he had nothing to trade. When Campbell, at Detroit, was ordered to refuse powder to the Indians he complained: " . . . I am certain if the Indians in this Country had the least hint that we intended to prevent them from the use of Ammunition, it would be impossible to keep them Quiet, I dare not trust even the Interpreters with the Secret . . . "[58]

In August of 1759, Bouquet wrote: "It is hoped that they [the Indians] will by degrees return to their former peaceable Way of living, Plant Corn, & Hunt, But in the present Circumstances we are Obliged to humor them tho' the Weight is almost intolerable."[59] Constant surveillance and caution were necessary to prevent the congregation of Indians in large numbers about the fort for fear of a surprise attack, their favorite ruse. It was also difficult to prevent the inhabitants from providing the Indians with rum and other unsanctioned trade articles.

Colonel Bouquet complained that the building of Fort Pitt was jeopardized "as long as all the Provisions forwarded are daily consumed by that Idle People [the Indians]." Bouquet wrote in September of 1759 that they had continually 400 to 500 Indians to feed at Pittsburgh and that if some aid from the Legislature was not forthcoming " . . ., we must loose all the Advantages obtained, with so much Pains, danger, & Expence, and the Peace with the Western Indians, and the building will remain imperfect." Bouquet ordered Croghan to put "an End to that useless Consumption; which is Our evident ruin." But Croghan, the Indian agent at the fort, did not apparently change his ways for Ecuyer wrote in April of 1763 "to think that in one month Mr. Croghan drew 17,000 pounds, half flour and half beef [for the Indians], makes one tremble . . . "[60]

Indians on the Communication

While the Indians were consuming the food at the forts they were at the same time, by attacks on the supply trains, adding to the tremendous task of transporting the food from the east. Gordon wrote Bouquet that in spite of the success at Niagara they could expect Indians "to infest the Communication, the Consequence of which is truly distressing as nothing is so wasteful and harrassing as large Escorts." In July of 1759 Major Tulleken advised Stanwix that "nothing can go safe with less than Five hundred men, . . . "[61] The success of the Indians in their frontier warfare is all the more impressive when one learns that the vast wooded stretches of the Alleghenies had a scant population of red men, even when numbers of western and northern Indians, urged by the French, joined the local savages in raiding the frontiers.

Before the area became the scene of international warfare, the English traders had enjoyed amicable relations with the Indians and had established trade of mutual satisfaction. The Indians when not aroused were a people of remarkable integrity and friendliness. Bouquet said of the Indians at the conference at Fort Loudoun in June of 1759: " . . . I was astonished to find so much spirit, imagination, strength, and dignity in savages." The translations of the speeches of the Indian chiefs may be ranked among the classics in their spirited imagery and directness of thought. From the Indian's point of view, it was a sad page in history when they finally recognized the white man as their nemesis. But when they did, they exhibited another facet of their character in their capacity for revenge. The almost incredible accounts of their delight in tortures of ingenious design, must be read against the background of a race facing expulsion from their lands, if not total extinction.

Once the savages had broken completely with the English and given provocation, the rancor of the English officers knew no bounds. In a memorandum of June 1763, Amherst made a suggestion of horrifying character: "Could it not be contrived to Send the Small Pox among those Disaffected Tribes of Indians? We must, on this occasion, Use Every Stratagem in our power to Reduce them." Bouquet readily agreed and the records contain a charge of £ 2, 13 and 6 for two blankets and two handkerchiefs "got from People in the Hospital to Convey the Small Pox to the Indians." Bouquet offered a counter-proposal to Amherst to make "use of the Spanish Method to hunt them with English Dogs, supported by Rangers and Some Light Horse, who would I think effectually extirpate or remove that Vermin."[62]

The pendulum had swung to the other extreme. The Indian trails had been made into roads for the armies, and were shortly to serve as highways for a migration of people over the mountains, seldom equaled in history. It is difficult to realize, as we walk about the streets of Pittsburgh today, that only two short centuries ago this was the forest home of another race. We hear far away, faintly, the voice of the Delaware chief who so plaintively voiced the predicament of his people: "The Frenchmen claim all the land above the Ohio, the Englishmen all the land below it; where is the Indian's land?" Nothing remains of this people but the beautiful Indian words we daily use, not the least musical of which are the Allegheny, the Monongahela and the Ohio.

IV. THE FIVE FORTS AT THE POINT

IN the five forts built at the Forks of the Ohio between 1754 and 1792, one may see almost all of the types of construction utilized by military engineers in North America in the eighteenth century. Fort Prince George provided a minimum defense, consisting merely of a squared-log house surrounded by a simple stockaded enclosure without ditch. Fort Duquesne was a timber and earth fort of common type with horizontal log front and palisaded rear face. Mercer's Fort presented a square arrangement of log houses which in themselves served as the curtain walls of the fort and which were joined by palisaded bastions. Fort Pitt, partly built of brick masonry, was a dirt fort with five bastions and distinguished by its uncommonly large size and extensive outworks. Fort Fayette was a bastioned stockade fort with double-storied blockhouses at the corners, a variation then becoming common on the frontier.

Of the five forts once standing in the triangle of modern Pittsburgh, Fort Duquesne and Fort Pitt are the only ones generally known to have existed and these two forts are commonly confused in the public mind. The only vestige which remains of all of these forts is the Blockhouse which generally passes for either Fort Duquesne or Fort Pitt but was not a part of either structure. Built as an outlying redoubt of Fort Pitt, this quaint structure remains the military symbol of triumph at the Forks. Bearing the scars of more than a century of use as a residence, the building was given in 1894 by Mrs. Mary Elizabeth Schenley to the Daughters of the American Revolution of Allegheny County. The restored Blockhouse remains the oldest authenticated building in Western Pennsylvania.

There are other remnants of the early forts beneath the ground as was learned when portions of the foundations and lower parts of the brick scarp wall of Fort Pitt were exposed to view in the archaeological investigations of 1943 and 1953. No other research of the kind has been made nor has the restoration of any of the forts been seriously planned. While full scale restoration of Fort Pitt is not feasible because of its great size, Point State Park will contain full size restorations of two of its bastions. These are the Monongahela and the Flag bastions. The Monongahela Bastion will contain a museum exhibiting scale models of the forts and related material.

Any realistic representation by restoration drawing or model of the forts built between 1753 and 1763 must necessarily be conjectural in many respects. Where feasible, digging at the site provides irrefutable evidence of the exact location and plan of the early structures, as well as fragments of the structure and artifacts. The ground at Fort Ligonier yielded some 450 articles ranging from uniform buttons and wagon hardware to gun flints and jew's-harps. But such archaeological research tells us little of the structure that once stood above ground. For this we must examine the various types of source material to be found in archives throughout this country and Europe.

As mentioned in Part Two, excellent eighteenth century drawings of all of the principal early forts in America are preserved in the libraries of the United States, Canada, France and England. The important drawings of the forts at the Point are illustrated in this article. None of these drawings provides adequate information to restore any of the forts completely and authentically. The drawings generally show only the plan and profile of the fort. However, there are occasional exceptions where somewhat more detailed plans give room arrangements and fireplace locations and occasionally elevations and sections of the buildings or even a section through a gun embrasure with the detail of a cannon platform. In a few rare instances perspective views of the completed fort were made, as in the case of Fort Ontario. (See Illustration 28.) It must be recognized that these plans and views may represent only the intention of the builders, not the completed result. Many of the forts were never finished, others suffered continual change. Gage complained that "One officer makes additions and the next pulls them down and there is no end to the different opinions of the Officers who relieve each other in the Command of the forts." The dates and signatures on the drawings do not necessarily indicate the time of construction or the person responsible for their design. The drawings are rarely accompanied by descriptive material that might answer these questions. There are many tantalizing references to surveys, plans, draughts, and other drawings in the military correspondence. Gordon requested Bouquet in January 4, 1759 to "Be so good as desire Capt Dudgeon to send the Survey of Pittsburgh by the First Opportunity." Mercer sent Bouquet "a Plan of Pittsbg," in a letter of January 19, 1759. Amherst thanked Stanwix in a letter of December 18, 1759 for "the Plan of Pittsburgh" he had just received. Some of these drawings undoubtedly exist today in the archives, but cannot be identified as they were not filed with the letters.[63]

Drawings, made by draftsmen working under the engineers, were submitted to the commanding officers and, if time permitted, were accompanied by careful cost estimates, some of which have been preserved. Such factors as limitations of material and money, changes in military plans, and adaptation to unanticipated site conditions could bring about changes in the plans when the forts were finally constructed. On the other hand, archaeological research has demonstrated that many of the more elaborate forts, notably Fort Pitt, followed the original drawings with great faithfulness. Surveying instruments were used with skill.

Our sources of knowledge of the early forts are limited to the contemporary fort drawings and maps and details gleaned from military papers, eye-witness accounts, and other written records of the time. It is soon learned that descriptions by travelers, spies and other lay observers are frequently as inaccurate and conflicting as the proverbial discrepancies between witnesses in court. This is not so much because of the reporter's unfamiliarity with building methods and terminology as his unconcern with the need for precise record. After a lifetime spent in ferreting out the innumerable pieces of this jig-saw puzzle it would still be necessary to supply the missing pieces by conjecture. This conjecture is rendered less hazardous by a knowledge of architecture and building, a study of the early handbooks on fortifications used by the military engineers and a liberal supply of common sense.

FORT PRINCE GEORGE

Virginia Takes the Initiative

The Indians, disturbed by the threatened occupation of the Ohio country by the French, urged the English at a conference in Logstown in May of 1751, to "build a strong House on the River Ohio, that if we should be obliged to engage in a War that we should have a Place to secure our Wives and Children, likewise to secure our Brothers that come to trade with us, for without our Brothers supply us with Goods we cannot live."[64] The government of Pennsylvania, to which this request was directed, failed to comply while

Virginia, eagerly awaiting the opportunity to exploit the western country by trade and settlement, took the initiative. The Ohio Company, a group of Virginia gentlemen and merchants, had sent Christopher Gist on two extensive survey trips through the Ohio country in 1751 and 1752, and in June of 1752 obtained an agreement with the Indians to build two forts and settlements on the south side of the Ohio River.

In July of 1753, Trent, Cresap and Gist were authorized by resolution of the Ohio Company to start work on a fort and settlement "on a hill just below Shertees [Chartier's] Creek upon the South East side the River Ohio." Even the details of construction had been anticipated, stipulating " . . . that the Walls of said Fort shall be twelve feet high to be built of Sawed or hewn Loggs and to inclose a piece of Ground Ninety feet Square, besides the four Bastions at the Corners of sixteen feet square each, with the houses in the middle for Stores Magazines &c." according to a plan entered in the Company's Books.[65]

The site of fort, marked on the Ohio Company map[66] made by George Mercer in 1753 and preserved in the Public Record Office in London, is readily identified as the hill, just below Brunot's Island, which terminates in the rocky cliff from which McKees Rocks took its name. A note on the drawing states: "This Hill is a very fine Situation for a Fort, being very Steep on the North and South Sides and River running at the Foot of it on the North Side, as it does at the East End which is inaccessible, being near 100 Feet high and large Rocks jutting one over the other to the Top. The West End has a gradual Descent down to the River." Another note on the same drawing is of interest: "There has been an Indian Fort there some Years ago. The Ditch is now to be seen. Here the Indians always fled upon an Alarm as it was reckoned the strongest Fort they had, several Thousands have lost their lives in the Attack of it but it never was yet taken." This elaborate project was never carried further, although the Company received four of the twenty swivel guns which had been ordered from England.

The above mentioned hill at McKees Rocks is shown in Illustration 12. This long whale-shaped protuberance, distinguished today by the stone cliffs on its up-stream face, made it a conspicuous and dramatic object in an otherwise flat river valley. It is therefore easy to understand why this natural acropolis at the head of the Ohio River attracted the attention of those seeking a site for a fort. In later days, the obvious protection from high water made it seem preferable to the low-lying lands of the Point. Though surrounded by industrial plants and congested dwelling areas, the hill remains today unoccupied by buildings. Large portions of the cliff at the eastern end have been quarried away so that we may not read the names said to have been carved there by English and French soldiers from the garrisons at the Point. Archaeological research has determined that this hill was an important Indian site as early as 1,000 B.C. The mound excavated there is of more recent origin.

Washington at the Site

In November of the same year, 1753, on his celebrated trip to Fort Le Boeuf, George Washington examined and took exception to this site proposed by the Ohio Company. He first "spent some Time in viewing the Rivers, and the Land in the Forks; which I think extremely well situated for a Fort, as it has the absolute Command of both Rivers. The Land at the Point is 20 or 25 Feet above the common Surface of the Water; and a considerable Bottom of flat, well-timbered Land all around it, very convenient for Building." The next day he continued downstream "About two Miles from this, on the South East Side of the River, at a Place where the Ohio Company intended to erect a Fort . . . . As I had taken a good deal of Notice Yesterday of the Situation at the Forks, my Curiosity led me to examine this [the McKees Rocks site] more particularly, and I think it greatly inferior, either for Defence or Advantages: especially the latter: For a Fort at the Forks would be equally well situated on the Ohio, and have the entire Command of the Monongahela; which runs up to our Settlements and is extremely well designed for Water Carriage, as it is of a deep still Nature. Besides a Fort at the Fork might be built at a much less Expence, than at the other Place." Washington thus describes the McKees Rocks site: "Nature has well contrived this lower Place, for Water Defence; but the Hill whereon it must stand being about a Quarter of a Mile in Length, and then descending gradually on the Land Side, will render it difficult and very expensive, to make a sufficient Fortification there; - The whole Flat upon the Hill must be taken-in, the Side next the Descent made extremely high, or else the Hill itself cut away: Otherwise the Enemy may raise Batteries within the Distance without being exposed to a single Shot from the Fort."

Whether or not this shrewd analysis would have altered its decision, the Ohio Company had decided, before Washington's return to Virginia, to abandon the proposed site at Chartier's Creek in favor of the site at the Forks. On his return trip, on January 6, Washington states in his journal that he "met 17 Horses loaded with Materials and Stores for a Fort at the Forks of Ohio, . . ."[67] Actually, this party was heading for the mouth of Redstone Creek on the Monongahela (Brownsville), where, in February, they erected a storehouse for the Ohio Company. It was "a strong Square Log house with Loop Holes sufficient to have made a good Defence with a few men and very Convenient for a store House where stores might be lodg'd in order to be transported by water."[68] Intended as a supply base for the ill-fated Fort Prince George, this was the first fort built by the English in western Pennsylvania.

Peril at the Forks

Some forty workmen under command of Captain William Trent arrived at the Point in February of 1754 to start the construction of Fort Prince George, so named for the future George III. The work began auspiciously with the Indian chief Half King, who laid the first log, saying: "The fort belonged to the English and them [the Indians] and whoever offered to prevent the building of it they [the Indians] would make war against them."[69] The Half King was later to be reminded of his futile promise when Ensign Ward surrendered the fort to the French.

No drawing remains of Fort Prince George. Little more than a crude sketch with general dimensions would have been needed by the frontier axe- and adzemen, adept in working timbers and long familiar with the structural requirements of such a simple building. Ward's depositions of 1754 and 1756[70] reveal only that the storehouse was made of squared logs. It is more than likely that Trent, who directed the work, duplicated the storehouse at Redstone Creek, described above. Even with a force numbering less than fifty the storehouse must have been finished by April 13 when the French were reliably reported on their way down the Allegheny. It was not thought possible that the enemy could manage to arrive so early in the year. But the alert French, in this race against time to occupy the Forks of the Ohio, did not await the spring opening of the rivers and lakes but had set out in early winter from Montreal on snowshoes, hauling their supplies on sledges over the ice. Reconnoitering parties of the French had earlier reported a building nearing completion at the Forks and had advised action immediately upon arrival of the army at Fort Machault (modern Franklin).

Ward was truly in a predicament. Reinforcements, led by George Washington, had not yet left Virginia. No fortifications had been built to defend the storehouse. The inadequate food stores brought from Virginia had been largely consumed by the idle Indians, in whose interests the fort was presumably being built. Ward not only lacked soldiers, defense and food but his leader, Captain Trent, was in Virginia seeking replacement supplies and food and unaware of the early arrival of the enemy.

Ensign Ward, in his quandary, went with the Half King to visit his next superior officer, "Lieutenant" John Fraser, who had gone to his trading post on Turtle Creek to put his affairs in order before the arrival of the French. The Half King suggested at this meeting the construction of a stockade fort. When Fraser refused to perform his duties as an officer at the expense of his private business affairs, Ward retorted he would build the stockade alone and "would hold out to the last Extremity before it should be said that the English retreated like Cowards before the French Forces appeared . . . and thus forever gave a bad example to the Indians." Matching words with deeds the little force hastily began the construction of a stockaded enclosure, the last gate of which was hung just as the French landed four days later.

Too Little, Too Late

When Contrecoeur arrived at the Forks with 500 men in 60 batteaus and 300 canoes, he landed his forces a short distance above the fort, mounted two of his 18 cannon, and sent forward an officer and drummer with a summons for surrender. As the French, who outnumbered the English about 50 to one, offered to use force if Ward delayed the surrender, the little garrison of 41 men capitulated. "As our men came out the French enter'd," a contemporary observer wrote, "but behaved with great civility said it might be their fate ere long to surrender it again so they would set (us) a good example."[71]

Contrecoeur must have been greatly relieved to find the English fort "no more than an enclosure of upright stakes." As England and France were not at war (war was not formally declared until 1756), Duquesne had hoped to avoid the use of force; this incident was to be treated as a mistaken notion of ownership. Although Contrecoeur, and his superior at Quebec, well knew the intentions of the English to fortify this strategic site, Contrecoeur feigned astonishment, with true Gallic effect, that the English would have presumed to establish a stronghold on lands known to belong to His Most Christian Majesty. In demanding the surrender of Ward, he carefully gave no insult or intimation of warlike intentions. "No doubt this violation of territory has been made only at the request of a company of traders to favor their commerce with the savages." As Duquesne had put it to Contrecoeur: " . . . the King my master only demands his rights. He has no intention of disturbing the fine harmony and friendship that exists between his Majesty and the King of Great Britain . . . " This is hardly to be equaled for gracious double-talk.

Ward mentions in his deposition that the Half King "stormed greatly at the French at the time they were obliged to march out of the Fort, and told them that he order'd that Fort and laid the first Log of it himself,"[72] but the Indian was brushed aside by the French.

Contrecoeur had Ward to dinner, but got no information from him nor would Ward agree to sell his building tools. The little garrison was permitted to leave the next day with their weapons. "J.C.B.", the chronicler who accompanied the French army, states that "We took possession of the fort in which there were only fifty men and four cannons, but no provisions at all. We distributed enough to the garrison to last them three days, and destroyed the fort, which was no more than an enclosure of upright stakes."[73]

This was not the first time, nor was it to be the last, that the poorly organized provincial forces, badly equipped and moving in a dilatory manner, found themselves no match for the alert French troops and their numerous Indian allies. It cannot be maintained that Fort Prince George was purely a commercial project of the Ohio Company to extend its settlements and the Indian trade, for this fort was authorized by the British government and the defrayment of its cost guaranteed by the Crown to Virginia. It was an unsuccessful stratagem of the "cold war" waged for possession of the Ohio Country.

FORT DUQUESNE

The French came to the Forks of the Ohio prepared to reduce any English fort at that site and immediately erect one of their own in its place. It had been Marquis Duquesne's firm intention to build a fort there in 1753, but the plans had miscarried. The French had considered other locations but, like the English, had finally determined that this land which positively commanded the confluence of the two rivers must be occupied, whatever its shortcomings, as the site for a fort.

Duquesne first instructed Contrecoeur to build the fort at Chiningué (Logstown), near modern Ambridge. Upon second thought, he wrote, "If it is true that there is a river [the Monongahela] six leagues on this side of Chiningué, which is said to be the usual route of the English in coming from Philadelphia, you will locate the fort at that site to block passage and prevent their commerce; I have been further advised that another advantage will be gained in placing the fort at the mouth of this river, in that Chiningué is almost without wood and that there is an abundance of it there [the Forks], which has persuaded me of this change which seems advantageous on all counts."[74] He adds that it would have been desirable to observe at close quarters the behavior of the Indians at Logstown by having built a fort there, but he hopes the Indians will move up to the new site when they see the fort being built. We see in these and other matters recorded in the Contrecoeur Papers the shrewd mind of Duquesne who directed French action with an application and intelligence lacking in the high levels of English government until the appearance of William Pitt four years later.

Now that the French were at last in possession of the strategic point of land, they "immediately went to work removing some of the logs as they complained the Fort was not to their liking, and by break of day next morning 50 men went off with Axes to hew Logs to enlarge it."[75] This does not necessarily mean that the fort was left in place. The witnesses departed from the scene the same day and could hardly report on the activities of the French thereafter. It is only natural that the French would have salvaged the materials from Fort Prince George. All of the wood was freshly cut and worked and would be immediately usable. Duquesne later wrote Contrecoeur: "... I am delighted that you have found a good supply of pickets and of wood well fitted, because the English are masters in wood and excell at handcraft."[76] To assume that any part of Prince George was left in its original location is not a reasonable conclusion. The tight and compact plan of Fort Duquesne, undoubtedly conceived in general layout to conform with site conditions sometime before the campaign, would not likely have been revised to include any storehouse or stockade left by the English.

The French Fort Described

It was not by choice that the French added a settlement at the Forks of the Ohio to their many widely separated and poorly developed communities in the new world. This new post diverted men and money badly needed to protect the Canadian lifeline at points much more accessible to the English. The imminent flood of settlers from Virginia into the Ohio country had forced their hand. It is significant that this threatened break in the dyke occurred in an area previously ignored by the French and well off their normally traveled routes. Céloron's map of 1750 bears an inscription across the southern shore of Lake Erie, "This shore is almost unknown."

It is not difficult to understand the inadequacy of Fort Duquesne, both in size and character, when we realize that practically all of the supplies and even some of the food had to be carried across the ocean to Quebec and then transported at great cost and with difficulty over hundreds of miles of rivers, lakes and portages to the Forks of the Ohio. Once ensconced in this tiny stronghold, the French may have felt an additional protection in the mountain barrier against attack by the English whom the French despised for their dilatory and poorly organized forces. Added to this was the insulation provided by the vast forest in which the numerous Indian allies of the French were a fearsome deterrent to English penetration. Vaudreuil boasted in 1756, "Messengers no longer come any further than Winchester because of our savages who are always in the field."[77]

The fact remained that Fort Duquesne was a poor fort, small and lacking in defense. Recognizing this, Contrecoeur sought aid when he learned of Braddock's approach. Engineer De Léry was summoned from Detroit to appraise and recommend ways of improving the fort. After careful examination he stated that the fort "can furnish but very little protection and mediocre quarters." His report[78] provided no constructive criticism and indicated that little or nothing could be done short of complete replacement. Time was too short for this. Contrecoeur, the commandant, recognizing the futility of resistance against the artillery and superior numbers of Braddock's army, prepared to abandon and destroy the fort. Only the remarkable and wholly unanticipated success of Daniel de Beaujeu's last minute ambush of the English army saved Fort Duquesne from certain destruction. Curiously enough, even after this demonstration

Favored by many as the site for Fort Pitt, this natural mound from which McKee's Rocks took its name was the subject of much controversy. As shown on the plan in Illustration 27, it is located on the Ohio River just below the mouth of Chartier's Creek.

Above: VIEW OF "THE ROCKS" AT THE UP-STREAM END IN 1896
Courtesy of the Carnegie Museum
Below: AERIAL VIEW LOOKING DOWN-STREAM TOWARD MCKEE'S ROCKS BRIDGE, MOUND ON THE LEFT

By Aerial Survey, Inc.

Ilustration 12

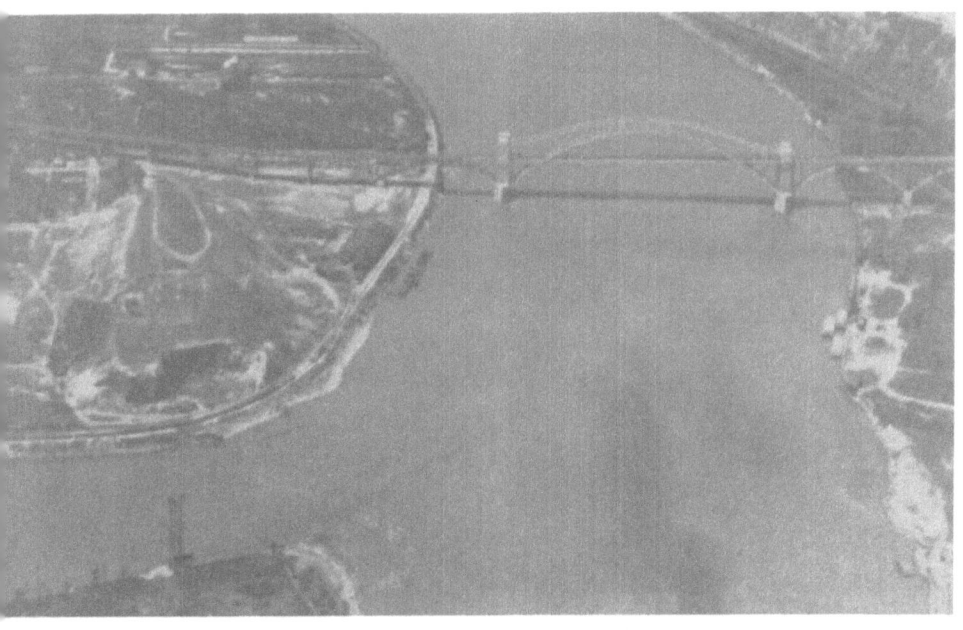

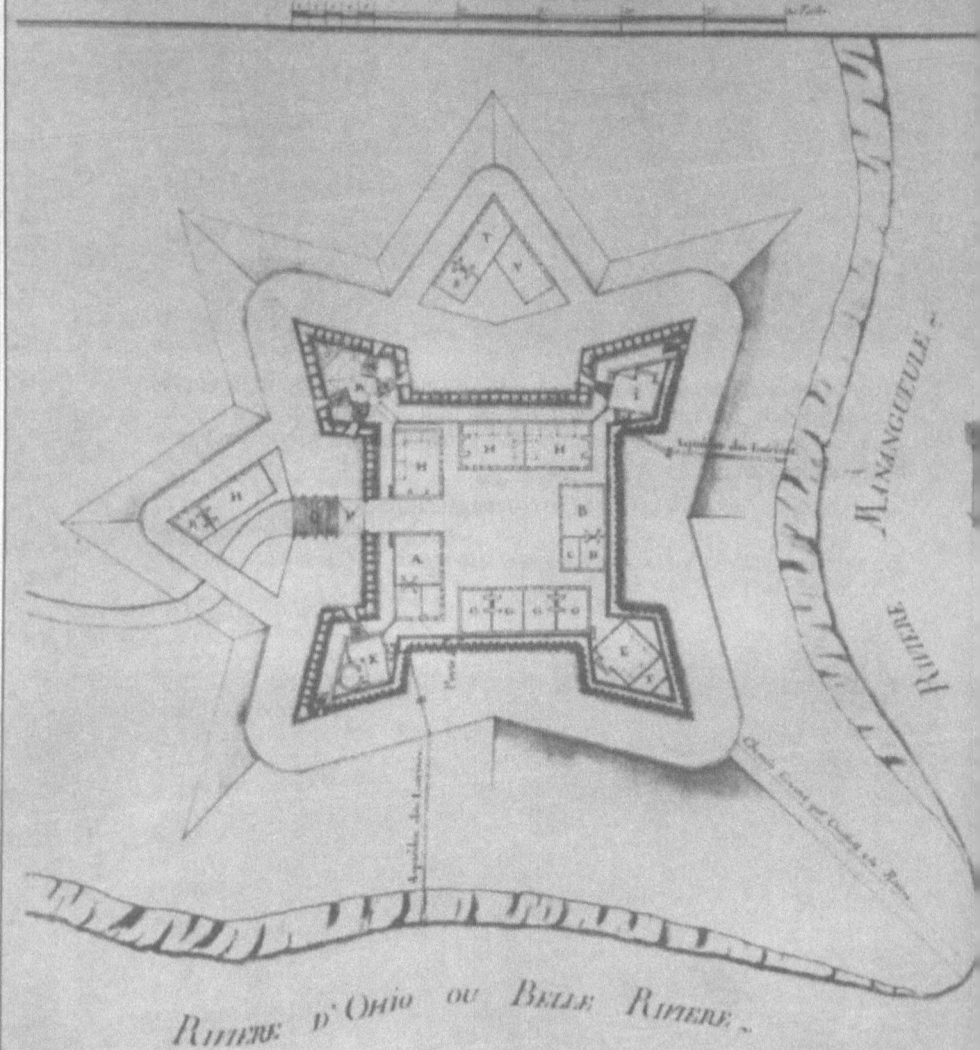

of its inadequacy, the fort was never materially improved. Vaudreuil wrote in 1757: "Fort Duquesne, in its present condition, could not resist the enemy. It is too small to lodge the garrison necessary for such a purpose. A single cannon shot would be sufficient to set it on fire, which could not be extinguished because the houses are too close together." He mentions also the menace of floods and concludes: "M. de Ligneris is having repairs made on this fort as well as possible, considering its wretched site; but that cannot diminish the necessity of erecting a new fort."[79] Subsequently a "second fort" was built along the Allegheny shore, but this was merely a cluster of log barracks surrounded by a stockaded wall and protected only by an advance battery at the eastern end. The inevitable consequence was that on the approach of Forbes' army in 1758, every attempt at ambush en route having failed, the fort was demolished and burned by the French and abandoned without show of defense.

The most important contemporary drawing of Fort Duquesne was obtained by the writer from the Bibliotheque Nationale in Paris. (Illustration 13.) No information is available to tell us when or by whom this drawing was made, though it is reasonable to assume that Francois Le Mercier, the engineer in charge of construction, would have been involved in its preparation. Duquesne had originally requested a fort "as solidly built as it is advantageously located." To this end he appointed Chevalier Le Mercier "to look after not only artillery and engineering duties" but also "provisioning the whole detachment." There is no other drawing of the fort of French origin known to the writer, except the small sketch, lacking in detail, which accompanied De Léry's report. The other drawings were made by English engineers at the site after the fort had been mined and burned. They therefore show only the plan and profile and none of the buildings within the fort. Captain Robert Stobo, taken as a hostage after the fall of Fort Necessity, was imprisoned in Fort Duquesne while it was under construction. He then made a rough sketch with descriptive material which was carried to Virginia by a friendly Indian. This sketch was recovered by the French at Braddock's defeat and used as evidence in Stobo's trial in Canada in 1756. After Stobo's escape he made other versions of the same sketch. John McKinney, a prisoner in 1756, left the fullest and apparently most reliable description[80] of the fort and, as such, it was deemed worthy of inclusion with the publication of the *Papiers Contrecoeur*, together with Stobo's descriptive sketch. Other English prisoners who will be quoted in the description of Fort Duquesne are Thomas Forbes and John Hogan. The statements of the ubiquitous "J.C.B." are taken with a grain of salt. Although he lived in the fort for some years as storemaster, his journal contains statements about the fort which are demonstrably incorrect and his veracity in other matters is under suspicion by general historians. The Contrecoeur Papers provide meager passages of graphic description or records of conditions beyond that of Chaussegros de Léry who qualifies his report by saying "an engineer would be needed to obtain more exact knowledge, . . ., since I have very little knowledge of this profession." The information gained from these drawings and descriptions is combined in Illustration 14, a perspective view of the fort.

Fort Duquesne followed the conventional pattern of many other French and English frontier forts in plan and construction. It was a square with bastions projecting at the corners and ravelins opposite two of the curtain walls. The eastern face of the fort measured about 154 feet from tip to tip of the bastions and about 160 feet in the other direction. It was surrounded by a dry ditch. The entrance road passed over the east ravelin and entered the fort by a fixed bridge (*pont dormant*) and a drawbridge (*pont levis*), which at night, McKinney informs us "is drawn up by iron chains and levers." The clear interior space or parade ground, according to De Léry, was only 34 feet (45 feet on the Paris plan) so small that "men cannot be quartered in tents." He adds, "The fort could, however, during a siege, with much inconvenience to them, hold two hundred men, especially since there would always be at least a third of the garrison on the ramparts and the number would always be lessened by accidents." He suggests that "If the fort is besieged, lines could be built to quarter those whom the fort could not hold."

There was a well in the center of the parade, "but the water bad," McKinney records. The parade was surrounded by five buildings. To the right, upon entering, stood the Commandant's House, on the left was the Guardhouse. Facing the entrance, across the parade, were the Storekeeper's quarters and shop. On the southern side stood the barracks and on the northern side the quarters for officers and chaplain. The chimneys, soldiers' bunks, doors and windows are shown on the drawing. The buildings were about 19 feet wide and the largest, the barracks, 54 feet in length. McKinney tells us that ". . . the eaves of the houses in the fort are about even with the top of the logs or wall of the fort; the houses are all covered with boards, as well the roof as the side that looks inside the fort, which they saw there by hand; . . . " De Léry suggested that "The roof of the houses which projected beyond the parapets could be taken off, as much to avoid the effects of the enemy's cannon as to guard against the fire they could set to it with fireworks, for then the granaries which are used as store-houses could no longer be of use either for food or for merchandise, except as these goods could be placed on the planks, which could, nevertheless, be covered with bear and buck skins." It is interesting to note that the roofs were removed on the approach of Forbes' army and placed against the walls as kindling. Stobo adds a significant comment. "None lodge in the fort but the guard [which he gives as forty men and five officers], except Contrecoeur, the rest in bark cabins around the fort."[81] There was a postern gate between the Commandant's House and the officers' barracks.

Three of the bastions of the fort contained buildings. In the Northeast Bastion were the kitchen and bake oven, which are shown on the Paris drawing as a round form. De Léry identified this as "Bakehouse with an oven, 40 loaves of six pounds." How unfortunate he was not equally explicit in other details. The Northwest Bastion contained the cadets barracks and behind it, the prison. A blacksmith shop occupied the Southwest Bastion. In all three of these bastions the buildings stood on the parade level. In the Southwest and Northeast Bastions a small strip of the bastion was elevated to rampart height to provide mountings for two cannons in each. The Southeast Bastion was the only one completely filled. It contained cannons on each face and a barbette, or elevated gun platform, at the point. As noted on the drawing made in 1758, Illustration 15, this was the "Bastion, under which was the Principal Magazine, entirely demolished." Another powder magazine was built "a little below the gate within the entrenchments; the magazine is made almost under ground, and of large logs and covered four feet thick with clay over it. It is about 10 feet wide, and about thirty five feet long," says McKinney. (See Illustration 15.) This is noted on the above drawing as the "Powder Magazine which was intended to have been blown up, but whose match went out before it reached the Powder." Contrecoeur reported in May of 1755 that the fort mounted six cannons of 6 pound balls and nine of two or three pound balls. James Hogan, a prisoner, in June of 1757 said there were "Six Guns five or six Pounders mounted and seven

Swivel guns." McKinney deposed that "each bastion has four carriage guns about four pound; no swivels, nor any mortars that he knows of; they have no cannon but at the bastions." It is obvious that only the full bastion could mount four cannons. The notes on Stobo's drawing show "there were 8 Pieces of Cannon in the Fort; 4 of which are 3 Pounders." He said there were two guns each on the partial bastions and four on the full bastion, as shown on the Paris drawing.

"The back of the barracks and buildings in the Fort are of logs placed about three feet distance from the logs of the Fort," says McKinney, "between the buildings and the logs of the Fort, it is filled with earth about eight feet high, and the logs of the Fort extend about four feet higher, so that the whole height of the Fort is about 12 feet." There is considerable variation in these reported figures, but the fort profiles on the English drawings confirm this height.

The east and south curtains of the fort and the three adjoining bastions were of horizontal log construction (See Illustration 11), laid as basketwork and filled with earth. The total thickness was about twelve feet. This log wall rose 14 feet above the bottom of the ditch, which was quite shallow. The parapet was also of log. McKinney noted that "There are no pickets or pallisadoes on the top of the fort to defend it against scaling." (These are fraises, described in Part Two.) The north and west curtains, the Northwest Bastion and half of the Southwest and Northeast Bastions were of stockades. McKinney said, "The stockadoes are round logs better than a foot over, and about eleven or twelve feet high; the joints are secured by split logs; in the stockadoes are loop holes made so as to fire slanting towards the ground." It will be noted on the drawing that a platform extended behind the palisades. These platforms were of plank with space beneath as we learn from one of Stobo's letters, in which he suggests that 100 Indians, carefully selected by the English, might surprise the garrison "by lodging themselves under the platform by day, and at night secure the guard with the tomahawks." This platform was somewhat lower than the portion of the bastions on which the guns were mounted as may be seen by examining the steps leading to them.

McKinney's report states that "Under the draw-bridge is a pit or well, the width of the gate, dug down deep to water; the pit is about eight or ten feet broad." The pit was dug to water to provide added protection at the entrance as the ditch itself was dry: "the gate is made of square logs; the back gate is made of logs also, and goes upon hinges, and has a wicket in it for the people to pass through in common; there is no ditch or pit at this gate." This door led to the magazine in the entrenchment and, as drawn and noted on Illustration 15, to a "Passage to the River, at the Mouth, a Small harbour." This was provided with a small breakwater and boat landing.

The ravelins, or demi-lunes as they were often miscalled, are the two arrow-shaped structures in the ditch before the east and south curtains. These were usually protected by parapets and served as "places of arms" or advance stations for soldiers in case of attack. The ravelins at Fort Duquesne, however, were occupied by buildings. That on the entrance ravelin housed the interpreter and soldiers and the south ravelin building contained stores, a hospital and surgeon's quarters. De Léry refers to these as "Houses of oak in place of the demi-lunes, which cannot be used for defense purposes since the moats have been dug." Apparently the desperate need for additional housing facilities led to this extraordinary expedient.

De Léry noted that " . . . ; it is not possible to put anyone on the edge of the counterscarp in the moat as it was thought, for the firing in the court would trouble them as much as that of the enemy." In the absence of the usual covered way and parapet on the counterscarp a stockaded entrenchment was built all around the fort. This feature is described by McKinney as follows: " . . . ; there are intrenchments cast up all around the Fort about 7 feet high, which consists of stockadoes drove into the ground near to each other, and wattled with poles like basket work, against which earth is thrown up, in a gradual ascent; the steep part is next the Fort, and has three steps along the intrenchment for the men to go up and down, to fire at an enemy—these intrenchments are about four rods from the Fort, and go all around, as well on the side next the water as the land; the outside of the intrenchment next the water, joins to the water." This entrenchment, on the Point side, stood at the top of the river bank and is noted on one unidentified drawing as a "Chevaux de Frise." This stockaded entrenchment was being built when Thomas Forbes arrived at the fort as a prisoner in 1754. Thomas Forbes states: "At our arrival at Fort DuQuesne (from Le Boeuf) we found the Garrison busily engaged in compleating that Fort and Stockadoing it round at some distance for the security of the Soldiers Barracks (against my Surprise) which are built between the Stockadoes and the Glacis of the Fort."[82] The "Soldiers Barracks" between the stockades and the glacis were undoubtedly the buildings on the ravelins mentioned above.

McKinney speaks of a building not shown on the plans. "About thirty yards from the Fort, without the intrenchments and picketing, is a house, which contains a great quantity of tools, such as broad and narrow axes, planes, chisels, hoes, mattocks, pickaxes, spades, shovels, etc., and a great quantity of wagon-wheels and tire."

Fort Duquesne weathered a bad flood in 1757. McKinney said: "The waters sometimes rise so high as that the whole Fort is surrounded with it, so that canoes may go around it; he imagines he saw it rise at one time near thirty feet." We know that the water rose high enough to float pirogues into the center of the fort to take off the garrison and supplies. There is no report in the records of serious damage to the fort structure.

Contemporary Descriptions

An interesting entry in the *Papiers Contrecoeur* presents an itemization of work on the fort and its cost between August 13th and November 27th of 1754: " . . . the ditches, glacis, fascines; moving of earth, cutting of wood; rooting out stumps and other work required to form the glacis and clear the fort also the works of the bakery; the ovens. Of a small barracks of 20 feet square located in the covered way of the little door in the northwest of the fort as well as a casemate [powder magazine] of 24 feet by 15, of an open shed of 80 feet by 7: of a small hospital beyond the glacis; of a pit of 13 feet of depth by 12 [see elsewhere pit before drawbridge]; of the cabins for Indian chiefs, of a conduit of 35 feet for the casemate serving as powder magazine mentioned above; and for the exhumation of 8 bodies; as well as the men who have been taken from the works to be employed in other labors as directed . . . " The totals show that 5,175 man days were required at a cost of 5,499 livres and 10 sol. and that Contrecoeur's salary for the year ending June 1755 was 3,000 livres.

De Léry was much concerned about the vulnerability of the fort to cannon fire. He describes Mount Washington as a "Mountain from which one can see into the fort, where musketry can be placed halfway up the slope, which, although out of range, plainly speaking, could cause trouble; a battery of cannon at the top of this mountain would command the side of the fort facing it, which is, like the one on the north, inclosed by a stockade without earth work." He must be mistaken in his last statement as the South Curtain was of horizontal logs, not stockades. McKinney likewise was aware of this hazard to the fort. He said: "Opposite the Fort, on the west side of the Monongahela, is a long, high mountain, about a quarter of a mile from the Fort, from which the Fort might very easily be bombarded and the bombarder be quite safe; from them the distance would not exceed a quarter of a mile; the mountain is said to extend six miles up the Monongahela, from the Fort; Monongahela, opposite the Fort, is not quite musket shot wide." De Léry was still more concerned about cannon fire from the northern side. The north shore of the Allegheny opposite the fort is noted on his drawing, "Island which is a peninsula when the water is at a medium, on which batteries can be placed to command the north side of the fort, which is inclosed by a simple stockade without earthwork." De Léry also examined the eastern, or land approach for defects in defense. He mentions the stream running from Hogg's Pond (about site of Kaufmann's store) into the Monongahela, well shown on Meyer's drawing of the environs of Fort Pitt (Illustration 25). He pointed out that this is "a coulee which protects those who are within [range] from the cannon of the fort; it is probably at this place that the enemy will open the trenches." Parallel trenches were dug by besiegers to approach a fort. From this shelter they could fire small arms and erect parapets to protect siege guns. This method was successfully used in the reduction of Fort Niagara by the English. De Léry concludes his report by saying: "It is to be hoped that they [the French] will be numerous enough to engage the enemy before the formation of a siege . . . "

We have much less information about the environs of Fort Duquesne than those of Fort Pitt. McKinney describes the area of the triangle before the fort in these words: "there are no bogs nor morasses near the fort, but good dry ground, which is cleared for some distance from the fort, and the stumps cut close to the ground; a little without musket shot of the fort, in the fork, is a thick wood of some bigness, full of large timber." We know that a fairly large settlement of cabins and Indian huts lay before the fort, extensive corn fields extended a quarter mile up both streams and there were pastures and gardens. In 1754 there was a harvest of nearly 800 bushels of Indian corn and in 1755 this was expected to reach 2,000 bushels. Duquesne boasted that sufficient produce could be grown at the fort to make it self-sustaining. He pointed to the fact that in 1755, "Peas are now planted, and they have two cows, one bull, some horses and 23 sows with young." Supplies from Canada were supplemented by those from the Illinois country. McKinney deposed that "While he was at Fort Duquesne, there came up the Ohio from the Mississippi, about thirty batteaux and about 150 men, ladened with pork, flour, brandy, tobacco, peas, and Indian corn; they were three months in coming to Fort Duquesne, and came all the way up the falls without unloading." Fort Duquesne was thus as remote from the Illinois country as from the lower St. Lawrence settlements.

"J.C.B." mentioned that "Opposite the fort, all along the bank in ascending the Ohio [the Allegheny was considered part of the Ohio], we had formed a sort of little village composed of about sixty cabins of wood, where a part of the garrison lodged." He notes that he had "a little cottage" there and recounts how, while asleep in it, he was nearly trapped by the flood which carried away fifteen of the buildings. He nonchalantly adds, "but we soone remedied this by constructing others and this was the work of two or three days . . . " McKinney spoke of "20 or 30 ordinary Indian cabins about the fort," and said that "There was about 250 Frenchmen in this Fort, besides Indians, which at one time amounted to 500; but the Indians were very uncertain; sometimes hardly any there."

These buildings were likely arranged without formal street patterns but the name of one commonly traveled way has been preserved. The path which led to the burying ground, known as L'Allée de la Viérge, later known as Virgin Way and now Oliver Avenue, was the first street named in western Pennsylvania. The French burying ground is said to have been located where the graveyard of Trinity Church is now located. Here Sieur de Beaujeu, French hero of Braddock defeat, was buried on the ninth of July, 1755. The cemetery was named L'Assomption de la s.^{te} Viérge a la belle Riviere.

The Second Fort, built along the Allegheny, is shown in the English drawings made after seizure of the fort, and must have been of late construction for it was reported still unfinished when the English came. One unidentified drawing of Mercer's Fort shows the Second Fort with the note "Horn Work and Barracks." (See

Illustration 18.) The English drawings describe this as "Hornwork, in which was the greatest part of the Soldiers' Barracks, & Ovens." This is the only drawing which shows the barrack within the enclosure. The Second Fort scales about 110 by 375 feet. The eastern extremity of the Second Fort was protected by two demi-bastions and a ravelin with ditch and glacis. This is the "Hornwork" mentioned above. The aerial view, Illustration 14, is a conjectural restoration. An eye-witness, Captain John Haslett, in a letter written on the day after the occupation, describes the scene thus: "There are two forts, about two hundred yards distant, the one built with immense labor, small, but a great deal of very strong works collected into very little room, and stands on the point of a narrow neck of land at the confluence of the two rivers. 'Tis square, and has two ravelins, gabions [bastions] on each corner, &c. The other fort stands on the bank of the Allegheny, in form of a parallelogram, but nothing so strong as the other; several of the outworks are lately begun and still unfinished."[83] We know that the wall of the Second Fort was formed of palisades, as described in Vaudreuil's description at the close of this section.

The Last Days of the Fort

In the last days of Fort Duquesne all previous predictions were confirmed; the fortification was hopelessly unequal to the challenge of Forbes' approaching army. The dramatic events were later reviewed in January of 1759 in a letter from Vaudreuil to the Minister: "M. de Ligneris immediately assembled the officers of his garrison to deliberate on the measures he should take under the circumstances to which he was reduced. He had less than 300 men, a third of whom at the most were capable of taking the field. All these gentlemen were of the opinion that they should prepare to evacuate the place. Accordingly, they began, from this day (November 19), to cut down the stakes around the new fort, in the part where there were no houses and where fire would not spread." This is the outer work or Second Fort. A French scout sent out on November 23rd reported the English 5 or 6 leagues from the fort and observed cutters making the road. "M. de Ligneris saw that there was no longer reason to flatter himself. He immediately ordered 8 days' provisions to be taken for the regulars and militia, who were intended to retreat with him to the Machault post." The small amount of goods remaining was packed up and sent to the Indians in Ohio

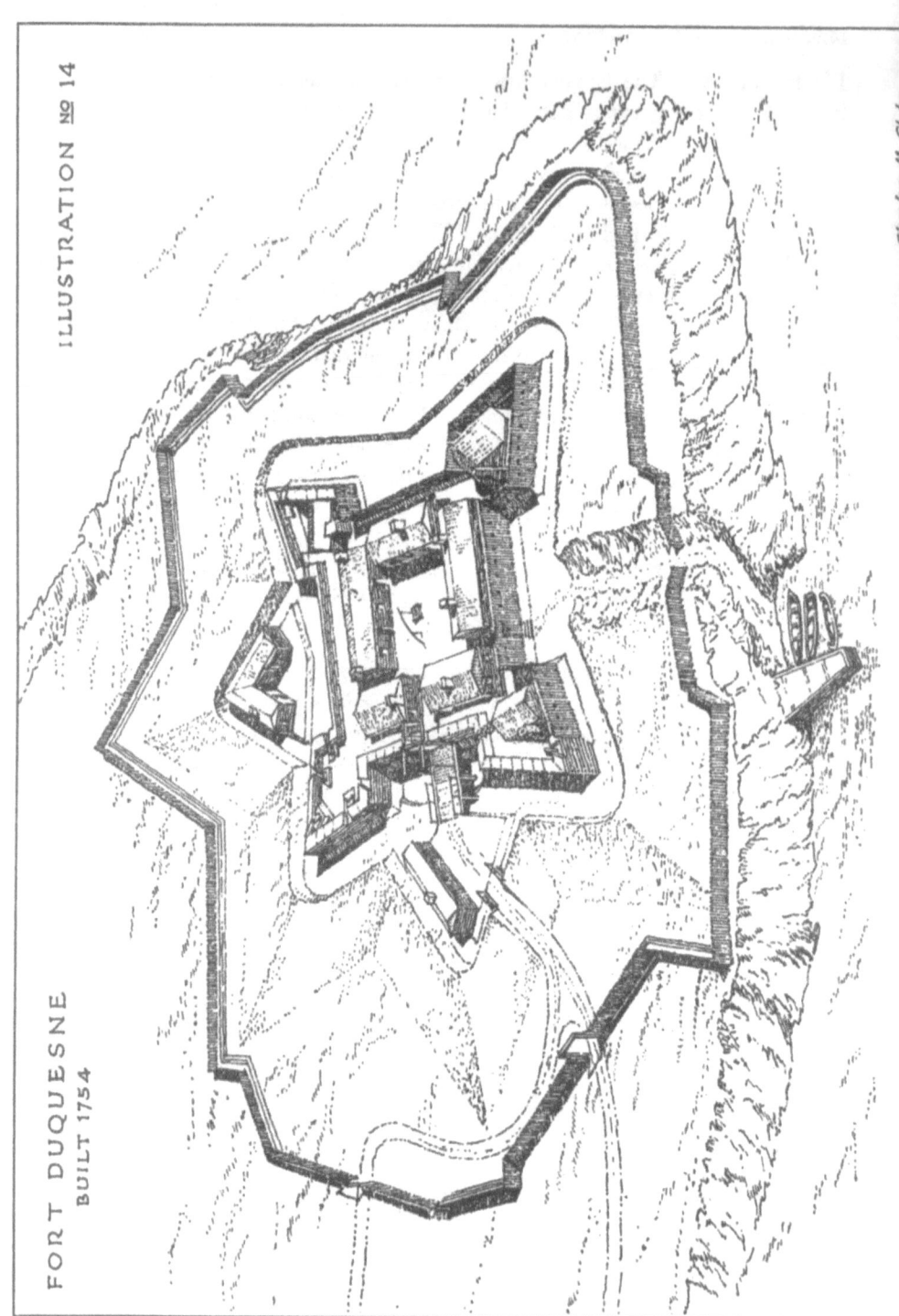

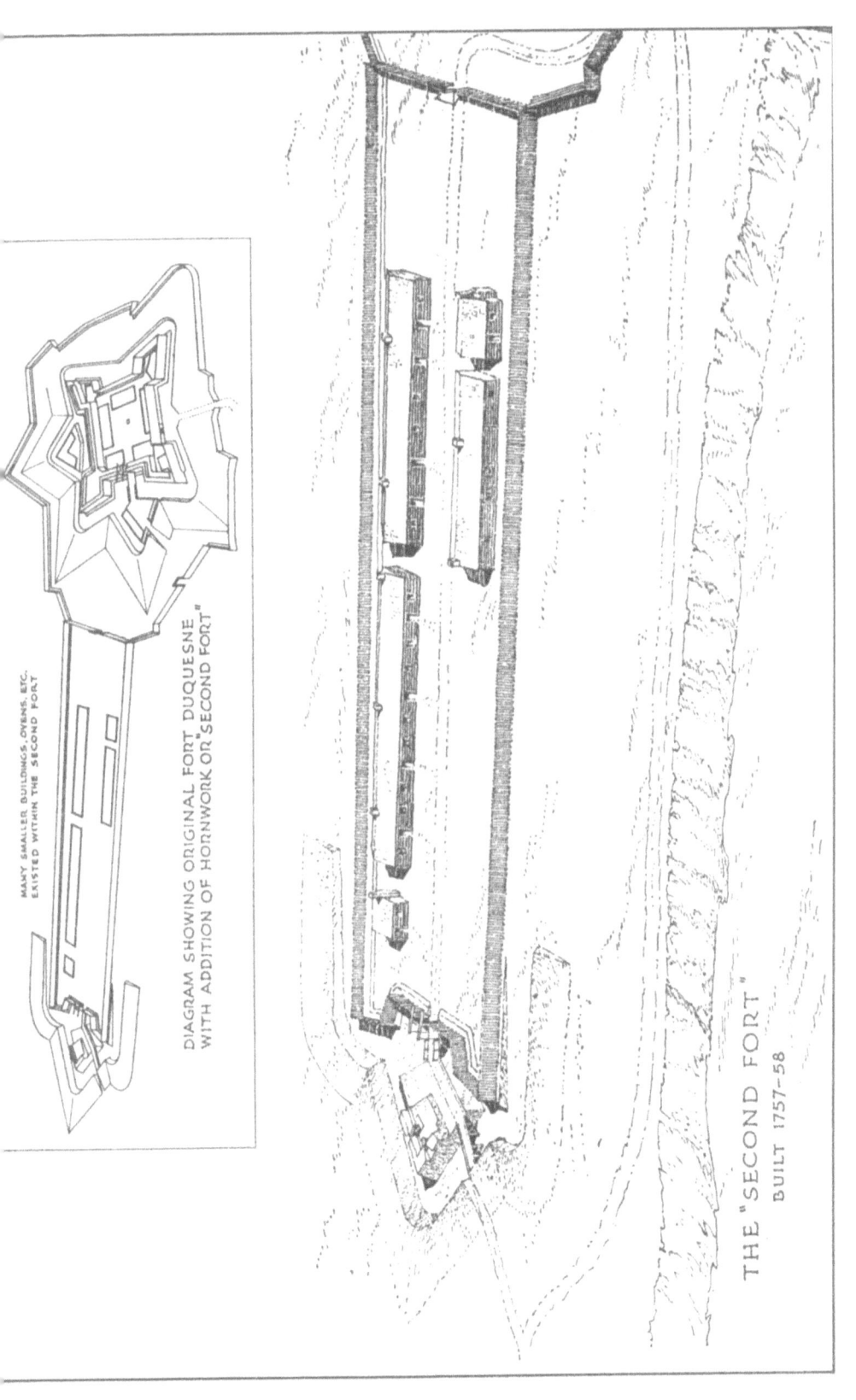

MANY SMALLER BUILDINGS, OVENS, ETC.
EXISTED WITHIN THE SECOND FORT

DIAGRAM SHOWING ORIGINAL FORT DUQUESNE
WITH ADDITION OF HORNWORK OR "SECOND FORT"

THE "SECOND FORT"
BUILT 1757-58

as insurance for future relations. "He has the cannon and munitions of war put in bateaux which he sent to the Illinois." With them went the prisoners. "This operation was accomplished in less than three hours."

"When everyone had embarked, when the scouts had returned, and when all the bateaux had left, except one which he had kept, he had the fort set on fire. After this, he embarked to join his force of 192 men, who had orders to wait for him about a league above the fort. To blow up the fort, 50 or 60 barrels of spoiled powder were left in the powder magazine. As soon as M. de Ligneris heard the roar of this mine, he sent three men by land to see what damage it had done. They reported that the fort was entirely reduced to ashes and that the enemy would fall heir to nothing but the ironwork of the community buildings."[84]

Any disturbance of the earth is difficult to eradicate. Hugh Henry Brackenridge, writing in the *Pittsburgh Gazette* in 1786, describes the last vestiges of Fort Duquesne: "The appearance of the ditch and mound, with the salient angles and bastions still remains, so as to prevent that perfect level of the ground which otherwise would exist. It has been long overgrown with the finest verdure, and depastured on by cattle; but since the town has been laid out it has been enclosed, and buildings are erected."

MERCER'S FORT

The explosion of the magazine of Fort Duquesne had been heard by Forbes' troops, encamped at Turtle Creek. Although a troop of light horses had been immediately dispatched to determine the cause of the sound, the body of the advance army did not arrive at the Point until late the next afternoon. As they emerged from the forest in the freezing cold of Saturday, November 25th, they viewed the same majestic panorama of rivers and wooded ridges that we know today, the hills at the distant turn of the Ohio a hazy blue before the low evening sun. But in the triangle of low ground immediately before the soldiers lay a prospect of complete desolation. In the foreground and extending up the rivers on either side lay the fenced grazing lands, corn fields and gardens, in sere autumn colors. To the left, along the Monongahela, the stone chimneys of the few more pretentious cabins rose among the charred remains of a haphazard settlement of huts and improvised shelters. On the right, near the Allegheny, the long rectangle of the Second Fort was defined by its

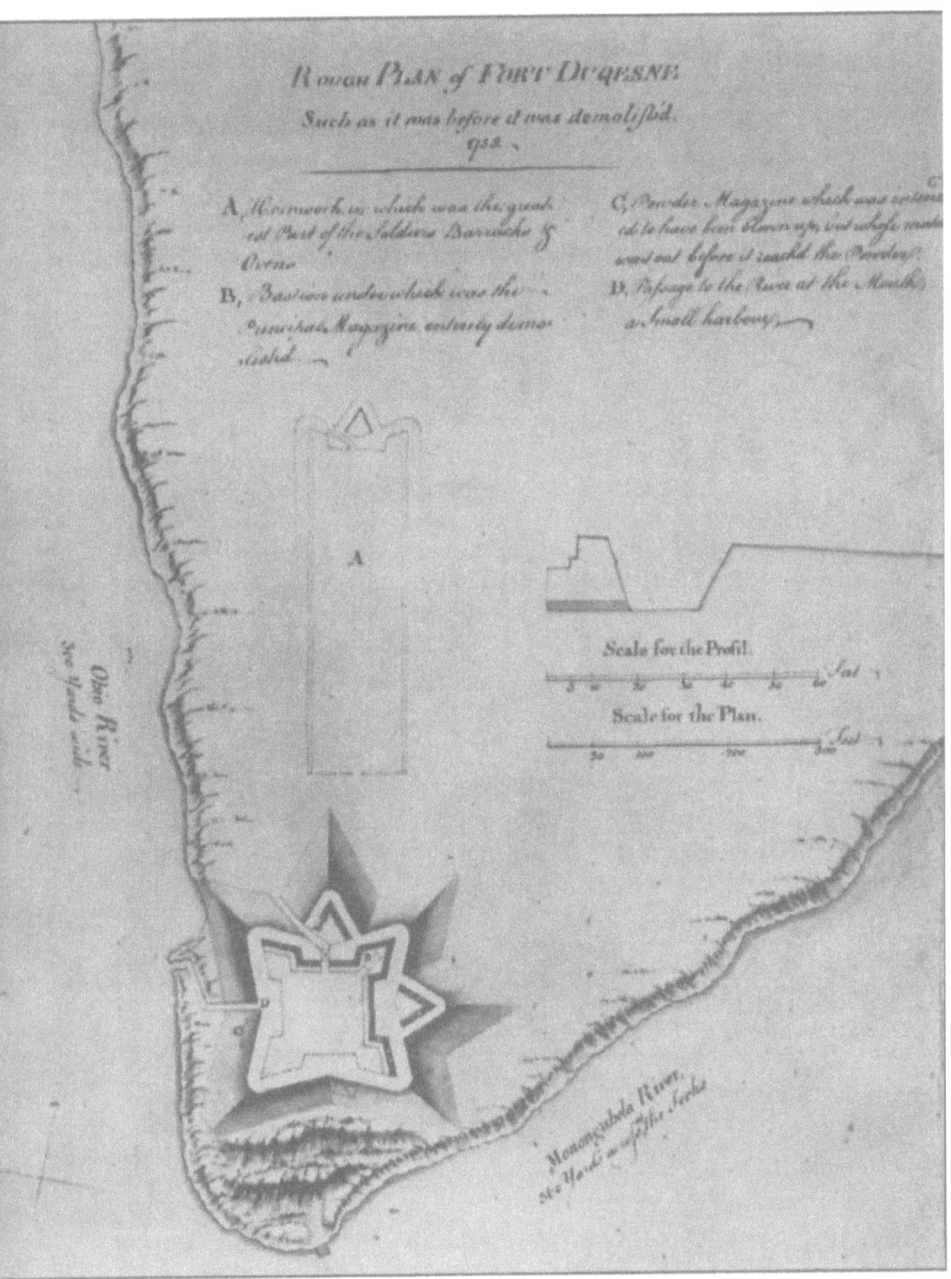

PLAN MADE BY ENGLISH MILITARY ENGINEERS OF FORT DUQUESNE
AFTER ITS CAPTURE BY FORBES

Illustration 15

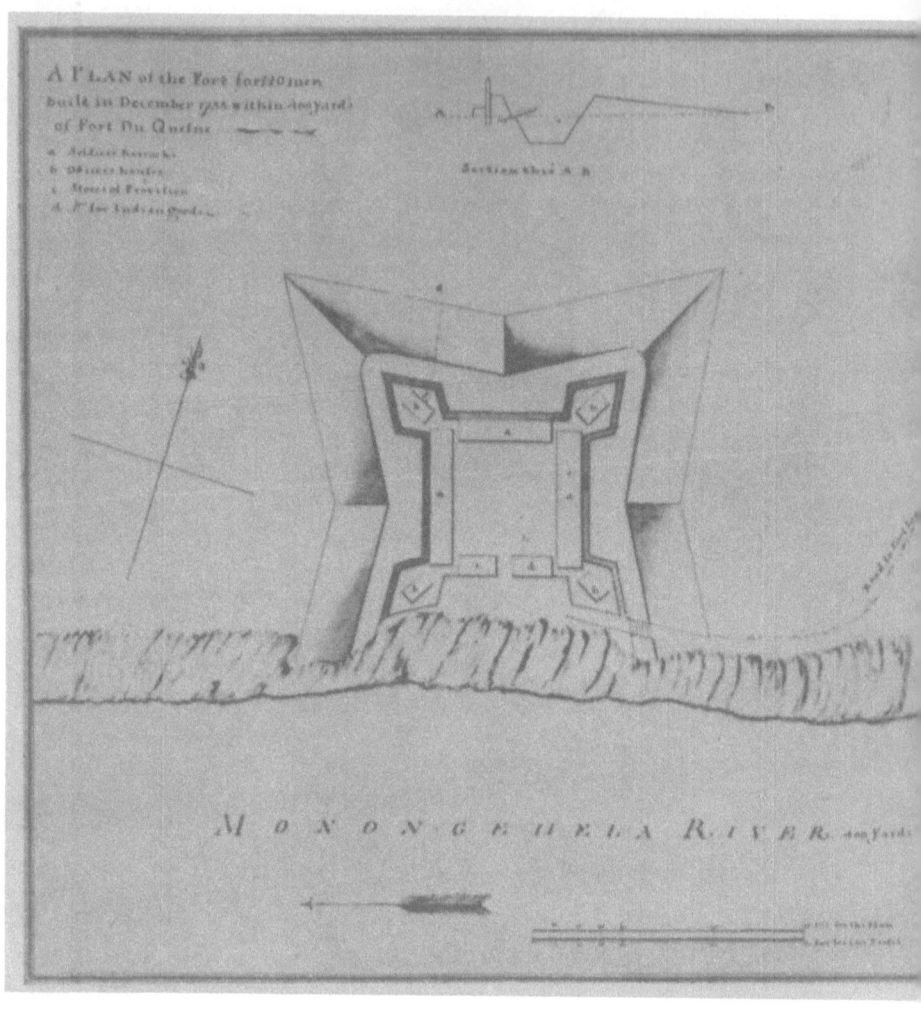

From a drawing in the British Museum, London

MERCER'S FORT

Illustration 16

border of shallow trenches and stumps of ruined palisades. Within this enclosure lay the remains of the outlying barracks. And at the very tip of the Point could be seen the dark mass of Fort Duquesne, which had been systematically destroyed by demolition, fire and explosion. The shape could be distinguished by the ditches around it and the horizontal log walls of the land front, which, because of their earth filling could not have been wholly consumed by fire. It must have been an anticlimax thus to grasp this dearly-bought prize without the clamor and dash of armed assault. For four years no words had been heard here but the many guttural dialects of the Indians, blended with those of the Canadian habitant provincials, the coureurs de bois and the gracious language of the French court. No longer would the Allegheny be known as La Belle Riviere, or the Monongahela as the Mal Engueulee. The brief civilization of New France at the Forks of the Ohio was now as dead as the smoking ruins of its tiny community.

Immediately upon arrival a guard was mounted in the fort to protect what might remain there and to put out all fires. The next day the soldiers were cautioned not to destroy any of the "Square Logs in or about the Camp," and a brigade was ordered "to sort the Iron Work in the Fort." "The Whole line" was ordered "to attend Divine Service at one o'Clock . . . to return Thanks to Almighty God for the remarkable Superiority of His Majesty's Arms over his Enemies, . . . " Thirty men were sent the next day to "bury the Bones upon the Field where General Braddock had his Engagement, . . . " Also a hundred men who had been in "Major Grant's Affair" were detailed to "search for & bury the Dead."[85]

Two hundred Virginian and Pennsylvanian soldiers under Colonel Hugh Mercer were left at Pittsburgh (formally named on December 1st) "to be employed in erecting their Barracks for which they will be paid." The remainder of the army left for Ligonier and the eastern posts, the greater number to return to their homes. We read in a letter written January 3rd from the new commandant, Colonel Hugh Mercer to Bouquet, that "Tho' the Ammunition is Removed from the Old Fort, the Guard Continues to keep a look out from the point . . . "[86]

It was unthinkable to attempt the restoration of Fort Duquesne which had occupied the extreme point of the triangle. (See Illustration 13.) Even had it been taken intact, the fort had proved to be inadequate and had suffered the ravages of weather and use for four years. We know, moreover, that an unusually large and elaborate fort was contemplated here by the English even before Braddock had set out from the east, three years before. While this ambitious project was being organized, the Point, through the next year or two, must be secured and the garrison housed by immediate construction, using the meager resources at hand, Bouquet ordered that "The Ammunition, and Stores actually in ye old Fort are to be removed in the New one as Soon as they can be Safely covered."[87] No name was ever formally given this temporary fort, built between December 1758 and late July 1759. Correspondence was addressed to and from "Pittsburgh." The name "Mercer's Fort" has been adopted as it is so designated on Meyer's drawing (Illustration 23) and occasionally elsewhere. However little Mercer may have had to do with its conception, he had apparently full responsibility as a contractor and commandant. Amherst considered the new English position at the Point in such little danger of reprisal by the French, that he wrote Forbes in December that a "blockhouse" would be adequate defense.[88] The plans and descriptions which he enclosed are not extant. Forbes' reactions to this suggestion are not known but on December 18th, 1758 he granted a warrant[89] "To Capt: Gordon Engineer, to be paid by him to the Officers who Contracted to Build a Fort at Pittsburgh, without Deduction . . . £ 124 13 2."

Fort Site and Design

Mercer's Fort was located a little over one thousand feet from Fort Duquesne, and hugged the bank of the Monongahela, thus keeping the point area clear for the large, permanent fort to be constructed later. The site also afforded ready escape to the south shore should the French return in overwhelming numbers, as was confidently anticipated.

The new fort was of the simplest sort, adapted to the readiest methods of construction. There was no time to build horizontal log ramparts or extensive palisaded walls. The log buildings on the four sides of the fort were made to serve as curtain walls between the palisaded bastions. The interior of these bastions was not elevated; all of the fort was on the level of the plane of site. The magazine was partially buried in the south bastion. The English recognized that this small palisaded fort might be adequate defense against Indians but could not withstand siege with artillery. Providentially, this test did not come.

MERCER'S FORT IN 1759 SHOWING LATER ADDITIONS
From a drawing in the Historical Society of Pennsylvania, Philadelphia
Illustration 1

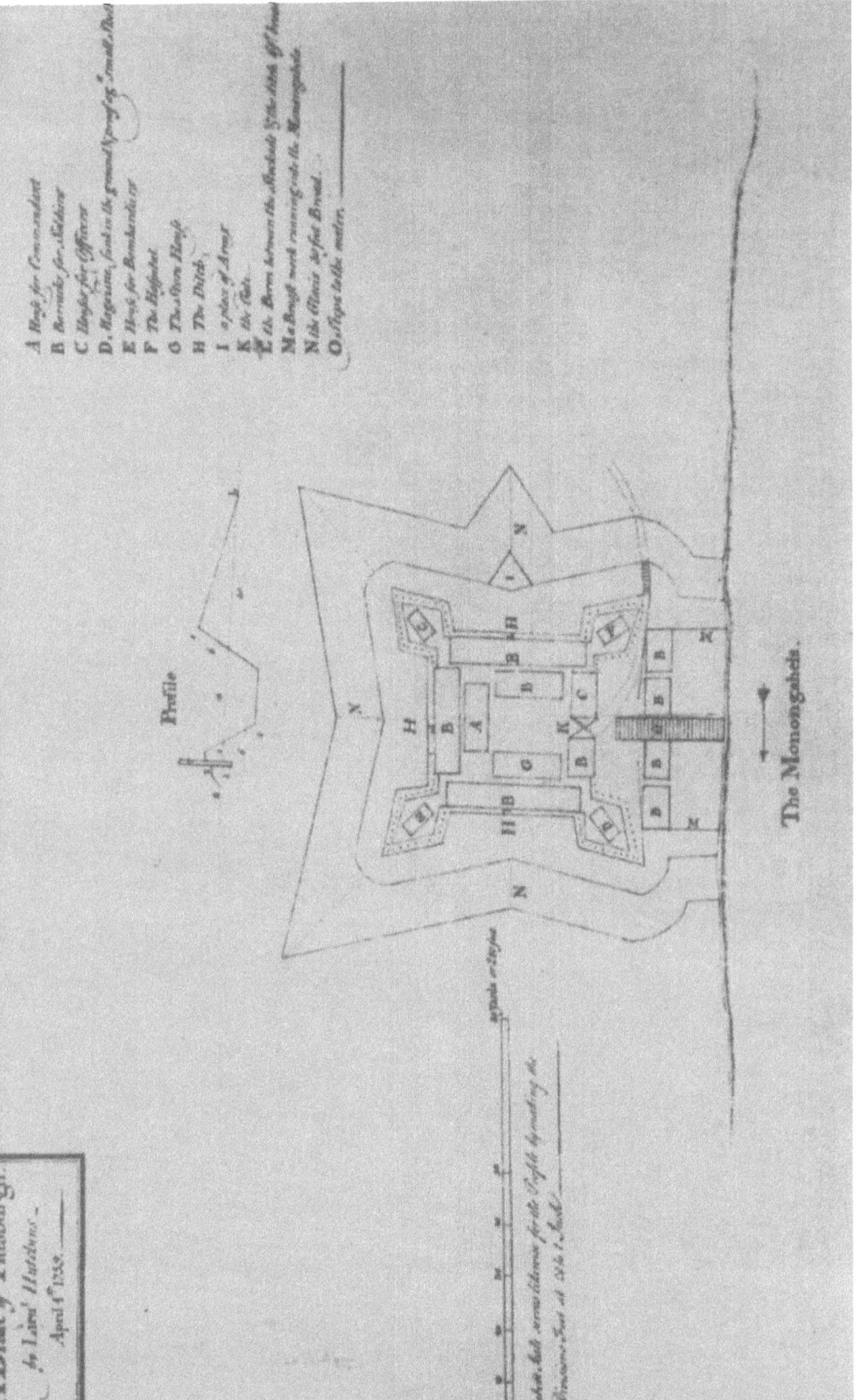

A Draft of Pittsburgh.
by Lieut. Hutchins —
April 1st 1758.

Profile

A House for Commandant
B Barracks for Soldiers
C House for Officers
D Magazine, sunk in the ground Nproof of Small Arms
E House for Bombardier &c
F The Hospital
G The Oven Bkh[o]p
H The Ditch
I a place of Arms
K the Gate
L the Barn known the Outside 5 in size of Pines
M a Bough work running into the Monongahela
N the Glacis sefest Broad
O Steps to the water

The Monongahela.

The Scale shels miscellaneous for the Profile by reading the
Dimensions Foot at Scale 1 foot

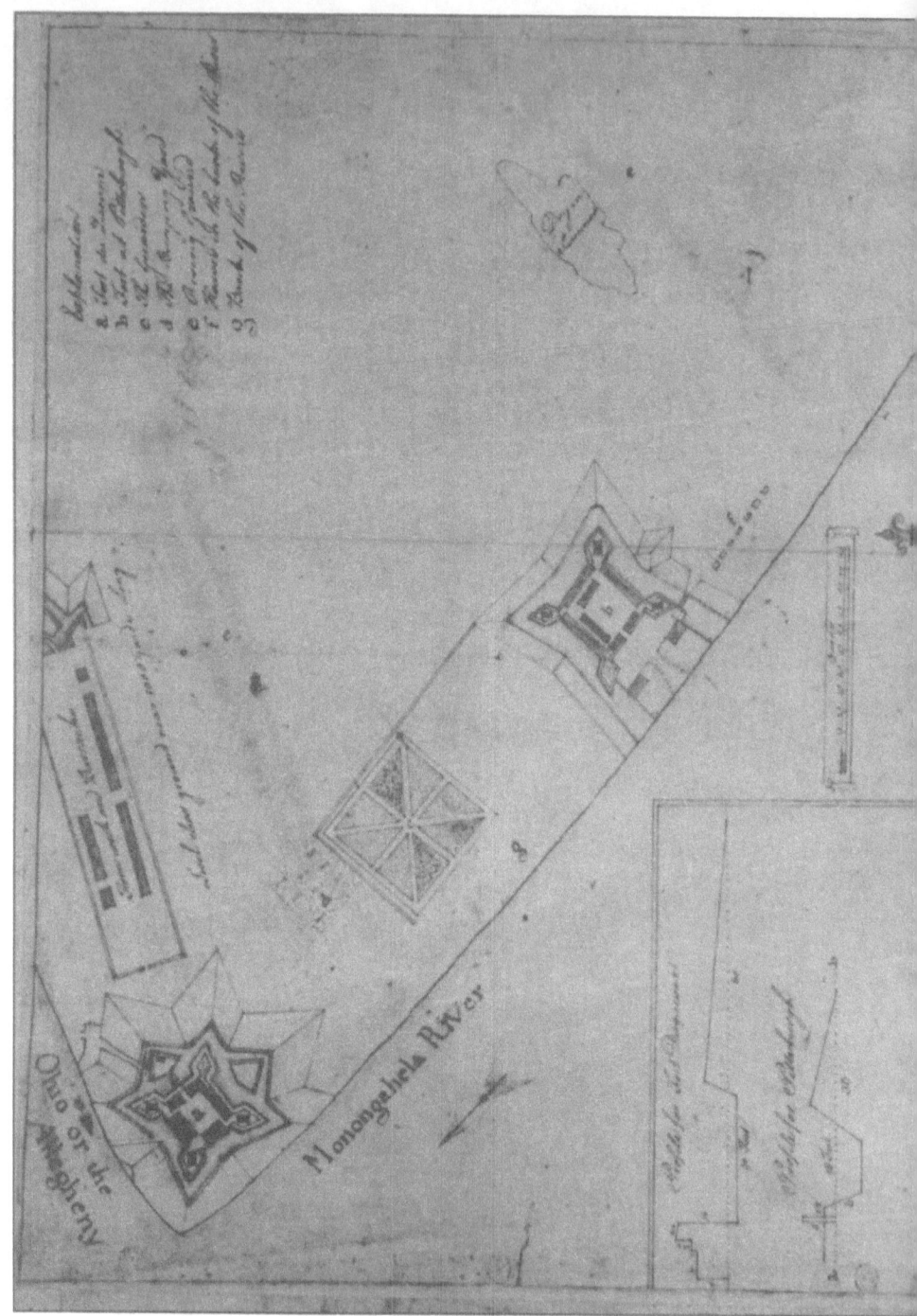

We have four drawings of Mercer's Fort. One of these, of which only half is preserved, was signed by Harry Gordon. This is the only sketch of any of the forts bearing Gordon's signature, though he undoubtedly made many such preliminary sketches in the field or in directing the draftsmen who prepared the finished drawings. This is apparently "the Plan of the Fort" enclosed in Gordon's letter to Bouquet of January fourth, 1759.[90] None of the later buildings or outworks on the river bank, ordered later in 1759, are shown on this drawing, further indicating it to be a preliminary draft. The same may be said of an unsigned drawing from the British Museum, entitled "A Plan of the Fort for 220 men built in December 1758 within 400 yard's of Fort Du Quesne." (Illustration 16.)

The third plan, drawn by Lieutenant Hutchins and entitled "A Draft of Pittsburgh," is dated April 4th, 1759 and is preserved in the Hutchins' Papers in the Historical Society of Pennsylvania. (Illustration 17.) It will be noted that the three buildings (10, 11, and 12) which were added within the parade to house the "artificers" and others needed in the building of Fort Pitt, created an unusually crowded condition. Four barracks (13, 14, 15, and 16) were also added outside the fort on the crest of the river bank. Breastworks were carried up the bank as additional protection for these new works and a ravelin was also installed on the eastern face.

A fourth drawing was found in the archives of the Historical Society of Pennsylvania. (Illustration 18.) No source, date or descriptive data for this rather crude drawing has been preserved. It shows the burying ground of Mercer's Fort and a garden surrounded by an entrenchment or palisade. This is the only drawing extant which shows the French barracks in the Second Fort of Fort Duquesne. Seven houses lay east of the fort on the bank of the Monongahela. One of these may be identified as the store conducted by James Kenny for the Indian Commissioners, as we learn from his Journal.[91] He identifies another building in an entry of July 10, 1759 as "ye Council house erected up ye river—from ours about 100 yds." All houses outside the fort were destroyed in July, 1759, when the French attack was expected, except the Council House which was used during that period by the guard.

Illustration 19 combines information obtained from both drawings and descriptions. The use and name of each building is shown. Illustration 20 is an aerial view of the fort and adjuncts.

ERCER'S FORT WITH FORT DUQUESNE AND ITS HORNWORK
om a drawing in the Historical Society of Pennsylvania, Philadelphia
'ustration 18

The Fort in Jeopardy

The need for shelter and defense sped the work in spite of conditions. The work progressed amazingly. Mercer reported on December 19th, 1758 "the Barracks being raisd & roofed & the Bastions almost inclosd. In a few more days the heaviest parts of our Work will be finish'd . . . " The reason for this great haste was Mercer's concern about an attack by the French. An Indian spy reported to him on the 23rd that the French were at work enlarging Fort Machault at Venango (modern Franklin) and also "fitting up a Number of Battoes, and preparing everything Necessary as the Com^g Officer told him to make a Descent on this Place & Loyalhanning (Ligonier); They have two Pieces of Cannon & about 300 Men at Wenango & expect a Reinforcement of Both from Priscile [Presqui'-Isle] . . . " This proved a false alarm but the ominous threat of attack hung over the garrison continuously until the climax in July.

Mercer goes on to report that the very cold weather retarded work and also made it impossible to dig a ditch in the frozen ground. Gordon wrote Mercer to break the ground with old axes, an expedient he had used successfully at Fort Edward. Mercer continued, "We are now employed in raising a Magazine, in hanging the Gate and raising the Bankets, I expect in four Days to have the Place made capable of a tolerable Defence, and am fully determined to maintain the Post, or at least, make it as dear a Purchase to the Enemy as possible." Food and supplies were desperately low. Mercer asked the authorities in the east if they were holding up delivery for fear the precious supplies would only augment the plunder when his fort was taken by the French. The corn field had been stripped by the Indians who, according to Mercer, were "eating us up too, especially in the Article of Flower." He was trying to persuade the Indians to send their "Young fry & Sqwas" home and leave only a few hunters to bring in fresh game.[92]

In a letter of December 26th, Bouquet advised Mercer to negotiate with the Indian heads to obtain their alliance in resisting any French attack, maintain an Indian spy system up and down the river, put his men on short rations until provisions should arrive, purchase corn from the Indians and expedite the building of boats. "As the Ennemy can not easily transport heavy Artillery, Try to mount 3 Cohorns to fire as Cannons horizontally, to dismount their Batteries," and another suggestion more easily said than done, "If practicable attempt in y^e Night to attack and nail their Cannon,

ILLUSTRATION No 19

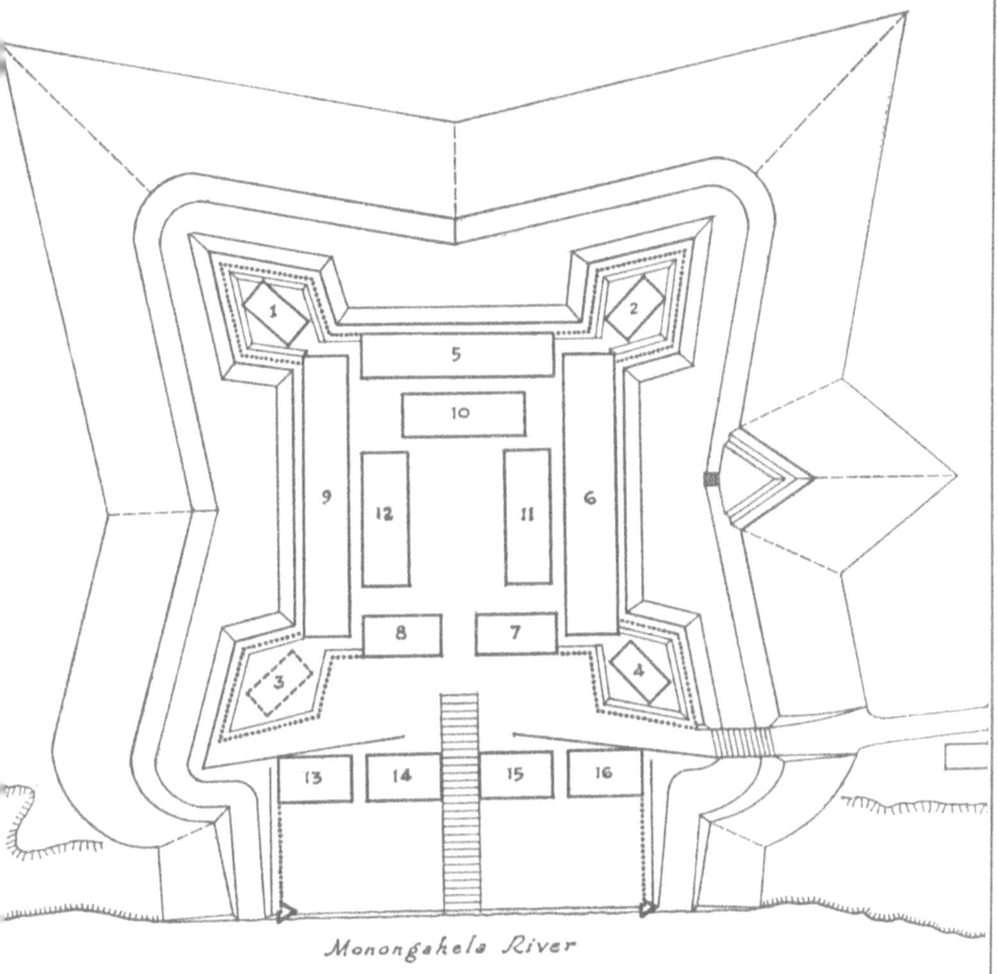

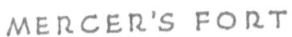

1
2
3
4
5
6
7
8
9
10
11
12
13
14
15
16
Monongahela River

MERCER'S FORT

BUILT 1758-59

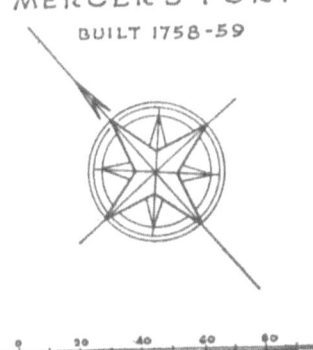

0
20
40
60
80
100
SCALE FOR PLAN

1 BOMBARDIERS QUARTERS
2 OFFICERS QUARTERS
3 POWDER MAGAZINE
4 HOSPITAL
5 SOLDIERS BARRACKS
6 SOLDIERS BARRACKS
7 OFFICERS QUARTERS
8 SOLDIERS BARRACKS
9 SOLDIERS BARRACKS
10 COMMANDANT'S HOUSE
11 STOREHOUSE
12 SOLDIERS BARRACKS
13 SOLDIERS BARRACKS
14 SOLDIERS BARRACKS
15 SOLDIERS BARRACKS
16 SOLDIERS BARRACKS

C.M.S.

having Steel nails and everything ready for it." Mercer had been taken by Indians to the spot in the river where the French were supposed to have sunk some of their cannon but none was found.

If faced by a superior force, Mercer was ordered not to capitulate, but to cross the river in the night, "Keeping a continual firing from ye Fort to mask your retreat," burn the fort and finally sink his boats. In anticipation of this extremity he was ordered to establish secretly a cache on the opposite shore of the Monongahela of "Cohorns, Ammunition, Arms, and stres, if you was forced to abandon the Fort." He was then to lead his forces to Fort Ligonier or Fort Cumberland.

Building Notes

Bouquet suggested in his letter of the 26th that Mercer "draw a Stockadoe, or any kind of Intrenchm^t from the two angels of ye Shoulder of the Bastions to the Water . . . to prevent the Ennemies taking advantage of the high banks of the River to surprise you in ye Night and it would be good cover for your Battoes, which are to be chained, and well Secured, I will send you Padlocks These Intrenchm^{ts} are defended by the faces of the Bastions." This accounts for the additional works mentioned above and shown on Illustration 17, and would indicate that Hutchins, an expert draftsman, was at Pittsburgh during this period.

There is another interesting item in this letter: "When your Works are finished, Would it not be of good Service to you to build a Redout (wth fraises) for 60 men on the Top of the Hill over Monongahela. It would prevent the Ennemies taking Post there and secure a Retreat."[93] The records contain no further mention of such a redoubt. The fort was substantially completed by January of 1759 when Mercer wrote that the fort could now provide some defense though hastily built under adverse weather conditions. There were 280 men in the garrison.

Mercer answered Bouquet January 3rd that the Indians made increasingly exorbitant demands for service as spies and their cooperation could only be expected if they thought Mercer's chances of success were better than the French. An attacking force of 500 French was expected if the attack were made in the winter and many more after the ice was out of the river. Batteau building proceeded slowly as Mercer was short of sawyers to make planks. He needed pitch and had enough tar for only one boat. He pleaded for a supply of black wampum, "the readiest traffick" with the Indians

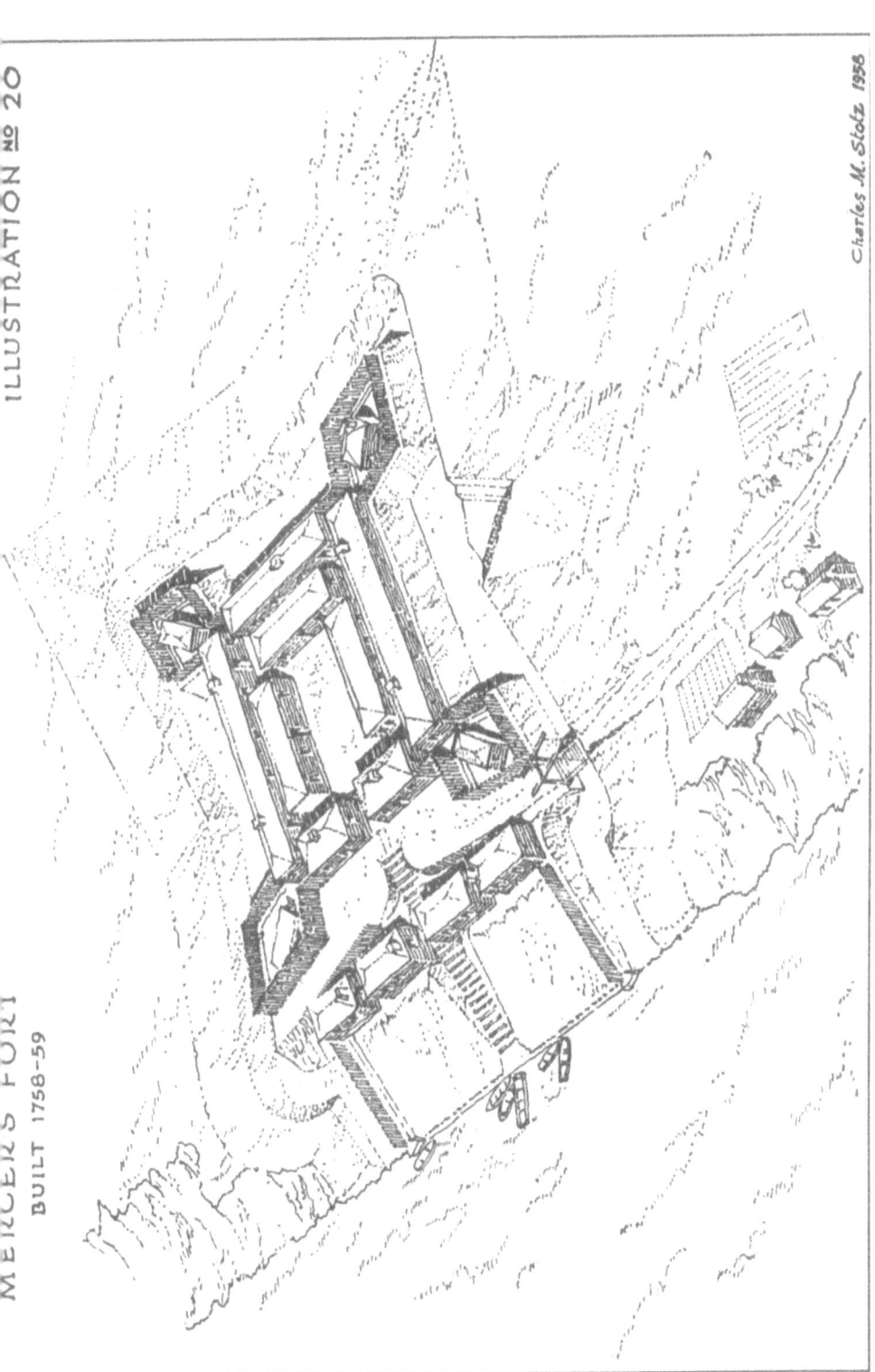

MERCERS FORT
BUILT 1758-59

ILLUSTRATION № 20

Charles M. Stotz 1958

for purchasing their canoes and game and paying spies. His supply of gold or Virginia currency was of no use as it was not tender among the Indians.

Mercer reported on January 3rd that "nine Hundred and fifty men May be Contained in the Fort by building Barracks opposite the Store houses [7 and 8] and hutts [13, 14, 15, and 16] might be Raised in the front within the Intrenchments you have Directed to be made, sufficient to Lodge 100 more."[94] The crowding of 1,050 men into this tiny fort was a desperate expedient. Mercer had but five artificers and needed a gunsmith with a set of tools. The badly needed supplies finally arrived, including a good supply of flour, of vital service in avoiding a break with the Indians. One hundred hogs, salt and other articles also arrived from Virginia.

On January 19th Mercer reported, "the Ditch is opened and would be compleated in two Days; I am glad to have Mr Gordons Directions and shall conform to them. Tho' I should think the Ditch too wide in our present weak state; .... Another Row of Barracks [proposed by Gordon] are now Raising, Opposite the Stores." Five batteaus were finished except for caulking. An additional blacksmith was needed to work for the Indians as "their little jobbs are perpetually empeding the Publick Work." Following Gordon's suggestion that part of the garrison could be housed outside the fort, Mercer suggested that "60 or 70 Men Could be extreamly well lodged, by running two Shades [crude sheds] along the Outside of the two Barracks fronting the River, and leave a flanker of Seven or eight feet; No Enemy can make an Approach on that side when the Works are compleated."[95] The plan shows that this was done.

In February logs were cut upstream but could not be brought to the fort because of ice in the river. The horses were too weak to be of service. Captain James Robertson, an engineer highly recommended by Gordon, arrived on the 28th with the new men, two howitzers, Indian goods, and other needed supplies. The new force of Highlanders and Royal Americans had arrived in such bad condition Mercer put them in the barracks and placed the Pennsylvanians outside in hospital tents. He now had 400 men.

In January the Indian Commissioners in Philadelphia authorized the construction of a Council House for Indian goods. A carpenter was sent from Philadelphia to build it with a supply of tools which included hand and whip saws for making boards, crosscut saws, falling and broad axes, frows and drawing knives to make shingles, augers of several sizes, nails for shingles, etc., locks, padlocks, hinges and other hardware, and horses and traces for hauling timber and boards. This building located outside the fort, was not completed until December 13 of 1759.

Deeply disturbed by French plans to retake the Forks, Bouquet wrote Amherst that the possession of the Ohio could not be secured with less than 1,000 or 1,500 men and that "no time should be lost in sending that force." Amherst, in his usual uncompromising style, answered Bouquet on March 16th: "I am sensible that the Fort at Pittsburgh is small but at the Same Time I am also convinced, that if Col.º Mercer and the Garrison it contains do their Duty, and in Case of an Attack, make the Defense they ought, no force the Enemy can be supposed to bring against it, if without Artillery, can oblige him to retire, and in my Opinion it is not likely, that, at this Season, the Enemy will be able to bring any with them, and as he can always be reinforced from Fort Ligonier, You must direct him to defend This Fort to the utmost Extremity, for if it is not, it might as well not have been built."96 Amherst would not have been so arbitrary had he known that only four months later 700 French soldiers with 750 Indian allies were to assemble at Fort Machault in preparation for an attack on Mercer's Fort. The sudden diversion of this great force to succor the besieged Fort Niagara saved Mercer's Fort from almost certain annihilation.

The ditch and glacis were completed by March 18th. The ammunition was made secure "from a few Small Shells, and the Other Works recommended are going on briskly." Scurvy began to develop from the winter's fare of salt meat, and the measles laid low many, including Lieutenant Hutchins. Mercer repeated his request for garden seeds and a seine "to catch the Catfish that now make their appearance." The boats already built could not be put in service as the pitch he had received was spoiled by having been carelessly mixed with dirt. Mercer was unable to locate pine in the vicinity of the fort from which to obtain pitch but did locate a good spot for a mill on the opposite shore. To add another specter to the mild nightmare in which he existed Mercer wrote of "the rising of the Monongahela in the Spring—but this I dread to mention lest you suspect that I take pleasure in sending frightfull stories down the Country."

By April living conditions had improved. Provisions were plentiful, the sick were eating fresh venison and greens were coming in. The seine was at last received; fish proved "an Immense ease to the Beef & Pork . . . " Bouquet promised shipments of cattle and vinegar for the scurvy victims and, most cheering of all, relief of the garrison who were to go back east to recover their health.

By late June well verified reports made it clear to the little garrison of Mercer's Fort that the French were now indeed massing at Venango and augmented daily by enormous numbers of Indian allies. The peril was real and immediate. One of the garrison, John Ormsby, writing of the incident later, said, "This information, you may be sure, struck a panic into our people, being 300 miles from any aid, and surrounded by the merciless savages, ... I must own I made my sincere application to the Almighty, to pardon my sins and extricate us from this deplorable situation . . . ."[97] James Kenny found his Quaker calm severely tested, writing in his journal on June 30th, "I am much exercised in mind, but toward evening got refreshed by quiet meditation." News of the precipitate departure of the French and Indians from Venango, on July 12th, to relieve Fort Niagara was brought to the garrison by an Indian spy on the 14th, but Kenny writes they "could not trust much to his report." That same morning "before we were out of bed ye Sergeant Major came and told us that our houses must be pulled down, only [except] ye house built for ye Provin[c]ial Commissioners where ye Guard is to be." Thus the little settlement was destroyed needlessly. A great sigh of relief must have been heard over the Forks of the Ohio on August 13th, the day Kenny wrote in his journal, "This day ye Indians bring intelligence that ye French have lost Niagara & that they have burnt Venango & Presque Isle & gone off."

After Kenny's store had been torn down he lived in a tent. His goods were temporarily stored in the "loft in ye Colonel's house" until he received permission to store them in "ye old magazine in ye old Fort [Fort Duquesne]." This was the magazine on the north side, described above, which had not been blown up. This is the only mention of any use made of the French fort structure.

By July 21st Mercer was able to report that " . . . The only additional Works for the Defence of the Place, which could be carried on, is a line of Pickets planted two feet within the Stockades to Strengthen the Bastion, by filling up the Interstice with Deer Skins, running a line of Chevaux de frize along the front of the fort, between the breast Works leading to the Monongahela, and strengthening these Breastworks with some Stockades."[98] We do not know whether these things were done because the emphasis in the correspondence was now passing from Mercer's Fort to the preliminary planning for the new fort. At any rate it may be stated with some assurance that little or no work was done on Mercer's Fort after late July of 1759.

Transition to the New Work

In anticipation of the needs of the new fort, Mercer was diligent in exploring the resources of the district. He discovered coal and limestone outcrops near the top of the hill across the river and built paths for pack horses to bring it down. Kenny described this coal mine: " . . . ye Mountain Side is so high & steep that its with Care & difficulty people gets up to it, . . . ye Coal is in a Bank fronting like a upright Wall in ye Hill side the^y put it into bags & tunbles them down ye hill." This coal mine, located near the crest of Mount Washington just west of the incline opposite the Point, was accidentally set afire and so described by the Reverend Charles Beatty in 1766. Coal was needed as a fuel and for making tar while the limestone was reduced in a kiln to provide lime for plaster and mortar. Kenny also mentions a visit to "ye French Lime Kiln & ye Coal Mine" which lay on a branch of Saw Mill Run about 1-1/4 miles from the Monongahela. Mercer, accompanied by Captain Robertson, searched the area for a better site for the new fort, as will be discussed in the next section.

As the buildings within the new Fort Pitt were made available to the garrison, those in and about Mercer's Fort were demolished, as we read in Kenny's journal entry of October 20, 1762: "where two years ago I have seen all ye Houses that were without ye Little Fort they had then, thrown Down, only One [the Indian Council House], which stands yet, also two that was within that little fort is now standing being ye Hospital now." Eventually its site was occupied by the Flag Bastion of Fort Pitt and the outworks east of it. The importance of the role played by Mercer's Fort in the history of the Point and the affairs of the British in America were in many respects equal to that of Fort Pitt itself. By the time Fort Pitt was completed, all possibility of French invasion of western Pennsylvania had passed. Mercer's Fort stood for a full year and a half as the tangible evidence of British possession of the Ohio country. This little stronghold and its garrison had no doubt deterred the menacing Indian population from any warlike effort.

But for the providential deflection of the French forces from Venango to Niagara, we would have known whether, in the event of attack, Mercer would have stood his ground as admonished by Amherst or have followed the counsel of discretion, destroyed the fort he had "huddled up in a very hasty manner" with such great labor and decamped across the Monongahela and thence to the south. In any event, the way was now clear for building a fort at the Point, which, in the words of William Pitt, would ensure "the undisputed possession of the Ohio."

FORT PITT
Site Considerations

The five forts that were constructed between 1754 and 1792 to defend the country at the headwaters of the Ohio were all built on the small triangle of land, known as the "Point" or the "Forks," at the confluence of the Monongahela and Allegheny Rivers. This site, which may seem an obviously desirable one to us, was the source of much controversy, as was discussed under Fort Prince George and Fort Duquesne. This uncertainty continued to plague those charged with the establishment of the new works.

The temporary Mercer's Fort was placed well up the bank of the Monongahela to leave ample space for the construction of a large new fort at the Point. Nevertheless Bouquet requested Mercer to determine if there was another, and possibly better site. Captain James Robertson, an engineer, was sent to Pittsburgh to assist in this search. Together with Mercer and a Robert Wright, he made a visit to "Chartres" (Chartier's) Hill. "Drafts" of the site were sent with a report to Bouquet on April 24, 1759. The drafts have been lost but from the description we know the site to have been the same as that proposed by the Ohio Company. (Illustration 12.) Mercer describes the spot as "Strong, convenient, healthfull and pleasant" but had the drawback of requiring " . . , a quantity of Iron Chain . . , for drawing up water, wood &c, either by Cranes or Windlasses." At the same time, Mercer calls attention to the chief defect of the Point as a fort site. "If it is judged proper to fortify the Point on the Ruins of Du Quesne, a foundation of Brick or Stone must be raised, several feet above its present level, the Ohio in its late rise, being all over the Plain where the Barracks [the Second Fort] stood, and covering, as I heard, the floor of the fort. 'Tis certain the french were once obliged to abandon it, and glad to escape to the high Grounds in their battoes."[99] Bouquet wrote Mercer in May that he had laid the matter before General Stanwix who, in spite of Mercer's enthusiasm for the new site, "will differ to take any determination upon the Choice of a ground for the new Fort, till he is himself on the Spot." Bouquet then quotes Stanwix with the persuasive consideration that seems to have finally swayed all authorities in finally settling upon the Point as a site for their forts, in spite of its obvious defects. "The difficulty of crossing the Monongahela Seems to be a great objection against the fine Place you describe, as well as the risk of loosing the Communication of that River, if we have not a Post upon it; The dangers and the advantages must be well weighed; and the Reasons for abandoning the Forks very prevailing to loose that convenient Station."[100] This corroborates Washington's analysis made five years before, that the strategic value of the Point as the site for a fort outweighed all other considerations.

Captain Harry Gordon arrived at Pittsburgh on August 1st with the advance group of workmen or "artificers" who proceeded with preparation of building materials. In the meantime, probably so ordered by Bouquet, Gordon also searched for an alternate site. He found nothing desirable up the rivers but caught some of Mercer's enthusiasm for the site at Chartier's Creek. However, Gordon made no decision but awaited Stanwix's arrival on August 29th. The records are silent on any further reference to site selection. Undoubtedly Stanwix was still convinced of the necessity of commanding the confluence of the rivers for construction was begun there on September third.

Although the site of Fort Pitt was irretrievably fixed by the construction of the fort itself, the location at the Forks again was to be sharply condemned three years later for its vulnerability to flood and cannon fire from the opposite shores. This final blast came from Lieutenant Colonel William Eyre in his report[101] to General Amherst in April of 1762. Eyre, described by Vaudreuil as "an officer of consummate experience in the art of War,"[102] had designed and had successfully defended Fort William Henry against an attack in March of 1757. Eyre had been instructed by Amherst to examine the damage sustained by Fort Pitt in the flood of the previous winter and to recommend means for rehabilitating the fort. Even though the fort was by then substantially completed, Eyre considered its plight so desperate that he spent much of his time searching for a better site. His first choice was the same as that first selected for the Ohio Company by George Mercer, and condemned by Washington and later recommended by Hugh Mercer, Robertson and Gordon. This was the long slender hill bordering the river at the mouth of Chartier's Creek below Brunot's Island and terminating in the cliff from which McKee's Rocks took its name. This he describes as "of very difficult Access on any Side, quite flatt at Top, and surrounded on one Side by the River, and the other by low Ground very even [known today as The Bottoms, this area was later used as pasturage for the horses of Fort Pitt], which would produce any Thing that a rich Soil could. No Hill [is] within Reach of it, so of Course the French here would have made a very formidable Post. A few Block Houses upon this Hill, join'd by a Stockade, would make it a difficult Task for any Army to force, was it made with Loggs, no Army that we could bring against it, could reduce it." (See Illustration 11.)

He considered this site incomparably the best in the neighborhood, saying, "Its amazing the French neglected this Situation, and chose so bad a one; but its still as Amazing that we repeated the Mistake by doing it in a more expensive Manner by building pretty nearly on the same Ground, in so formidable a Manner when it could be so easily avoided."

Further to discomfit the builders of Fort Pitt, he pointed out that a better site existed within little more than a stone's throw from the Point, namely the crest on which Duquesne University stands today. The early drawings name this as Ayre's Hill, probably for the Colonel. He said this "very high Eminence . . . domineers over every Thing within Cannon Shot, is only attackable in one Part. All the rest being either very steep or a Precipice, particularly on the Side of the River." He mentions Suke's Run which then partially encircled the hill. These features may clearly be seen on Meyer's Map, Illustration 25. Eyre admits the lack of water but thought a well would reach water in 70 or 80 feet. He claimed that a temporary fort of a "few Block Houses . . , join'd by a strong Stockade" could be built here in one summer "with the greatest Ease," until the "Fate of War settled our Frontiers," after which a permanent one could be erected there or elsewhere as the "Events of War" might dictate. He believed that "a Work built here well dispos'd would be out of the Power of all Canada, with the Force of Louisiana to reduce." To command the "Passage of the Rivers" he proposed to build no more than a blockhouse at the Point for 18 or 20 men. This was to be supplemented by a blockhouse "at the lower Point of Grants Hill, and another close to the Allegheny River, which twelve Men, would well defend each." He adds a pleasant note: "There is the most delightfull Prospect from this Hill of the three Rivers, as also of the Country round; the Air must be most pleasant and healthfull and always clean and dry."

A fort of the size and complication of Fort Pitt could not have been laid out without a ground plan from which to survey and establish its various features. Bouquet wrote to Mercer in August of 1759 "to leave Capt. Gordon at Pittsburgh to commence the execution of *his Plan*, . . ."[103] We cannot identify this plan among those extant. All of the existing plans of the fort apparently were made later than September of 1759. No earlier layout of any kind remains except those which are the subject of the following paragraph.

New Evidence on Site and Design

Most of the writers on Fort Pitt ascribe its design to Captain Harry Gordon. Stanwix, who had constructed Fort Stanwix in New York in 1758, came to Pittsburgh in the summer of 1759 to rule on site selection and it is presumed that he had something to do with matters of design. Dahlinger gives the credit to Lieutenant Bernard Ratzer whose name appears on one of the most important drawings. However, this drawing was made in 1761, after the fort was substantially completed. Furthermore it was common, then as now, for draftsmen to make and sign drawings prepared under the direction of those who designed the work.

To the writer, all of these speculations were cast in doubt, when he came upon two sketch drawings preserved in the Huntington Library in San Marino, California. One drawing shows the Forks of the Ohio and adjacent territory with obviously inaccurate indications of tributary streams. The other drawing (Illustration 21) shows the point area with a fort somewhat more carefully drawn with a ruled ink line. The layout, and practically every main feature, is immediately identifiable as that of Fort Pitt, though neither the name Fort Pitt nor Pittsburgh appears on it. The title in the upper right-hand corner reads, "New Work at Fort Du Quesne." There is a note in the upper left-hand corner: "Ref'd to Genl Braddock. Thos Gage." The clue to the significance of this important document is found in the inscription in French in the lower right-hand corner: "Trouvi dans le caisse militaire du General Braddock, ainsi que ses plans de campagne et instructions." It is signed "Dumas, Capt" and dated "10 Juillet 1755." Captain Jean Dumas had taken command when Captain Daniel Beaujeu fell in the battle. Following the defeat Dumas seized Braddock's military portfolio of preciously guarded plans and instructions, countersigned the drawings and sent them to Canada. Here is conclusive evidence that the design had been determined before Gordon had received his engineer's commission on August 18, 1756, although he had accompanied Braddock's army. Further, that Braddock had been prepared to proceed with the erection of a major fort at the Forks, had he not been waylaid by the French and Indians when almost within sight of his goal.

These drawings, when found by the writer, were recognized as crude representations of Fort Pitt, improperly designated as Fort Duquesne and were filed with other questionable material. A year later, upon more careful examination, the electrifying inscription in French by Dumas was first noticed and the significance of the drawings realized.

When the British government officials granted the request of the Ohio Company to build a fortified storehouse at the Forks of the Ohio, those in England were not fully aware of the value of the Ohio country and of its importance to the French. By the time Ward's tiny garrison had been overwhelmed by an alert, determined French force, the English at last realized what they had lost by this feeble gesture of defense. They were determined not to make the same mistake the second time. As Braddock's campaign was being organized, it is only reasonable to suppose that the English carefully considered measures to fortify the Forks after the French had been driven out. A general knowledge of the site and its topography could readily be gained from Washington, Gist, Mercer and others who had visited there. In contrast to the tiny fortified storehouse erected by Trent, Braddock was supplied with a tentative sketch and possibly specific orders, for building what was for those days, a mighty fortress.

The many unintelligible notes and indications on these two drawings apparently were intended to inform Braddock of conditions in the area as reported by spies and scouts, but are not pertinent to the primary concern of this article. While Harry Gordon was not commissioned an engineer until August 18, 1756, he accompanied

PLAN OF FUTURE FORT PITT SEIZED WITH BRADDOCK'S BAGGAGE BY DUMAS
From a drawing in the Henry E. Huntington Library, San Marino, California
Illustration 21

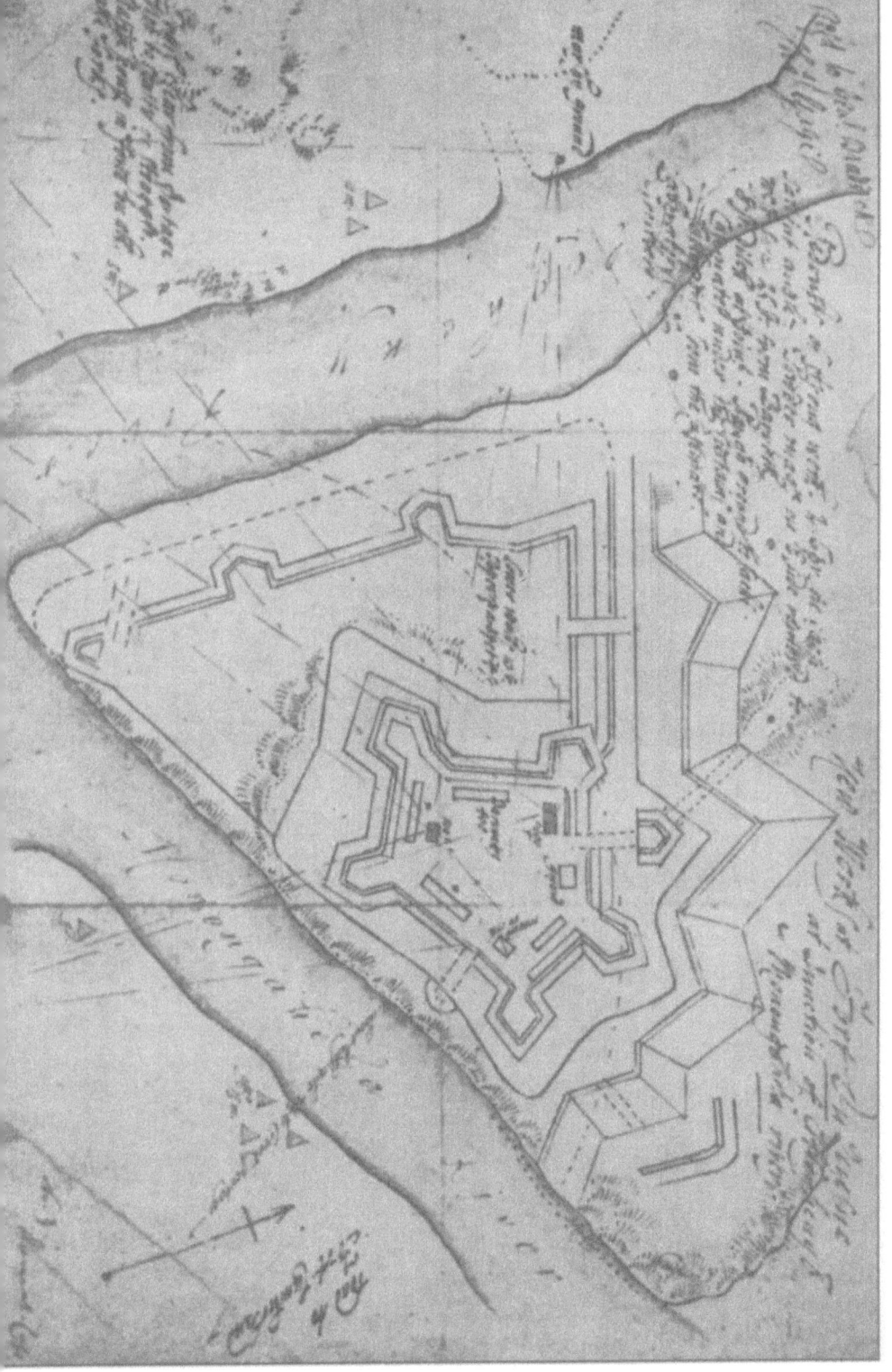

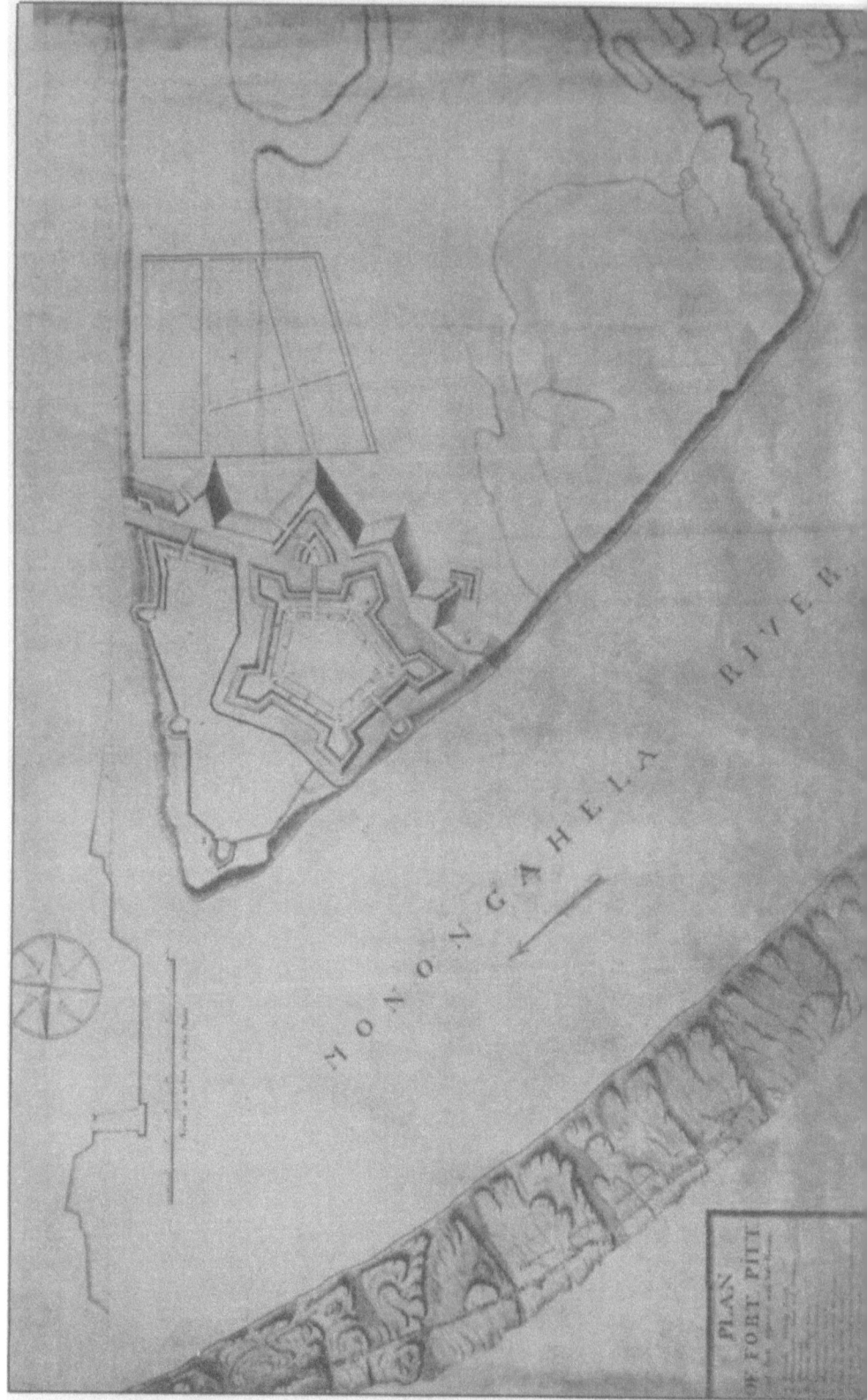

Braddock on his expedition, as had Colonel Thomas Gage. Gordon may well have known of these drawings, "referred" by Gage to Braddock, but makes no mention of them in subsequent correspondence. It remains only to say that the Point area was the first and the final choice as the site of Fort Pitt. If Gordon was not actually the designer, he was the man personally charged with the construction of the Fort. Bouquet wrote Gordon from Bedford in August of 1759: " . . . he [General Stanwix] recommends that all your Works be Part of *your Plan* of the Pentagone."[104] This certainly indicates that Gordon was credited with authorship of the plan for Fort Pitt and may possibly mean he had had a hand in the sketch carried by Braddock. Stanwix reported to Amherst in September 1759: " . . . The Fort begun is a pentigon that Figure best Suiting with our ground near the Old Fort which when finish'd is judged will be of Sufficient Strength and every way adequate to the great importance of its several Objects . . . "[105]

Contemporary Fort Plans

There are some fifteen contemporary drawings of Fort Pitt extant, of which the drawing made by Bernard Ratzer (Illustration 22) and that by Lieutenant Elias Meyer (Illustration 23) in 1761 are the most informative. These are large drawings, excellently drawn in ink on a good grade of heavy paper. Since the fort was near completion in 1761 they presumably comprise our best record. Another drawing made by Meyer (Illustration 25) shows the entire point area as far east as modern Oakland and as far down the Ohio as Brunot's Island, then known as Shurtee's Island. This drawing is unsigned but Bouquet's correspondence reveals that Meyer was at work on the survey in May of 1762 for Colonel Eyre. The reconstruction drawings are based on the evidence of these three important documents.

There is another group of four smaller drawings, all uniform in wording and subject matter except for minor details, though differing in character of draftsmanship. They all are entitled "Plan of the New Fort at Pittsburgh, November 1759." This was not necessarily intended as the date the drawings were completed but rather the month in which work was substantially under way. In fact two of these drawings show work completed at a later date. Only one of the drawings is signed, "G. Wright, Fecit." In addition to these seven drawings, there are others of minor

PLAN OF FORT PITT DRAWN BY BERNARD RATZER IN 1761
From a drawing in the British Museum, London
Illustration 22

interest, among them two crude sketches made in the last days of the fort when its ownership was in dispute. These drawings are valuable in showing the location of three of the five redoubts constructed in 1764 and 1765, including the existing Blockhouse. They also contribute to our knowledge of the buildings within the fort.

Information gleaned from these drawings and all other sources is combined in the drawing (Illustration 25) which shows Fort Pitt as completely and accurately as may be managed. The aerial view, Illustration 27, will assist in visualizing the fort structure. Limitation of space in this article permits reference only to the more important items in the military correspondence, journals and other written source material.

Modern Investigations at the Point

An archaeological study was conducted by Wesley L. Bliss[106] for the Point Park Commission of Pittsburgh in 1942-43 with a view to establishing the Point as a national park to be administered by the National Park Service. It was not intended to restore the fort but only to preserve the features exposed by excavation. Although the park project was eventually abandoned, much valuable information was gained about Fort Pitt.

In 1945 the Regional Planning Association commissioned Ralph E. Griswold, landscape architect, Donald J. McNeil, traffic engineer, and the writer as architect, to make a study for a park at the Point with such traffic revisions as might be needed to make it an integral part of the "living city." Their findings, submitted in November of that year, established substantially all of the main features of the Point State Park as well as the relocation of the bridges and traffic routes now under construction. In the course of the above study it was determined that the full size restoration of Fort Pitt was impractical because of prohibitive encroachments on the city and interference with an acceptable solution to the traffic problem. James L. Swauger, of the Carnegie Institute, conducted additional archaeological research in excavations made when construction was begun on Point State Park in 1953.

During the Bliss survey, a number of test pits and trenches were dug on city-owned streets, as much of the former fort site was occupied by private property and lands of the railroad terminal, since removed. The lower part of the brick walls and foundations of Fort Pitt were uncovered in several places and the exact levels of

PLAN OF FORT PITT PREPARED BY ELIAS MEYER IN 1761
From a drawing in the Public Record Office, London
Illustration 23

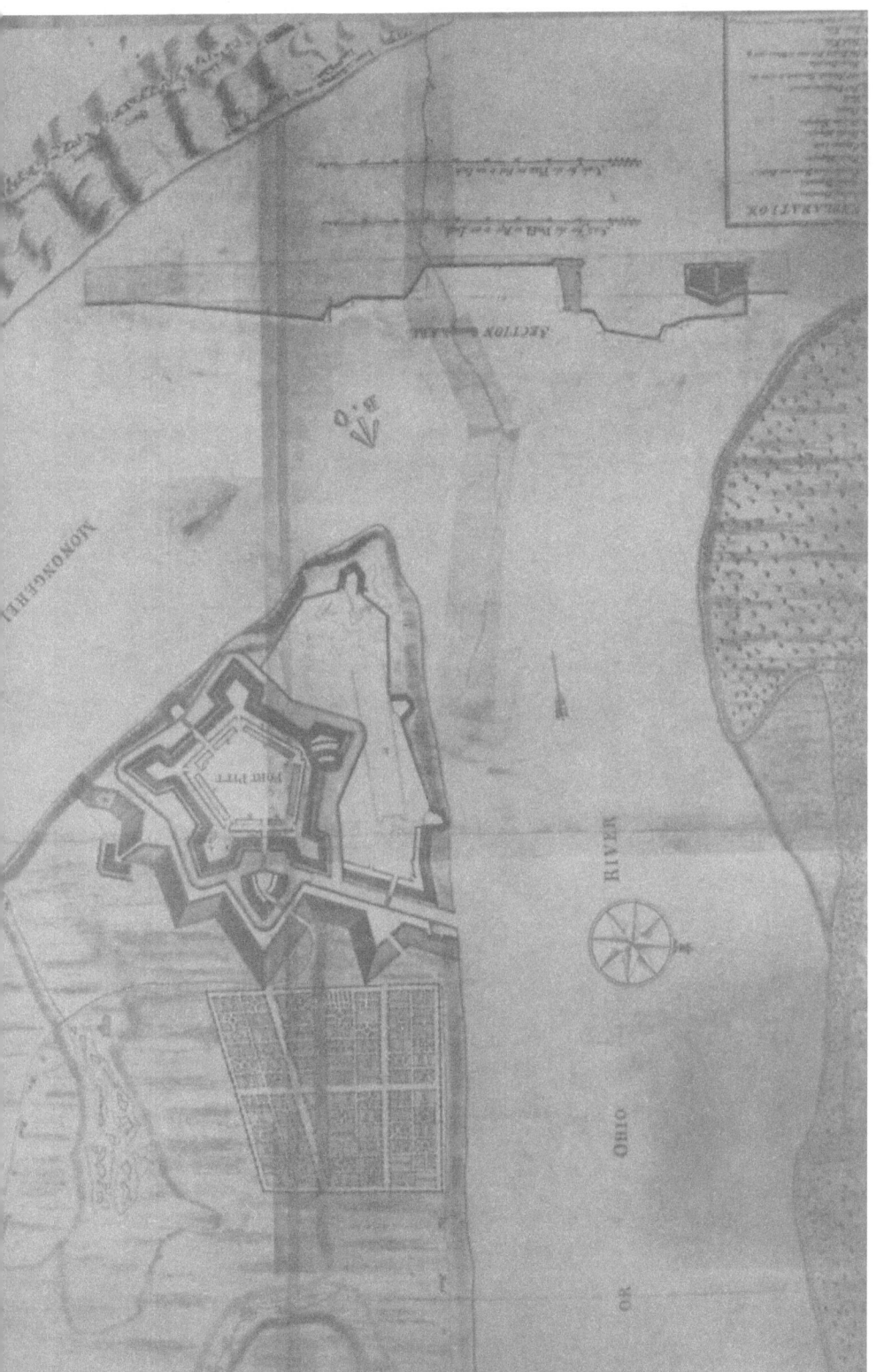

the parade ground, covered way and ditch were established. It was likewise proved that the fort plan conformed, with only minor variations, to the eighteenth-century Ratzer and Meyer plans. The plane of site, or parade ground level, was found to average 728.4 feet above sea level and the top of the stone foundations 718.4, which corresponded exactly with the ten foot depth of ditch shown on the eighteenth-century drawings. Further reference will subsequently be made to these important findings.

Description of the Fort

In topography, the Point was a slightly undulating plane. A terrace about five feet high, parallel with the Allegheny River and about 400 feet from it, is indicated on most of the early drawings as a shaded strip. This lower level along the Allegheny was the plane on which Fort Duquesne was built. The northern extremity of Fort Pitt bordered this terrace and only the Ohio Bastion extended beyond it, on to the lower ground and, for this reason, was termed the "low bastion." This bastion, built entirely of earth, was never completely finished and suffered much from floods as it projected beyond the protecting masonry walls of the fort front, thus receiving the full force of the current. Because of the lower level on which the Ohio Bastion was constructed, its top also was lower than those of the other bastions.

The area of the triangle was then much less, as the shore lines have been pushed out into the rivers in modern times. The Point itself lay just short of the present day junction of the Manchester and Point Bridges. The Allegheny River bank now lies about 250 feet and the Monongahela bank about 150 feet beyond their original locations. The old banks were about fifteen to twenty feet high and rutted by erosion, exposing the clay, sand and gravel that composed the soil. According to the Bliss Report the flood of 1762 rose about 4.8 feet above the parade ground level of Fort Pitt and that of 1763 about 6.7 feet, as compared with 11.6 feet in the flood of 1936. Illustration 24 shows the relation of the five eighteenth century forts to the modern city. Note that the early shore line is some distance inside that of today.

The pentagonal shape of Fort Pitt was admirably adapted to the triangular shape of the Point, as General Stanwix, quoted above, observed. The fort proper lay very close to the Monongahela bank to provide space between the fort and the Allegheny River for the

THE FIVE FORTS AT THE POINT SUPERIMPOSED ON A 1958 PHOTOGRAPH
Photograph by the Aerial Map Service Company
Illustration 24

protected building area, known as the Lower Town, outside the fort walls. The Lower Town, comprising about 4.8 acres, was protected by a fortified embankment, known as the Epaulement, on the Allegheny shore. A continuous ditch, known as "The Isthmus," extended in front of the land side of the fort from the Allegheny almost to the Monongahela River. The ditch around the fort joined the isthmus at two points. The ditch was filled with water only at high stages of the river. The isthmus provided a continuous advance line of defense across the Point with a covered way where a line of soldiers could fire from the protection of earth embankments. The entrance road to the fort crossed the ditch at two points by bridges, each protected at their inner end by drawbridges that were lifted at night. The triangular island or ravelin between these bridges served as added protection for the entrance and contained an underground guardroom for prisoners. There was another ravelin of simpler type between the Grenadier and Flag Bastions and still another which commanded the Monongahela River opposite the Monongahela Curtain.

Bastions projected from each of the five corners of the fort proper. The five bastions, as well as the five curtain walls between them, are designated by names for convenience in reference. The bastion names are of uncertain modern origin but to abandon them would only create confusion. The only bastion names found by the writer in the early records are the Monongahela Bastion (now called the Flag Bastion), the Lower Monongahela Bastion (now called the Monongahela Bastion) and the Cavalier Bastion (now called the Ohio Bastion). The Flag Bastion undoubtedly earned its title by the single reference to its use taken from Kenny's Journal: "on ye South East Bastion stands a High Poal like a Mast & top Mast to Hoist ye flag (on) which is Hoisted on every first Day [Sunday] of ye Week from about Eleven to One o'clock & on State Days &c." The names for the curtains are taken from various references in the contemporary records. It may be of interest that the perimeter of the bastions varied from 233 feet (Flag) to 255 feet (Ohio). The length of the curtains varied from 188 feet (Upper Town) to 272 feet (Monongahela). From tip to tip of bastions was 416 feet on the entrance front and 476 feet on the face paralleling the Monongahela River. The total area within the ramparts contained 2.1 acres, the parade ground itself 1.3 acres. The entire fort, with its outworks, not including the gardens, occupied 17.6 acres of the

SURVEY OF FORT PITT AND ENVIRONS MADE BY ELIAS MEYER IN 1762
From a drawing in the Public Record Office, London
Illustration 25

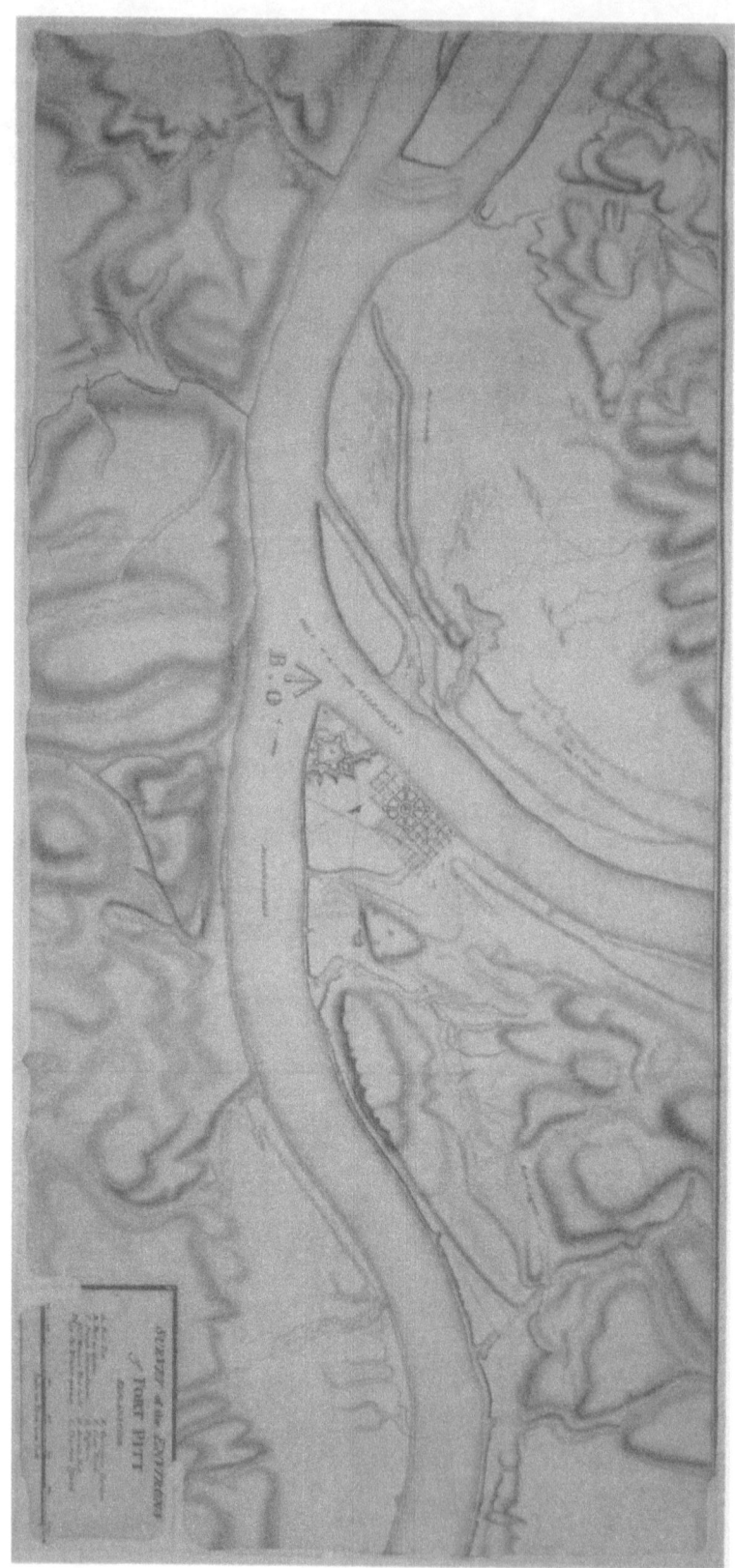

Point. Fort Pitt and Fort Duquesne have been mistakenly described as "star" forts. This appellation was reserved for star-shaped works "whose faces present a series of salient and re-entering angles" and would therefore lack bastions. Forts Brewerton and Oswego were star forts and a star redoubt may be seen on the plan of Fort Bedford. (See Illustration 4.)

Fort Pitt, with its outworks, was the most elaborate fortification built by the British on their frontiers in America. However, it shared many characteristics with two other five-bastioned forts of pentagonal shape. Only slightly smaller, Fort Ontario, built on Lake Ontario in 1763, was of inferior horizontal log construction and lacked extensive outworks. The existing restored Fort Ontario is of later vintage. In 1759 Amherst built Fort Crown Point on Lake Champlain close by the abandoned French Fort Frederick. It is said that 3,000 men worked two years to build the stone barracks and stone-revetted scarp wall, using the limestone chiseled out to create the ditch. The ruins of Crown Point are most impressive. About the same size as Fort Pitt, sentries on the ramparts of both forts walked nearly a half mile in making a complete circuit. The aerial perspective of Fort Ontario, drawn by Francis Pfister, is most unusual among early drawings for its informative realism. (See Illustration 28.)

Earthwork Construction

Fort Pitt was a "dirt fort." In simplest terms it was a five sided parade ground, bordered by five rows of buildings, which, in turn, were protected by five parallel mounds of earth shaped to the contours of the conventional rampart of the day. On the two sides toward the land these earth ramparts were supported by heavy masonry retaining walls built of brick with stone foundations and a coping or cap piece of stone. This fifteen foot high brick facing or revetment enclosed the Music Bastion and extended southward around the Flag Bastion. The tips of the bastions were trimmed with hewn stone, as we learn from Kenny's Diary of 1761. This is the same treatment as seen in Illustration 28 of Fort McHenry and provided needed strength at the sharp angles of the bastion points. The brick facing also extended along the scarp wall of the isthmus or ditch from the Music Bastion to the Allegheny River. This wall was somewhat lower than the wall of the fort proper. Earth parapets were built above the masonry scarp walls. The terre plein, a 20 foot wide terrace behind the parapet, provided space for movement of the soldiers in action. The gun platforms were placed on this level.

We are apt to think of earth as commonplace material for the construction of a fort, yet Harry Gordon, when he learned that General Stanwix had ordered the fort "to be made of Earth instead of Logs," said that he thought it would "turn out much Better." Gordon had learned from experience that the horizontal log walls and wood palisades used on practically all of the other frontier forts deteriorated rapidly. Earthworks of ample size were more easily maintained and gave excellent protection from cannon fire.

As earth-moving in those days was done entirely by hand with picks, shovels, handbarrows and wheelbarrows, no earth was moved farther than absolutely necessary. Therefore, on a level site, the size of the earth walls which formed the curtains, ramparts and the bastions were, of necessity, determined by the amount of earth taken out of the ditch. This calculation must be made beforehand by the engineer with great care. Any error could be corrected only by a reduction in the size of the structure or an increase in width and depth of the ditch. A careful measurement of the plans shows that some 66,000 cubic yards of earth were removed in the construction of Fort Pitt, a formidable building operation for those days. This study also confirmed that the cut (earth dug away) almost exactly balanced the fill (earth used in the structure).

A considerable saving in the earth needed for the structure was effected by the construction of casemates and magazines within the curtains and the bastions. These underground structures were sunk from five to seven feet below the level of the parade ground. The three provision casemates, under the Lower Town, Ohio and Upper Town Curtains, were about 20 feet wide and had a total lineal footage of 475 feet. The casemates under the Monongahela and Gate Curtains were reserved for the use of artillery supplies and workshops. There were four of these, each about 24 by 45 feet in size. The two powder magazines, each 15 by 45 feet, were under the Grenadier Bastion. The three "wall'd" wells within the fort are shown on the plan. To meet the level of the terre plein the powder magazines were covered with about 4 feet of earth to render them bombproof and the casemates, which needed less protection, with about one and one-half feet of earth. Kenny describes these underground rooms in picturesque language: " . . , at y^e Bank Side of y^e Barracks open y^e Doors of y^e Magazines Vaults & Dungeons lying under y^e Great Banks of Earth thrown out of y^e Great Trinches all

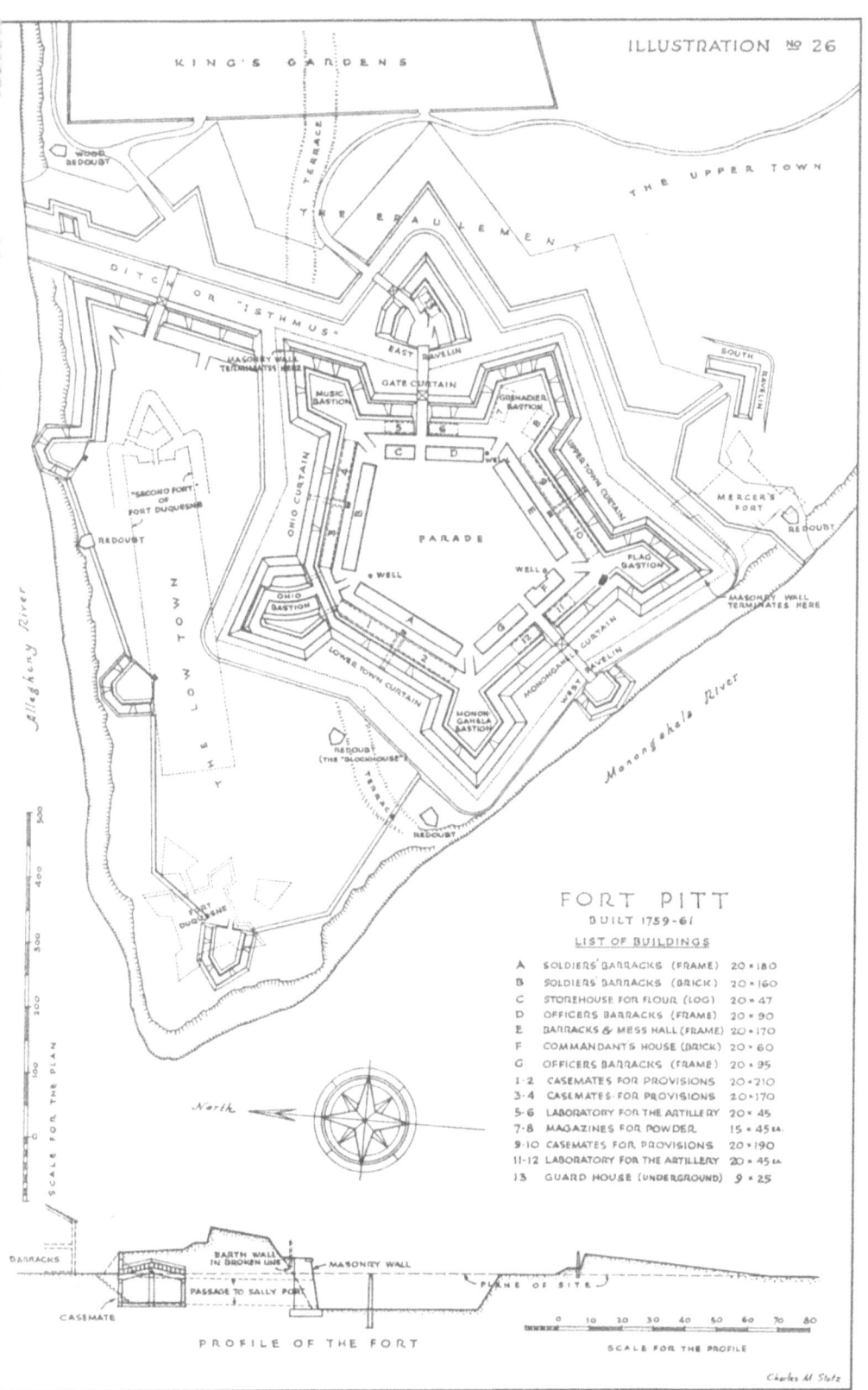

Round in these are kep y^e Stores of Ammunition &c & Prisoners that are to be tried for their Lives, in these Vaults are no light but as they carry Lanthorns, . . . " The great capacity of the provision casemates and storehouses of the fort may be judged by the return of provisions from Pittsburgh in December 1759 which lists the following food stuffs on hand: 146,740 pounds (667 barrels) of flour, 212 beef cattle, 66,415 pounds of salted beef, 22 barrels of pork, 64 barrels of salt, 5,800 pounds of butter, 3,285 pounds of cheese and 525 pounds of tobacco.[107]

Earthwork forts were subject to serious deterioration not only from frosts, thaws and rain but from grazing horses and cattle as well as smaller animals. The records contain many references to this subject. Chickens and hogs were forbidden in the ditches and banks of the fort, and, in the late days, the inhabitants were even prohibited from digging for worms. Bouquet ordered that after February 15, 1764 "all dogs & fowls seen upon the Rampart to be Killed."[108] The earth walls of the western end of Fort Pitt were never fully repaired after the floods and eventually the cattle would roam with ease over the formless mounds. This difficulty was experienced with the forts in England as well. An edict, beautifully printed and decorated with the royal arms, was issued by "His MAJESTY's Command" and signed by Egremont from the Court of St. James in 1761. Preserved in the Public Record Office in London, this says in part: " . . . and that no Person whatsoever do presume to plough on our Ground or Covered-Ways, or in any of the Ditches or Out-Works, or to permit any Beasts or Cattle to graze or feed on the same, or to plant or make any Gardens in the Bastions or Out-Works, or to make any Inclosures, or to erect any Sort of Building whatsoever . . . "

The brick covering of the front face gave the fort a distinction which was not intended for architectural effect but rather for its greater resistance to artillery fire. As cannon could not likely be brought to bear on the western sides of the fort next the water, the costly masonry was abandoned in favor of earth ramparts. As matters turned out, the brick front proved its value in an unanticipated way during the floods of 1762 and 1763 by serving as a buffer for the strong currents of the river filled with ice and debris. This protection probably saved the fort from destruction. The earth ramparts above the walls were badly eroded by flood water. The Ohio Bastion which projected beyond the shelter of the brick wall of the

Music Bastion was almost completely carried away and was never entirely replaced thereafter. Those in command later regretted that the entire fort was not faced with brick. The original builders, who well knew of the flood perils the fort might have to face, deemed a full masonry construction too costly for the uncertain advantages it might possess. The brick scarp walls of Fort McHenry (Illustration 28), built in 1800, are almost identical with those of Fort Pitt.

After the Canadian "life line" had been cut at Frontenac and Niagara, the lessened importance of Fort Pitt as a frontier defense precluded any thought of extending the brick revetment, or indeed, making any but the most drastically needed repairs and improvements. Ecuyer was hard pressed during the siege of Fort Pitt in 1763 to make his badly damaged parapets proof even against the poor fire and arrows of the Indians. By this time pickets had replaced the missing parapets on the earth ramparts and an improvised parapet of planks was used on the brick front. In some places Ecuyer was reduced to the expedient of placing his men behind bales of furs and skins taken from the trading store. For further protection stockades were placed at the base of the earth scarp walls.

The three barracks within the fort were two stories high. The barracks behind the Lower Town Curtain, the only one built of brick, was 190 feet long and 20 feet wide. This was used for many years after the other two weatherboard barracks, one behind the Ohio Curtain (168 feet long), the other behind the Upper Town Curtain (176 feet long), had become untenantable. These barracks housed between 700 and 1,000 men. As one entered the parade the squared log building for bulk storage of flour stood on the right and the frame Officers' Barracks on the left. Behind the Monongahela Curtain stood a frame officers' barracks on the right and the Commandant's House on the left. This latter was of brick and excited Kenny's admiration for its "fine Steps at ye Door of Hewn free Stone, a Cellar all under it . . . " This was the only building of architectural pretension, as will be described later, but so taxed the resources of the builders that it seems never to have been entirely completed.

Contemporary Records of Construction

The story of progress on the fort is told in letters that came to and went from Pittsburgh. Though the fort was not officially named by General Stanwix until November of 1759, work had started on September 3rd. By the 12th the earthworks were well along, though retarded somewhat by a shortage of shovels and lack of wheelbarrows. General Stanwix wrote Amherst on March 17, 1760 that he had "finish'd the works all round in a very defensible manner" leaving the garrison "in excellent Barracks." He felt that a creditable showing had been made in the first six months and was relieved that "the rest of the works may now be finished under cover, and be only obliged to work in proper weather, which has been very far from our case this hard winter and dirty spring."[109] An unidentified writer amplifies this statement in a letter written four days later: "The works are now quite perfected, according to plan, from the Ohio to the Monongahela, and eighteen pieces of artillery mounted on the bastions that cover the isthmus; and casemates, barracks, and storehouses are also completed for a garrison of 1,000 men and officers, so that it may now be asserted with very great truth, that the British dominion is established on the Ohio."[110]

This seems good progress for seven months but Gordon, short of workers, allowed no pause in the work. It was not until the summer of 1760 that the men were allowed to rest on Sundays. Gordon found difficulty in obtaining currency to pay the men but he was able to supply them with daily rations of liquor, by which he was able to "cut a great figure" in the works. Until the rum and whisky were available there had been illness "owing to drinking Quantities of bad Water." The artificers worked under a yearly contract. We do not have a detailed knowledge of their number throughout the period but we know that in the middle of August of 1759 Gordon had but 55 workers. The fall of the next year there were 128 artificers, including one master carpenter, three assistant carpenters, fifty-eight house carpenters, twenty-three bricklayers, one master smith, three blacksmiths, four wheelwrights, three brickmakers, ten masons, fourteen miners, three limeburners and five sawyers.[111] A least 128 artificers were still at work after October of 1760. Men were at first housed in Mercer's Fort but were gradually moved into tents to make room for the precious supplies and building tools arriving from the east.

Activity Outside the Fort

The area about the fort was a beehive of activity. The preparation of materials and building of boats spread operations a great distance from the building site and necessitated covering parties to protect the men while at work. Desirable timber within easy reach of the Point had long since been cut. Three hundred trees were cut in the fall of 1759 and left to cure for use in the spring. Forage brought in for the horses had to be supplemented with hay and grain locally grown some distance up the rivers. Miners were at work on the slopes of Mount Washington and Ayres Hill excavating coal and limestone. Clays and shales were taken from the hills on the eastern extremity of the Point and many hands were required to reduce this material into workable form, fill the molds and make and fire the brick kilns. The limestone was broken down and fired in kilns for the lime necessary in making plaster and mortar. These activities were confined to the open triangular area already largely taken up by the fort itself, the gardens and fields, pastures for cattle, sheep, hogs and horses, Mercer's Fort and numerous huts and cabins to house tradesmen, suppliers, artificers and their families as well as Indians. Outdoor ovens, forges, blacksmith and cooper shops and many other structures were needed to house the workers. In addition, piles of squared timbers, boards and planks were stacked to cure in the open air and near them, space for sawyers, including a pit in which nine saws were operated, two men to a saw, one above and one below. Hand production was slow but in the fall of 1759 a water powered sawmill was constructed on the south bank of the Monongahela River and fitted with machinery carried across the mountains. According to some accounts this sawmill was visible from the fort, but as we see on Meyer's drawing of the environs of Fort Pitt, Illustration 25, the mill was located about a quarter of a mile from the Monongahela on Saw Mill Run. This name remains today. An additional area of some size was set aside on the margins of the Monongahela for the construction of batteaus. These were needed for many purposes, but principally for the conveyance of men and goods from the supply depot at Redstone Creek (modern Brownsville) by which the slow and costly land carriage from Virginia was decreased by some forty miles. In and among all of this activity moved great numbers of idle, curious Indians, restrained with difficulty from seriously obstructing the work and viewed warily by the officers and the soldiers as an ever present hazard to their safety. The efficient and harmonious direction of this motley organization was a challenge to both the engineers and the officers who directed them. Gordon not only was charged with the direction of the work but also had to make trips to the east to select and purchase materials and equipment and to recruit additional artificers to supplement or replace those working in Pittsburgh.

Harry Gordon's Report

The most complete progress report on the fort was made by Gordon in Philadelphia on December 24, 1760.[112] He notes that the brick revetment was completed and the drawbridge installed. The earth parapets had been erected on the top of these masonry walls but had not yet had sodwork applied to their face to secure them in place, a process shown in Illustration 11. The banquettes had been placed behind the parapets and the three front bastions filled with earth. The eastern face of the fort was completed first to afford some degree of defense in case of need, after which work on the rear ramparts toward the Point could proceed. Proceeding clockwise, the earth ramparts of the Monongahela Curtain and Monongahela Bastion had been built and their scarp walls sodded, as well as half of the Lower Town Curtain. The casemate under this curtain had been built and covered with two feet of earth, and the sally port to the Lower Town and passage leading to it were completed. However, the sodding had been carried only ten feet high from the center of the Lower Town Curtain and around the Ohio, or "low" bastion. This bastion had then been half filled with earth. From this bastion, the Ohio Curtain was sodded a full twenty feet high to where it met the Music Bastion, the point at which the description started. The casemate under the Ohio Curtain had been carried up to within a few feet of the top.

The excavation of the ditch on the land front was then in progress and the glacis before it. The retrenchment or epaulement extending from the Music Bastion to the Allegheny was "in a defensible State with its Banquet, and the Bridge across the Ditch" which led into the Lower Town. The long brick barracks behind the Town Curtain and the wooden barracks behind the Ohio Curtain were finished, "with a Closet in each Room, and other accomodations for the Officers." The frame barracks behind the Upper Town Curtain were "shingled and weather Boarded, with a Chimney that serves four Rooms, that are floored and in order for Kitchens." This building thus apparently housed feeding facilities for the garrison. Seven carpenters were at work flooring and setting windows in this building as well as "compleating the Stair Case and other Furniture of the Commandants' House." It contained a full cellar. This and the barracks mentioned above were the only brick buildings. "The Flour Storehouse was being constructed of squared logs."

The bastions and curtains on the west side, until they were

fully completed and parapets set, offered little defense. In the interim, protection was gained by closing the gorges (the narrow ramped access leading from the parade to the top of the bastion) with stockades, a condition that persisted as late as June of 1761. However, the powder magazines with a capacity of 2,000 barrels each had then been finished. A colorful picture of activities at Fort Pitt is provided by the storekeeper, James Kenny, in his journal entry of July 21, 1761. His request for "one of ye Provincials to assist in this Store" had been refused by the Colonel who could not spare a man from the work on the fort. "I think they are very diligent ye Drum beats as its light in ye morning to set all to Work and holds it untill ye Gun fires late after sun Down. Mostly ye works going on are ye fort Banks raising higher, a fine Stone House, a Building in ye S.E. Corner for a Governor's House, Stone quarring & Squairing for the House, quarying for Lime & Burning ye Same, Making & Burning Brick, & farming & gardening, having a fine Incloasure under Indian Corn & divers things, Mowing & Haymaking abroad up both Rivers." The "Stone House" mentioned above must have been an error as the records and plans do not refer to any stone building in the fort. Later Kenny speaks of this as a brick building.

The Siege of Water

The account of the flood of January 9, 1762 tells us more about the fort structure. This flood exceeded any remembered by the oldest Indian. The water first entered the fort through the sally ports and the drains of the casemates, the bottoms of which lay some seven feet below parade level. Vats for salting meat were sunk in the floor of the casemates and covered with planks upon which the recently salted meat was stored in bulk and in headless barrels. Although soaked with silt-laden flood water, the meat was too much needed to be discarded. We read that " . . . it must be salted all over again . . . "

The casemates, or magazines, containing the powder were likewise flooded. The water rose so rapidly that, after a few barrels were removed, the doors were closed and barricaded. This loss was not greatly lamented as the powder had been damaged from storage in the damp magazines of Bedford and Ligonier.

Because of the porous nature of the soil at the Point, the water, then as now, built up underground pressure and boiled up through the surface of the parade ground in several places. Finally the flood rose to its peak, more than four feet above the parade ground.

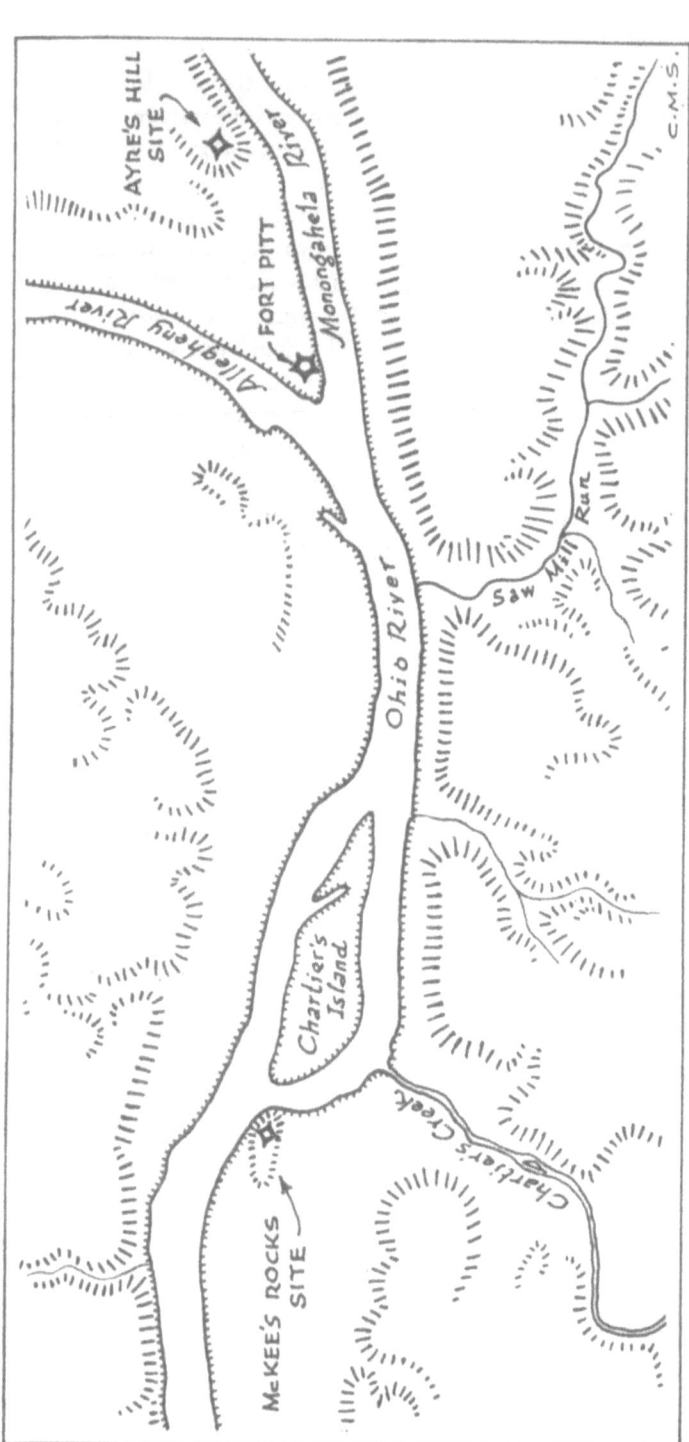

MAP OF THE RIVERS NEAR "THE TRIANGLE" OF MODERN PITTSBURGH

This map shows the rival sites for Fort Pitt. The mound at McKee's Rocks, preferred by most, is shown in Illustration 12. Colonel Eyre, chief engineer, also recommended Ayre's Hill, today occupied by Duquesne University. The Point site was chosen by General Stanwix for its positive command of the rivers.

Illustration 27

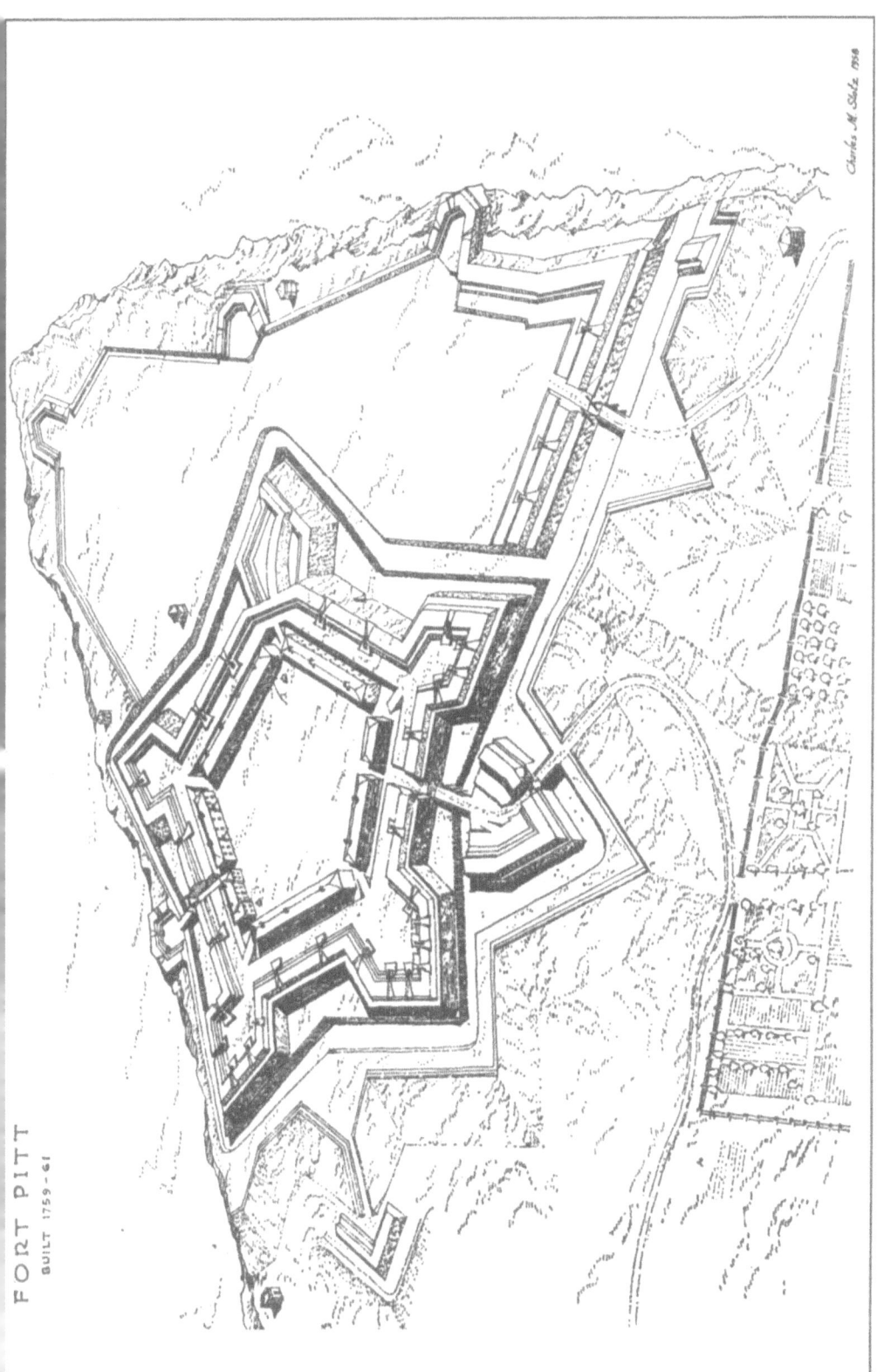

FORT PITT
BUILT 1759-61

Batteaus were floated into the fort. Provisions were loaded in them and sent away with part of the garrison to high land in the Upper Town. Only those men were kept in the fort who could be accommodated in the available boats so that they could abandon the fort in the last extremity.

The fort was saved from complete destruction by the brick facing on the land side which took the direct force of the current. Had these walls been built of earth they would have washed away with little resistance, weakened as they were by frost. At one in the morning, the water at its crest was on a level with the top of the rampart of the Ohio Bastion where there was as yet no parapet. The water did not fall until ten o'clock the next day and within twelve hours the parade of the fort was dry, though the casemates still contained water.

After the water had receded it was found that half of the sod had washed away from the scarp wall of the Ohio Curtain which suffered less than the Lower Town and Monongahela Curtains which were also of earth. Pickets, which had been installed on these uncompleted earth ramparts, were "laid down or Carried off, which leaved one half of the Fort open & defenceless." The earth parapet of the brick faced bastions and curtains was ruined. The artillery barracks and houses, one fifty feet long, that stood on the Monongahela bank were carried away as well as some buildings in Lower Town.

Chief Engineer Colonel Eyre was sent to Pittsburgh by Amherst, as mentioned above, to examine the flood damage and make recommendations. In his report,[113] dated April 28, 1762, he stated that the damage of the earthworks "might be easily remedied if one was Sure the like Flood would not happen again, but as that may be the Case it appears to me that there is no alternative, Either to revet the whole Scarp and Counter-Scarp with Brick, pretty much in the Same Manner that two of the Exterior Sides of the Pentagon are already done, or Suffer it to wash away by Degrees as the Floods happen.

"The Buildings within Side may be raised high, Particularly the Storehouses, so that the first Floor may be five feet above the Parade, and a Magazine for Powder, as also for fixt Ammunition may be of Brick arch'd in one of Bastions least Exposed to an attack, the Floor of which may be five or Six feet above the Level of the Parade. In this Building the Powder and fixt Ammunition may be

Lodg'd, and in Case of Siege, it may then be removed into those under the Bastion which are Bomb-proof.

"The present Interior buildings cannot be fit long to receive the Troops, so that there is but one in the Fort (which is designed for the Commandant), that's good for much, and that is yet not finish'd.

"The compleating the Fort in the Manner I have above Observed, I believe would amount to about Seven thousand Pounds Sterling." Amherst, much disturbed by Eyre's report, expressed doubt that it was worth while to send any more men to carry on the work, and ordered Bouquet to do what he could with his own force until he (Amherst) could get authority from England. The Engineer, Captain Bassett, who had previously reported to Colonel Eyre, wrote from Philadelphia that no expense could be incurred, "save as arise from setting up the Pickets thrown down by the Flood, and making of Bricks which he orders to be continued." In reviewing the flood damage, Ecuyer makes a remark of interest: " . . . I have noticed two things regarding the way in which this fort was sodded . . . The first is, that in laying the sod they neglected to drive into each, 4 or 5 pickets of dry thin wood . . . about two feet long; this wood would certainly hold and not rot until the grass had taken root. The second is that the grass soaks up much more water, and consequently its weight pulls the sod loose." It will be remembered from the discussion on fort construction that these pickets were considered a necessity in sod work.[114] (See Illustration 11.)

The following year still another flood all but submerged Fort Pitt. This time the garrison was better prepared. Ecuyer wrote Amherst March 11, 1763: "On the morning of the 7th, the two rivers having risen very high, I gave orders to transport the provisions and the ammunition into the upper stories . . . " On the 8th at 4 p.m. there were six inches of water in the fort. On the 9th at 8 a.m. the water was at crest. "The berm on the side which is not reveted collapsed into the ditch. I am busy repairing all the little damages in the interior as well as the exterior of the fort. They are only trifles." This flood, higher than the first by 22 inches, did much less damage. Nevertheless, Amherst declares, "The Situation of Fort Pitt seems to be so Liable to Destruction from the Floods, that I conclude it will be Judged necessary to Change the Design: . . . "[115]

The coincidence of two successive record floods must have been a source of embarrassment to the proponents of the Point site.

There is little doubt that the damage thus caused precluded any hope of fully completing the fort according to its original design.

The Indian Siege

Serious changes were made in the town and fort when the Pontiac war struck. Ecuyer wrote in June that he had "collected all the cattle of the settlers and placed them under our watch, I have demolished the lower town and brought the wood into the fort. I have had the upper town burned. Every body is in the fort where I have had two ovens and a forge built." During the siege, "shades," or sheds, had been built in the narrow space between the barracks and the terre plein wall. Ecuyer continues: "I have surrounded our bastions with barrels full of earth, made good entrenchment and embrasures for our cannons. I have a good entrenchment on the mined bastion, and on the two curtains left and right of it; all around the rampart my men are covered by strong planks fastened by stakes with an opening between two for rifle fire without being exposed in any way. If there were any unprotected places, I would cover them with the bales of deer skin belonging to the merchants; I have likewise made batteries at the neck of the bastions which connect with the barracks . . . The rascals are burning the surrounding houses, they have burned the saw mill . . . "[116] During the siege Ecuyer built a small hospital under the drawbridge for the smallpox victims.

Ecuyer also wrote in June: "My fort is formidable now with 16 pieces mounted on good platforms. I have quite a good entrenchment together with fraising wherever it is not revetted. It is not quite so regular as it should be, but being without an engineer and much hurried, it should do, and I believe is good enough against this rabble, so that I begin to breathe again." Concerned with Indians who prowled about the fort, he reports an ingenious desire: "I have collected all the beaver traps which our merchants had and they were set in the evening outside the palisades. I would be happy to send you one, with a savage's leg in it, but they haven't given me that satisfaction." He also indicates the unsuitability of the fort for Indian warfare: "The Extensive & open Works of Ft. Pitt require more Men than would otherwise be necessary against an Enemy who has no Chance but by Surprise."[117]

Upon Bouquet's arrival on August 11th, he praised Ecuyer's work: " . . . without Engineer or any other Artificers than a few

Shipwrights he had raised a Parapet of logs round the Fort above the old one which having not been finished was too low & Enfiladed. He has Frased the whole, Palisadoes on the Inside of the Aria [Area or Ditch]."[118]

The Beginning of the End

From this time forward, there are numerous entries that throw light on the nature of the fort structure. However, the heyday of Fort Pitt had passed. The once highly vaunted stronghold of the Ohio country was henceforth accorded scant attention from military headquarters in the east. Only those measures of repair and maintenance were sanctioned that were absolutely unavoidable and those commandants who proceeded with work on their own initiative were subject to censure. We read continually of the bad repair into which the buildings within the fort had fallen. The frame barracks had so deteriorated by the fall of 1763 that an occupant mentions that he was housed in a room where he was "almost Afloat Whenever a Showr of Rain falls; Neither the Roof nor Walls of it Screen its Inhabitants from any Inclemency of Weather; ... And between every Board of the Walls the hand may Enter."[119]

Bouquet wrote to Gage in December of 1763: "Three Sides of this Fort which are not reveted having been rendered almost defenceless by Two successive Floods in 1762, and 1763, I have caused Three Redouts to be built on the glacis, to cover them. Two are compleated, and the Third going on, as fast as the Weather will permit."[120] Unfortunately we do not know the sites of the other two, but one of these redoubts, located midway between the Monongahela and Ohio Bastions, is the "Blockhouse"[121] which remains today. The term "blockhouse" was then applied to wooden redoubts, constructed of squared timbers, or "blocks." The Blockhouse is the only early structure remaining in western Pennsylvania with true "loop-holes," or horizontal slots, for rifle fire. It is interesting to note that this building is five sided, like the fort itself. Three of the sides are set in square plan, the other two project in a V-shape toward the northwest. The photograph and measured drawings of the Blockhouse shown in Illustrations 30 and 31 are from *The Early Architecture of Western Pennsylvania.*

Captain William Grant reported to Bouquet in February of 1764 that these redoubts were finished and that he had just begun "the one you traced out upon the banks of the Monongahela." Hutchins describes this as "... the Redoubt that was Marked on the rising Ground near where the upper Town Stood Captain Grant has built near two Story high with Brick, with a Battlement on the Top that Commands the Bank of the River and the Ground a great way round it." We read that these redoubts were plastered inside. A fifth redoubt, of wood construction, was built on the banks of the Allegheny. Hutchins reports in May of 1764 that: "I have Picketted round the Woodden Redoubt Situate in the Angle of the Epaulement and put a Cheveaux de Frize at the entrance ..." The location of the two redoubts east of the fort are confirmed on the crude sketch made about 1785 during the dispute on ownership of the fort property. These redoubts, according to Grant, put the fort "in a better state of defence than it ever was befor ..."[122]

Grant also states in May of 1764 that "the two pompes and the well are well repaired, as is also the Water Engine [Pittsburgh's first fire engine!], it has been tried in my presence, and throws water up to the top of the Governour's house." He reports that Indian spies were frequently in the neighborhood, shots were occasionally heard and any work parties sent out had to be well covered by soldiers. One of these "Corporal's guards" was killed May 27th while protecting ploughmen "at work in Capt Phillip's field." To add to the uneasiness of the garrison, they heard "fourteen death hollows 'tother side of the Allegany River."[123]

June 25th Grant reports, "we have finished the pavement around the barracks under the piazza [an interesting refinement not revealed on any drawings], and are now carrying on a proper parade, from the entry of the great gate, all the way to the corner of your room." This was in Building F, the Commandant's house. Colonel John Reid wrote Bouquet in September with compliments for Grant's work on the redoubts and the "Parade which is an ornament to the Place."[124]

The "Return of Ordnance and Stores at Fort Pitt"[125] of September 17, 1764 reveals that Fort Pitt was then protected by six 12 pound and ten 6 pound cannons, two 8 inch and two 5-1/2 inch howitzers; that is, a short cannon, intermediate between the gun and mortar, and three types of mortars. These included one 8 inch mortar, two Royal mortars and twelve Coehorn mortars. There were also three "Pattereroes" and two iron swivel guns.

Another "Return of Ordnance and Stores," for June 24, 1766, found in the Public Record Office in London is of further interest in indicating the materials of the cannon at Fort Pitt. Listed under light brass ordnance, there were six twelve-pound cannon and ten six-pounders. There were two eight-inch howitzers and two five-and-a-half-inch howitzers, all of brass. There were three sizes of brass mortars, one eight-inch, two five-and-a-half-inch and twelve four-and-two-fifth-inch. There was no iron ordnance.

It is curious that the drawings of Fort Pitt, unlike most of the early fort plans, show no embrasures for the cannons. The height and thickness of the parapet would have precluded any possibility of mounting cannons on elevated platforms or barbettes to fire over it. After consultation with authorities on the subject of early armament, it was decided to supply conjectural embrasures on the restoration drawings.

With the apparent feeling that Fort Pitt was no longer needed, Bouquet recommended to Gage on March 4th, 1765: "In point of economy I should think it best to build a Spacious and Strong Blockhouse of Bricks at Pittsburgh, out of the Reach of Inundations, and convert the Fort in to a trading Place, . . ."[126] This was not done.

Harry Gordon ordered April 2, 1765 that no "Works" were to be carried on at Fort Pitt until further orders. On February 3, 1766 Gage wrote Sir William Johnson that "On the Pennsylvania side. I must keep Fort Pitt, and a few men possibly at Ligonier, all the rest will go, . . . " This was in response to a plea from Sir William Johnson, the New York Indian agent, to improve Indian relations by abandoning some of the posts. A report to Gage in 1766 indicates that the barracks were in need of repairs that would require five carpenters for 180 days, and 5,000 feet of board. Repair of chimneys would need two masons working 130 days. Also limestone was to be quarried and burned in two kilns to produce the needed 500 bushels of lime. This report contained the statement that "The under Ground Wooden Magazines are mostly decayed, but there will be spare Barracks enough to hold Provisions and every thing but Powder."[127] When the two original powder magazines, built of logs and buried in the earth of the Grenadier Bastion had become unusable, Major Isaac Craig built a single stone magazine above ground. This remained intact until about 1840 and was the subject of a well-known water color sketch made by Russell Smith in the 1830's. He ascribes the building to Fort Duquesne. Smith also made a painting of the Blockhouse, then the residence of Isaac Craig, and also mistakenly associated with Fort Duquesne.

Gordon made a visit of inspection on June 15, 1766 as the new chief engineer. He suggested a variety of repairs needed to return the fort to usable condition but thought much of the work to be "too considerable to take Place." He concluded, "But if it is to be less than that there will be no Safety in the present Place, and something new should be done." A few of his suggestions, such as new picketing in the ditch and repair of the roofs of the storehouses, were subsequently carried out by Edmonstone and later by General Irvine, but the condition of the fort rapidly went from bad to worse. The final disposition of the land and materials dragged on for years and does not seem a proper subject for discussion here. The late days of the Fort are fully described in Charles W. Dahlinger's *Fort Pitt.*

In the issue of the *Pittsburgh Gazette* for July 29, 1786, Hugh Henry Brackenridge reminisces of Fort Pitt as he knew it when he first came to Pittsburgh in 1781. He speaks of a "row of houses, elegant and neat, not unworthy of the European taste, . . . " that once stood on the margins of the Allegheny River. These he said were "the receptacles of the ancient Indian Trade" and that they were standing twenty years before. One of these may have been the trading house erected by Samuel Young in the summer of 1762. There remains a receipted bill for £ 64/5/6, certified by Bouquet, that George Croghan had paid this sum to Young, which reads, "I do Certify that in the summer 1762 Mr Croghan had a House built at this Post, intended for Conferences with the Indians. Fort Pitt 11th October 1762. H. Bouquet."[128] The detailed bill reveals that the house was built of hewn logs, two stories high, with stone chimney and mantel, plastered inside on lath, two windows with shutters, one door, divided by a partition, a closet, stud partitions covered with boards, and a shingle roof.

All searches of early records to determine the total cost of Fort Pitt to the British government have been fruitless. The writer examined the declared accounts of Harry Gordon in the Public Record Office in London without success. These accounts show that Gordon authorized the expenditure of £ 28,321/0/4 (New York currency) during the period of his commission on the many forts in his charge but provided no total cost for any of them. The writer has heard but could not verify the statement that the treasury records in London place the cost of Fort Pitt at £ 7,000. This amount would probably not include the tremendous contribution of common labor by the hundreds of soldiers engaged in the work. It is said that £ 7,000 or $35,000 in mid-eighteenth century would be equivalent to $350,000 in 1958. The great latitude of error in such conversions of money value provides an artificial cost estimate that is probably no more dependable than the many speculations that have been contributed by modern writers.

As the reader can judge only by comparison with present day prices, the writer has prepared a reasonably careful cost analysis of the fort structure as shown in the contemporary drawings. It is estimated that to reproduce the fort and its outworks by modern building methods would cost not less than $1,400,000.00. More than half of this total is assigned to the brick and stone scarp wall.

Another question frequently asked is, "Why did the British government build a fort here of such great size?" Judging by informed hindsight, Fort Pitt was unreasonably large. But one must recognize that positive and permanent control of the upper Ohio Valley appeared a desperately important objective to William Pitt when he ordered the building of a fort in "every way adequate to the great importance of the sever¹ objects."[129] England had been waging a losing war for five years; bold strokes were necessary. Had this shrewd leader foreseen the swift changes of fortune that lay ahead for England he might have been more conservative in his instructions. But if Pitt ever regretted this fine gesture of defense, it was probably seventeen years later when those for whom the fort was built, declared their independence from England.

GARDENS AND GARDENING AT FORT PITT

The cultivation of the land about the forts at the Point was a necessity, not an amenity. No mention of flowers was found in the records, even those of the later, less hectic years. No doubt there were flower plots but the first concern was for the life of the indispensable domestic animals. Those horses that managed to survive the grueling transport over the mountains suffered from malnutrition and fatigue, the fodder carried with them having been consumed long since. The cattle and other animals that had been driven over the mountains also required pasturage. Grazing lands were established in the limited space near the fort and in the few open unforested strips of land along the river margins. Among these river sites was that which George Croghan many years before had used for pasturing his numerous pack horses at his post on the site of modern Etna. The horses of Fort Pitt were later pastured on the rich bottom lands on the Ohio at Chartiers Creek, where a special "grass guard" was stationed. From these and other fields stocks of hay and grain were brought to the Point to tide the animals over the winter.

As the army had arrived in late November, Colonel Hugh Mercer had a very difficult time the first winter, lacking both hay stock and pasturage. In February of 1759 he was unable to bring in logs which had been cut on the Monongahela for the barracks as the river was frozen, and he said, "We have no Horses that can draw a Pound,.."[130] As additional horses were being brought in to work on the fort, the problem became critical. Bouquet wrote Mercer in May of 1759 that "As we shall want the Grass about the Fort, for the Number of Horses to be Kept, for the Works,.. no Grass [is] to be Eaten within four Miles of Pittsburgh, and if it is Possible to make any Hay that you will please to Collect, as much as you Can."[131] The development of adequate pasturage and grain fields was slow work, for even in March of 1760, Mercer wrote that the horses could do no more work until forage was brought over the mountains. In 1760 Bouquet ordered the placing of farmers at all the western posts to raise oats, Indian corn, wheat and rye.

The monotonous and unhealthful diet of salted beef and pork with bread made in the field was an unavoidable necessity on the march. It was not possible to procure enough game in the forests or to drive enough cattle with the army to maintain adequate supplies of fresh meat. This inevitably resulted in continuous outbreaks of scurvy. Once permanent posts had been established no time was lost in planting vegetable gardens and building "bullock pens."

Bouquet forwarded seeds to Mercer from Philadelphia in April of 1759 to "make as large a Garden, and Turnips Field as may serve the whole Army."[132] In the meantime grain was carried in from the east and stored in Mercer's Fort in the spring of 1759. Granaries were then built for flour and two for corn and oats. Bouquet ordered Mercer to establish adequate storage facilities for an 18 month wheat supply, since flour was more perishable. "Land Mills" were to be built for use in time of siege when the outlying water-mills could not be used.

We do not know when the cultivated area, known as the King's Gardens, was established east of the fort along the Allegheny shore.

The gardens as shown on the two drawings made in 1761 by Ratzer and Meyer agree in shape and size, but Meyer's drawing gives considerably more detail. There are 77 separate plots averaging 40 by 90 feet each and divided into geometrical patterns. The main paths are bordered with trees and one plot was occupied by an orchard. The terrace paralleling the Allegheny River, mentioned in the discussion of Fort Pitt, is shown passing through the center of the garden. The entire plot, containing a little over 10 acres, is surrounded by what appears to be an ornamental fence, with posts at regular intervals. The drawing undoubtedly shows this ambitious project as its designers hoped it might some day appear. This view is supported by a letter written by John Langdale in March of 1761: "That as a great deal of Land taken into the Kings Garden lays uncultivated he would . . . order the Gardiner to admit a portion of about 45 or 50 yards square adjacent to what is cultivated to be by us Cultivated for ye Use of ye Store."[133]

The Survey of the Environs of Fort Pitt (Illustration 25), made in the summer of 1762, presents a quite different garden layout. We may assume that the flood of the previous winter which carried away the houses of the adjacent Upper Town, the Artillery Barracks and most of the Lower Town, likewise so nearly obliterated the old garden as to require a fresh start. Bouquet complained in April that "we have suffered much, by the total want of Fresh Provisions, and Greens" and adds that the flood waters "spoiled our winter stores . . ."[134] At any rate here we have a central plot with radial tree-lined paths which is marked the Garrison's Garden. The outside dimensions of 600 feet square enclose about eight and one-quarter acres. On either side, reaching to the top of the Allegheny River bank, lie two additional garden areas. That to the west is divided into eight rectangular plots, each about 120 by 150 feet in size with trees planted at the corners of the paths separating them. To the east lies another plot about 600 feet square, divided into 16 square plots separated by paths. The corners of the four central squares are cut away by a central circular plot 180 feet in diameter. Trees are planted at the corners of the small plots. To the east of the gardens a square pasture containing about 20 acres extends up the Allegheny beyond Grant's Hill. To the south, bordering the gardens, is an eight acre corn field. In addition to this considerable area laid out for cultivation, we learn from orders issued in 1762 that there were private gardens attached to many of the numerous houses outside the fort. There are references also to a "Bullock Pen" for the cattle brought to the fort.

The new garden of 1762 seems to have flourished. "Our Oats Indian Corn &c^a goes on very well and Denotes a plentifull Crop," writes Captain Thomas Barnsley in June, "Except the Carrots & Parsnips in the Lower part of the Garden which does not make much Appearance yet, . . " He adds, "I got two Battoe Load of Hay down the Allegheny Yesterday and this morning sent them of for more, . . " This hay was likely cut at Croghan's former plantation mentioned above. Barnsley mentions that the pasture had just been fenced and continues with the first mention of non-utilitarian use of land: "wee are now going on With the Deer Park" as well as "the New Fence . . . across the Big Garden which is to be done very Elegantly . . . "[135] Thus with the comparatively calm days following the completion of the fort, Pittsburgh was experiencing its first hint of refinement. Many of the civilians residing at the fort acquired animals of their own which they allowed to forage for their food. The inhabitants were ordered to yoke their hogs but we read, "they still continue to break thro' the Fences, And are Continualy in the Kings Garden and Fields adjoining . . . " As conditions did not improve the people were told that "no hogs can be kept within three miles of the fort after December 1st or they will be killed and confiscated for use of the King's Troops."[136]

Work in the fields and gardens provided one of the few escapes from the confining life at the fort. Bouquet mentions his pleasure in "the Farming way" to St. Clair "as the only Recreation I can have here, where I am likely to Continue long Enough to try further Experiments upon paitence and weeds . . . " And again, "The return of the nice weather has rendered my garden my only pleasure."[137]

One gardener and two assistants appeared in the "list of Artificers" of January 1763. Apparently the people were provided with seeds each year but in February they were told that "Seeds for the Publick garden are to be preserved, and hereafter None will be furnished."[138] The "Publick garden" may have been the large plot, described above, to the east of the Garrison or King's Garden. In the same month Sergeant Burent recorded that " . . . The Trees are all Planted (Except in the Fort, which the Season will not permit) Last Fall." The trees shown in the garden layouts were probably included among these. The trees "in the Fort" must have been located in the Lower Town, within the Epaulement although the Parade

Ground within the fort was large enough to accommodate trees without being crowded. Burent also mentioned that "most the new pasture Cleard, and as soon as the Weather will permit I shall set about Mauling Rails for it . . . "[139] All agricultural activities were rudely interrupted on March 8th when the Point was covered with six to seven feet of flood water, higher than the crest of the previous winter. Reporting on the flood damage he adds, "The Inclosures of Gardens & Fields . . . have been carried off," the same "elegant" fence built with such care. "The poor deer's leg was broken . . . and I believe our gardening equipment was lost . . . "[140] However, much less damage was done by the second flood and only eleven days later Colonel Simeon Ecuyer, the commandant, writes that "I have ordered our trees replanted, and the garden enclosed simply to prevent the cows, etc., from completely destroying it, as it appears we will not enjoy any of it . . . "

The useful and pleasant activities in the fields and gardens were again interrupted in June, this time from a much more terrifying cause than flood water; the long expected Indian uprising drove everyone within the ramparts. The outlying works and animals were easy prey for the Indians. Ecuyer wrote in June, "the savages came across the garden, fired on the fort and our oxen and cows which were in the enclosure where the deer were . . . " There are few entries concerning the gardens during the siege and subsequent days of rehabilitation until January of 1764 when we read that " . . . the Garden and Fields are again to be fenced and as soon as the Frost is out of the ground; They must be ploughed, and sowed with Garden seeds, Corn, Oats, & Speltz." The notes of April, 1764, reveal some new refinements: " . . . , ploughing, gardening, makeing fences, . . . " "the deer park, the little garden, and the bowling green, I am just now making into one garding, it will be extreamly pretty and very useful to this garrison, the Kings garden will be put in proper order in due time we want seeds very much, and we have no potatoes at all." And by the middle of April: "things are very forward in the New garden, we eat sallad from it already several times and Sparrow grass every day from the King's garden. Nixt week we'll begin to sow corn seed . . . " At the end of April: "We are very busy . . . plowing, and sowing, the fields."[141]

Bouquet compliments Captain William Grant in May of 1764: "The Improvements you have made in the Fortifications and Garden are extreamly proper . . . I hope the Men will recover from the

Scurvy by the use of such Greens as the Gardens can afford them. I wish they would make Gardens for every Mess in the lower Town where they would not be exposed and would be at hand in case of necessity." Grant found this suggestion difficult to carry out. He wrote Bouquet in May: "The lower Town I have ordered to be divided into small lotts for gardens, but the men don't seem much inclined that way, they have indeed no seeds, .. the men are quite recovered from the Scurvey, I send them to the woods sometimes for greens with covering parties." To Indian wars and floods was added another threat to the gardens: " . . . the new gardens thrive wonderfully well, but the locust and grasshoppers, have hitherto defeated all our endeavours and industry with respect to the Kings garden, having entirely destroyed in it already 5,000 Cabbage plants, and a great many Seeds of different kinds, which is supposed to be owing to the very remarkable driness of the season, for indeed we have had hardly any rains at all this summer." Grant declared war on the insects and reports in July: " . . . now no Enemy disturbs us except grasshoppers, the locusts and Indians have quite disappeared, . . . "; "we have again planted 10,000 cabbages in the Kings garden, and this week 10,000 more will be added. we have parties constantly in it from 8 in the Morning till 7 in the afternoon to keep off the grasshoppers, nevertheless they do a world of mischief to the plants . . . " Grant found the garden a great comfort: " . . . we have nothing of any kind to drink except whiskey and water, with the assistance of the garden we make shift to live pretty well . . . "[142]

In spite of the insects Colonel John Reid reported to Bouquet in September that "The Gardens are extensive and full of Vegetables, which will be more than sufficient to supply the Garrison during the Winter . . . There are Fields of Indian Corn which by computation will yield about 400 Bushells; and there is a Stack of Spelts and Rye secured below the Shade within the Fort. I have given directions to have some Hay made, & the Mowers are now at Work; they tell me there is grass enough within a Mile of the Fort to make Seven or eight Cart loads." Reid adds, though, that "This season was very backward, and the vermine very pernicious, else we should have had ten times the quaintity at least."[143]

After 1764 there are few references to the garden. Because of Bouquet's decisive action in that year against the Indians, the usefulness of Fort Pitt was greatly lessened and its maintenance was correspondingly relaxed.

Brackenridge, writing in 1786, describes an orchard of apple trees, with some pear trees among them, on the bank of the Allegheny which he said were planted by a British officer in the early days of the fort. The trees still bore good fruit in abundance. He mentions the King's artillery gardens, "cultivated highly to usefulness and pleasure, the soil favoring the growth of plants and flowers, . . ."[144] These gardens, long since vanished, existed only in his romantic fancy. Zadok Cramer's *Navigator* for 1808 recalls the "most elegant gardens, called the Kings and Artillery Gardens; near to these they planted an orchard of excellent bearing apple trees, some of which still bear fruit, . . ."[145]

FORT FAYETTE

With the passing of Fort Pitt came many other changes in the Ohio country. The French had departed the stage forever. The lands south of the Ohio were being steadily occupied by settlers from the south and, to a lesser degree, from the east. After the Revolution, the British had withdrawn their forces to the western posts at Sandusky, Miami and Detroit which they continued to occupy after peace had been signed. There they maintained a "despicable affiliation . . . with the Indians in the last hope of limiting the territories of the upstart colonies to the land east of the mountains . . ."[146] With this substantial backing, the Indians once more instituted a reign of terror on the borderlands. The people of Pittsburgh, having protested the demolition of Fort Pitt, now demanded protection of their new government. This demand became more insistent after the demoralizing defeats of two expeditions sent into the Ohio country against the Indians, that of General Josiah Harmar in 1790 and of Major General Arthur St. Clair in 1791. Furthermore there was fear of an Indian attack against Fort Franklin at Venango (modern Franklin).[147] President George Washington doubtless recalled his concern 38 years before with the first little fort at the Point as he instructed his Secretary of War, General Knox, to order the construction of the fifth and last fort to be built on the site of the Triangle of modern Pittsburgh.

General Knox advised Governor Mifflin on December 16th, 1791 that he had issued orders to Major Isaac Craig "to build a blockhouse at Fort Pitt and surround it with palisades, so as to contain about 100 men, . . ." and the same day wrote Craig to select a site "in such part of Pittsburgh as shall be the best position to cover the town as well as the public stores which shall be forwarded from time to time. As you have been an artillery officer during the late war, I request you to act as engineer. I give you a sketch of the work generally, which you must adapt to the nature of the ground." Two weeks later, Craig replied: "By the next post, I shall inclose you a sketch of the ground and the work, that I have judged necessary. It will be erected on eight lots, . . ."[148] Space was reserved for gardens for the garrison. Craig engaged Turnbull and Marmie's Furnace, blown in in November of 1790, to make 400 cannon balls.

The site chosen lay across Penn Avenue at Hand (Tenth) Street. Work proceeded without delay, as we learn from a letter to Knox, written May 18, 1792: "Captain Hughes, with his detachment, has occupied the barracks in the new fort since the 1st instant. Two of the six pounders are very well mounted in the second story of one of the block-houses. The others will be mounted in a few days. The work, if you have no objections, I will name Fort La Fayette."[149] Although the Secretary approved this name, it was always thereafter known as Fort Fayette. The dedication of Fort Fayette was reported in the *Maryland Journal and Baltimore Advertiser* under the Pittsburgh dateline of May 19, 1792: "The fort begun last winter, at this place, stands on the Allegheny River, within about one hundred yards of the bank, on a beautiful rising ground, about one quarter of a mile up than the old garrison at Fort Pitt. It is completely stockaded in, and one range of barracks built, a blockhouse in one of the angles finished, and the remainder in forwardness." The fort was officially named Fort Fayette and "At the first toast, two pieces of ordnance were discharged, old double-fortified 12 pounders brought to this place originally by the French . . ." Earlier records show that none of the French cannon was ever recovered.

The drawing of Fort Fayette shown in Illustration 29, owned by the William L. Clements Library, is a rough sketch bearing fold marks and may be Craig's own sketch mentioned above. It is titled "Plan of Works erecting at Pittsburg," and there's a note, "Transmitted enclosed in letter 15th January 1792." The fort lay almost square with the compass, producing an irregular garden shape between Liberty Street and the entrance on the southern side of the fort. The entire fort, including the bastions at the corners, was composed of pickets twelve feet high. Three of these bastions enclosed pentag-

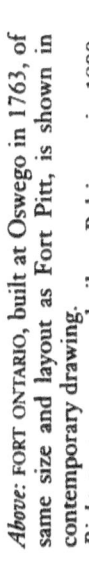

Above: FORT ONTARIO, built at Oswego in 1763, of same size and layout as Fort Pitt, is shown in contemporary drawing.
Right: FORT MCHENRY, built at Baltimore in 1800, has masonry scarp walls similar to Fort Pitt.

Illustration 29

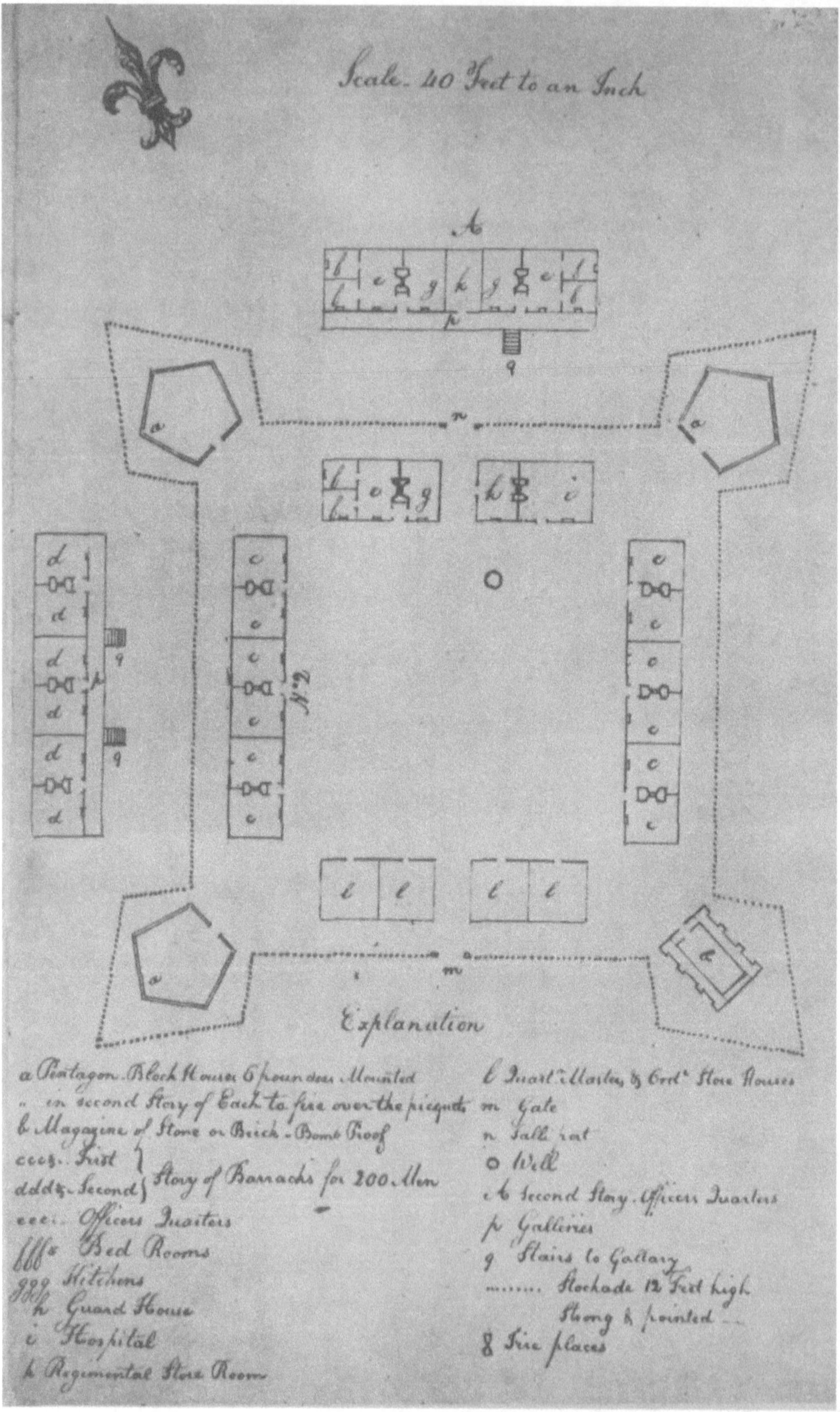

Scale 40 Feet to an Inch

Explanation

a Pentagon Block House 6 pounders Mounted in second Story of Each to fire over the picquets
b Magazine of Stone or Brick – Bomb Proof
cccc. First } Story of Barracks for 200 Men
dddd. Second }
eeee. Officers Quarters
fff. Bed Rooms
ggg. Kitchens
h Guard House
i Hospital
k Regimental Store Room
l Quarter Masters & Cont.ᵉ Store Houses
m Gate
n Sally Port
o Well
k Second Story Officers Quarters
p Galleries
q Stairs to Gallery
.... Stockade 12 Feet high Strong & pointed
8 Fire places

onal two-story log blockhouses, the southeastern bastion a brick powder magazine. The officers' quarters on the eastern side were of brick. The remainder of the buildings were of logs, and two of them, the commandant's and staff quarters on the northern side and the barracks for 200 soldiers on the western side, were two stories in height. A well stood in the northern end of the parade grounds. A fort of such frail character could not have been intended to withstand artillery and it seems a remote possibility that an Indian attack within the town could have been expected. At any rate, Victor Collot, who visited the fort in 1796, spoke slightingly of it in the account of his travels. He stated that on "a dark night four grenadiers, with a dozen faggots of dry wood, might burn the fort and all the garrison, and not a single individual escape."[150]

The only other drawing of Fort Fayette known to the writer is reproduced on page ten of *Fleming's Views of Old Pittsburgh*. This drawing, made in 1800 and owned by the War Department, is mentioned by Mrs. Elvert M. Davis in an article, "Fort Fayette," in the *Western Pennsylvania Historical Magazine*. The disposition of buildings differs somewhat from the drawing from the Clements Library, discussed above.

Mrs. Davis states that "As described by travellers a few years later, and according to the map furnished by the war department, the fort stood within an inclosure composed of large pointed stakes fifteen or sixteen feet high. Through the center of this inclosure Penn Avenue would now extend. There were four wooden hexagonal towers, on three of which were blockhouses; on the fourth, which looked toward the town, was a powder magazine of brick. [The brick magazine stood on the ground in the southeast bastion. There were only three blockhouses.] Within were two sets of barracks, one for the use of the officers, built of brick, on the side toward what is now Liberty Avenue, with a garden space between the road and the fort. The barracks, toward the river side, was built of logs, and housed the men. A guard-house at the entrance toward the town (about where Penn Avenue would cut through), a dungeon next it, and an artificers shop back of that, all making toward the river; and a well over toward the north corner (for according to the map of the war department, the fort sat almost exactly cornerwise to the points of the compass), complete the picture. The line of the fort did not accord with the line of the road (according to the map) and that gave an irregular shape to the garden, . . . "[151]

FORT FAYETTE
From a drawing in the William L. Clements Library, Ann Arbor, Michigan
Illustration 29

It does not seem possible to resolve the discrepancies between the two drawings described above with the information now available. It would appear, however, that revisions were found advisable after the first drawing was made and before construction was begun. Whether the second drawing is an accurate record of the fort as built must remain, as is so often the case, a matter of conjecture.

General Anthony Wayne was chosen by President Washington to organize and train an army that would, once and for all, end the Indian menace. His troops were assembled in Pittsburgh in 1792. The men were quartered near the fort on Suke's Run and some across the Allegheny River. Wayne set up headquarters on the southeast corner of Liberty and West Streets. It was deemed wise to establish a camp outside the town for the intensive training of the troops before proceeding against the Indians in Ohio. Accordingly, in November of 1792, Wayne moved his men to the new camp at Legionville, just below Ambridge, leaving a small garrison in the fort.

Attention was again focused on Fort Fayette during the Whiskey Insurrection of 1794. Bradford, the leader of the whiskey rebels, promoted a coup to take the fort but found the officers of the garrison uncooperative. He then marched his men without demonstration through the town, keeping a respectful distance from Fort Fayette which was thus spared its only risk of seizure by an enemy force. Soldiers from the fort were sent out to defend John Neville's house when attacked by the "whiskey boys." Until 1812 there was only a handful of men in the garrison. An English traveler, named Cuming, reported in 1807-08, "The surrounding grounds of the fort handsomely laid out, planted and ornamented by General Wilkinson [commandant during this peaceful period] some years ago, considering the smallness of the field, show much taste and are an ornament to the eastern and principal approach to the town."[152]

Fort Fayette was a busy place during the War of 1812, rendering assistance to Commodore Perry as headquarters for supplies, purchase of horses and training of soldiers. Many British prisoners were sent to the fort after Perry's victory and the commandant was hard pressed to prevent their escape as well as to prevent the desertion of his own men. This was the last service rendered by the post. The lots were sold and the garrison removed in the spring of 1815. Captain Jacob Carmack, the commandant, secured his discharge and the next year advertised that he would thereafter "keep tavern at the Turk's Head" in Pittsburgh.

THE BLOCKHOUSE OF FORT PITT. ONE OF FIVE REDOUBTS BUILT IN 1764-65 BY ORDER OF COLONEL HENRY BOUQUET.
Illustration 30

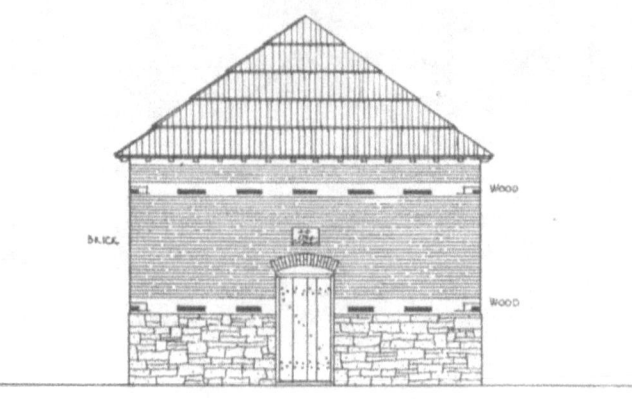

SOUTH EAST ELEVATION
SCALE

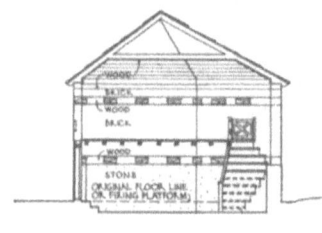

SECTION

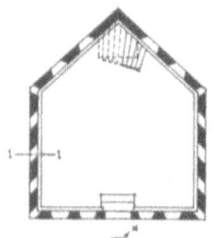

PLAN
AT FIRST STORY LOOP HOLES
SCALE

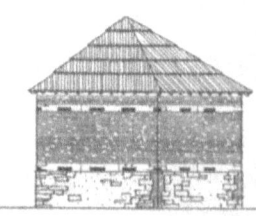

N·E· ELEVATION

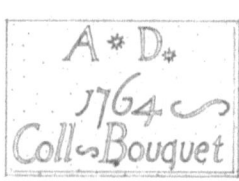

TABLET OVER DOOR
SCALE

SANDSTONE SUNDIAL
FOUND ON PREMISES
SCALE

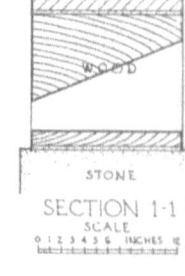

SECTION 1-1
SCALE

THE BLOCK HOUSE
PITTSBURGH ALLEGHENY COUNTY

EPILOGUE

From the spring day in 1754 when the little band of Virginians began the erection of Fort Prince George until the spring day in 1815 when the last garrison marched out of Fort Fayette, sixty-one years in all, the Forks of the Ohio was continuously guarded by a military post. Modern catastrophic weapons against which there is no defense save retreat underground give an air of quaintness to these rude forts of a mere 200 years ago. They are "a reminder . . . of the character of war when it was still a relatively gentlemanly way of settling disputes."[153] Although no decisive military action occurred at the Forks and none of these five forts was tested by cannon fire, each was built under duress and each played a worthy role in history. Three of the forts flew the flag of Britain, one the French flag, and the last, the new flag of the United States.

Even impotent Fort Prince George justified its brief existence in creating a diversion of troops and supplies that New France could ill spare from the defense of her life line. This frail stockade was the symbol of the inexorable westward movement of the English colonists and, as such, could not be tolerated. The English fort must be taken and a new one built in its place. New France did not choose to add any load to her precarious economic structure nor add to the armament of her defensive ring around the English. Fort Duquesne exacted a killing toll on her resources because of its remoteness from Montreal and its inaccessibility from the Illinois country. The Ohio flowed in the wrong direction for the French, the right way for the English. For one it was a barrier, for the other a natural highway. The enormous cost in money and man power needed to supply their little fort at the Point may explain why the French never replaced it with a structure adequate to insure possession of the country.

Had France in 1754 relinquished her claim on the Ohio country, we might well have her as our Canadian neighbor today. The English had not challenged her rights to the lands above the St. Lawrence and the Lakes. Longueuil in 1739 and Céloron in 1749, on their expeditions down the Allegheny and Ohio, had found themselves in

MEASURED DRAWINGS OF THE BLOCKHOUSE OF FORT PITT
From The Early Architecture of Western Pennsylvania
Illustration 31

unfamiliar and hostile country. They reported the English traders well entrenched and the occupation of the land by Virginia settlers to be imminent. The French, who had too much land for their people, did not seem to anticipate the glacier-like pressures that were to be exerted by the English colonies that had abundant people for their land. Instead of avoiding this diversion of her energies, New France pressed her ancestral claims to the headwaters of the Ohio and precipitated the conflict. After four years of occupation, the French had made no appreciable progress at the Point in perfecting its defense or in colonizing the land, in spite of the glowing prophecies of the Marquis de Duquesne. How then, after the abandonment of Fort Duquesne to Forbes' army, in the fall of 1758, can we account for the French determination to retake the Point the following spring?

The answer lies in the fact that France with her superior military force was confident of her ability to establish her empire in America as evidenced by the succession of defeats inflicted on the English in America through the preceding four years. Obviously the English could not fortify the Point effectively before the spring of 1759 as no work could be started before December of 1758. Mercer's Fort was indeed little more than an improvised shelter. Supplies were inadequate for more than a minimum garrison; construction in winter months was necessarily limited. The unquenchable energy of the French led them to collect by late spring a formidable force at Venango that would have been more than a match for Mercer's men. But, as events proved, the French again had made the mistake of diverting their strength from the Canadian frontier. The unanticipated siege of the weakened garrison at Fort Niagara forced the recall of the army at Venango, which was defeated en route. As a result, the French lost Niagara and failed to retake the Point.

The English who had for four years planned the construction of a truly worthwhile fort at the Point, one which would firmly secure this strategic post of their Empire in America, were now determined to carry out a major fort building project. For the first time, circumstances were favorable. Although the need for such elaborate defense against the French had passed, before the fort was finished, a new need had arisen, one not of so much consequence to the mother government in England as to the colonists. The land west of the mountains had been established by royal proclamation as Indian territory, and settlement within it was forbidden. The Indians realized that this was a hollow promise which was being daily proved by the steady encroachment of the settlers. Fort Pitt, originally regarded by the Indians as a symbol of defiance to French ownership, was now seen as a symbol of the white man's aggression. Thus, for the first and only time, a fort at the Point was attacked, not by cannon for which it was built but by musket and arrow. After Bouquet's expedition in 1764 the importance of Fort Pitt largely ceased and, with it, any adequate attention from military authorities.

The Reverend David McClure, who visited Pittsburgh in 1772, preached to the soldiers of the garrison. On October 9th, he wrote, "In consequence of orders from General Gage, the garrison are preparing to depart, They have begun to destroy the fortress. This is a matter of surprise and grief to the people around who have requested that the fortress may stand as a place of security to them in case of an Indian invasion. I asked one of the officers, the reason of their destroying the fort, so necessary to the safety of the frontier. He replied, 'The Americans will not submit to the British Parliament and they may now defend themselves'."[154]

The fort continued in use for many more years. As it became dilapidated and unserviceable the public demand for protection from Indian invasion persisted. This culminated in 1792 in the construction of the last of the five forts at the Point. Fort Fayette was the physical expression of fear, not conquest. It is ironic that this fort would ultimately serve in 1812 as the base of operations against the British, whose professional troops and military initiative largely affected the winning of the West for the Anglo-Saxon residents of America.

The victory of the British here determined that we should be an English speaking people. This statement frequently is made with the sense that we were spared providentially from having been absorbed into a French civilization. It seems idle to speculate on what manner of country America might have become under the French flag. But, as the frontier moved steadily westward and Fort Pitt crumbled away and was forgotten, the young nation finally learned what the French had known for a century—the rich interior of the continent was a prize worth having, at any price.

SELECTED DEFINITIONS OF FORT TERMS

(From *The Concise Oxford Dictionary, Fourth Edition,* 1951, and *The Oxford English Dictionary*)

Banquette—A raised way running along the inside of a rampart or parapet, or bottom of a trench, on which soldiers stand to fire at the enemy.

Bastion—Projecting part of fortification, irregular pentagon with its base in the line (or at an angle) of the main works.

Berme—Ledge in fortification between ditch and base of parapet.

Blockhouse—Detached fort (orig. one blocking passage), sometimes one of connected chain of posts, also one storeyed timber building with loopholes, also house of squared logs.

Casemate—Vaulted chamber in thickness of wall of fortress, with embrasures. [Cannon were not placed in casemates of the frontier forts.]

Counterscarp—Outer wall or slope of ditch, supporting covered way.

Covered way—The Covert or close way . . . left above the Moat next the open Field.

Demilune—An outwork resembling a bastion with a crescent-shaped gorge, constructed to protect a bastion or curtain.

Epaulement—A covering mass raised to protect from the fire of the enemy, but differing from a parapet in having no arrangement made for the convenient firing over it by defenders.

Exterior Slope—An inclined surface of the nature of a bank, one artificially constructed, as in fortification or engineering.

Fraise—Horizontal or down-sloping palisade round berme.

Glacis—The parapet of the covered way extended in a long slope to meet the natural surface of the ground, so that every part of it could be swept by the fire of the ramparts.

Hornwork—Outwork consisting of two demi-bastions joined by a curtain.

Magazine—Store for arms, ammunition, and provisions, in time of war; store for gunpowder or other explosives.

Palisade—A fence made of poles or stakes fixed in the ground, forming an enclosure or defense.

Parapet—Defense of earth or stone to conceal and protect troops, esp. mound along front of trench.

Ravelin—Outwork of two faces forming salient angle outside main ditch before curtain.

Redoubt—Outwork or fieldwork usually square or polygonal and without flanking defenses.

Revetment—A retaining wall (of masonry or other material) supporting the face of an earthen rampart on the side of a ditch.

Salient Angle—Pointing outward, as an ordinary angle of a polygon (opposed to re-entrant).

Sally-port—Opening in fortification for making sally from.

Scarp—Steep bank immediately in front of and below rampart; similar natural formation.

Stockade—A barricade for entrenchments and redoubts, usually made of timber, furnished with loopholes for gunfire.

Terreplein—Surface of rampart behind parapet, where guns are mounted.

BIBLIOGRAPHY

DEFENSE IN THE WILDERNESS

Manuscript Materials

Amherst Papers
>In the British Museum. Photostats in the Library of Congress, Washington, D. C.

Bouquet Orderly Book
>In the Henry E. Huntington Library, San Marino, California. Printed in *The Papers of Henry Bouquet,* II, 656-690.

Bouquet Papers
>The Library of Congress, Manuscripts Division, has photostatic reproductions of almost all of Bouquet Papers in the British Museum.
>*The Papers of . . . . Prepared by Frontier Forts and Trails Survey.* Edited by S. K. Stevens and D. H. Kent. Harrisburg, Pennsylvania Historical Commission, 1940-41. 19 vols.

Chatham Papers
>In the Public Record Office, London.

Draper Manuscripts
>In the Wisconsin Historical Society Library, Madison, Wisconsin.

Forbes Orderly Book, Marching Journal
>In the Manuscript Division, Library of Congress, Washington, D. C. This is No. 414 of the George Washington military papers. Photostat of 45 pages in the library of the Historical Society of Western Pennsylvania.

Gage Papers
>In the William L. Clements Library, Ann Arbor, Michigan.

Harmar Papers
>In the William L. Clements Library, Ann Arbor, Michigan.

Hutchins Papers
>In the Historical Society of Pennsylvania, Philadelphia, Pennsylvania.

Loudoun Papers
>In the Henry E. Huntington Library, San Marino, California.

Monckton Papers
>Microfilm collection at the Historical and Museum Commission, Harrisburg.

Shippen Orderly Book
American Philosophical Society, Philadelphia, Pa. Photostat in the library of the Historical Society of Western Pennsylvania.

PRINTED MATERIALS

Bailey, Kenneth. *Ohio Company Papers*. Privately printed. Arcata, California.
Baldwin, Leland D. *Pittsburgh—The Story of a City*. University of Pittsburgh Press, 1938.
Brackenridge, H. H. *Gazette Publications*. Carlisle, Pa., 1806.
Buck, Solon J. and Elizabeth. *The Planting of Civilization in Western Pennsylvania*. University of Pittsburgh Press, 1939.
Collot, Victor. *A Journey in North America* (1796). Paris, 1826. Reprinted, Florence, 1924, in English and French.
Craig, Neville B. *The History of Pittsburgh*. J. R. Weldin Co. Pittsburgh, 1917.
Cramer, Zadok. *The Navigator*. Pittsburgh, 1808.
Cuming, Fortescue. *Sketches of a Tour in the Western Country*. Pittsburgh, 1810.
Dahlinger, Charles W. "Fort Pitt," *Western Pennsylvania Historical Magazine*, V(1922), 1-44, 87-122.
Dahlinger, Charles W. "The Marquis Duquesne," *Western Pennsylvania Historical Magazine*, XV(1932), 3-33, 121-151, 262.
Davis, Mrs. Elvert M. "Fort Fayette," *Western Pennsylvania Historical Magazine*, X(1927), 65-84.
Documents Relative to the Colonial History of the State of New York. Albany, Weed, Parsons and Company, printers. 1853-87. 15 vols.
Downes, Randolph C. *Council Fires on the Upper Ohio*. University of Pittsburgh Press, 1940.
"Colonel Eyre's Journal of his Trip from New York to Pittsburgh, 1762," *Western Pennsylvania Historical Magazine*, XXVII (1944), 37-38.
Fleming, George Thornton. *History of Pittsburgh and Environs*. I. The American Historical Society, Inc., New York and Chicago. 1922.
Fleming's Views of Old Pittsburgh. Collected by George T. Fleming. The Crescent Press. Pittsburgh, Pennsylvania, 1932.

Fort Duquesne and Fort Pitt, 8th edition. Fort Pitt Society, Daughters of the American Revolution of Allegheny County, Pennsylvania, Pittsburgh, 1931.

Fort Pitt and Letters from the Frontier. Compiled by Mary Carson (O'Hara) Darlington. J. R. Weldin & Co. Pittsburgh, 1892.

Gipson, Lawrence Henry. *The British Empire Before the American Revolution.* IV-IX. Alfred A. Knopf, 1949.

Gist, Christopher. *Christopher Gist's Journals with Historical, Geographical, and Ethnological Notes and Biographies of His Contemporaries,* by William M. Darlington. Pittsburgh, J. R. Weldin & Co., 1893.

An Historical Account of the Expedition Against the Ohio Indians. London, 1783.

Hulbert, Archer B. *The Crown Collection of Photographs of American Maps.* Series 1, 2, and 9. Library of Congress.

Hulbert, Archer B. *Historic Highways of America.* III-V. Arthur H. Clark Co., Cleveland, Ohio, 1903.

James, Alfred Procter. *Writings of General Forbes.* Collegiate Press. Menasha, Wisconsin, 1938.

J. C. B. *Travels in New France* (1751-61). S. K. Stevens, et al., eds. Harrisburg, 1941.

"Journal of James Kenny." *The Pennsylvania Magazine of History and Biography.* XXXVII(1913), 1-47; 152-201. Historical Society of Pennsylvania. Philadelphia, Pennsylvania.

Kent, Donald H. *The French Invasion of Western Pennsylvania.* Pennsylvania Historical and Museum Commission. Harrisburg, 1954.

Letters of General John Forbes Relating to the Expedition Against Fort Duquesne in 1758. Compiled by Irene Stewart for the Allegheny Committee of the Pennsylvania Society of the Colonial Dames of America. Pittsburgh. Allegheny County Committee. 1927.

Life and Reminiscences from Birth to Manhood of Wm. G. Johnston. Pittsburgh, 1901.

Lochee, Lewis. *Elements of Field Fortifications,* London, 1783.

Makers of Modern Strategy. Section 1, Chapter 2. "Vauban" by Henry Guerlac. Princeton University Press, 1943.

Mauncy, Albert and Peterson, Harold L. *Artillery Through the Ages.* U. S. Government Printing Office, National Park Service Interpretive Series. Washington, 1949.

McClure, Rev. David. *Diary.* Franklin B. Dext , ed. New York, 1899.
George Mercer Papers Relating to the Ohio Company of Virginia. Compiled and edited by Lois Mulkearn. University of Pittsburgh Press, 1954.
Montgomery, Thomas Lynch. *Frontier Forts of Pennsylvania I and II,* Second Edition, Harrisburg, 1916.
Muller, John. *Attack and Defense of Fortified Places.* London, 1757.
Muller, John. *A Treatise Containing the Elementary Part of Fortification.* London, 1755.
Muller, John. *A Treatise Containing the Elementary Part of Fortification.* London, 1774.
Nixon, Lily Lee. *James Burd—Frontier Defender* 1726-1793. University of Pennsylvania Press, Philadelphia, 1941.
Olden Time. II. Edited by Neville B. Craig. Wright and Charlton, N. E. Corner of the Diamond. Pittsburgh, 1848.
The Papers of Sir William Johnson. Prepared for publication by The Division of Archives and History. Alexander C. Flick, Ph.D., Litt.D.V. Albany. The University of the State of New York. 12 vols. 1927——.
Papiers Contrecoeur. Edits par Fernand Grenier. Les Presses Universitaires Laval. Quebec, 1952.
Pen Pictures of Early Western Pennsylvania. Edited by John W. Harpster. University of Pittsburgh Press, 1938.
Stotz, Charles Morse. *The Early Architecture of Western Pennsylvania.* Helburn, New York, 1936.
Stotz, Charles Morse. *The Story of Fort Ligonier.* Fort Ligonier Memorial Foundation, 1954.
Viollet-le-Duc, E. *Dictionnaire Raisonne de l'Architecture Francais.* Paris, 1875.
Wilderness Chronicles of Northwestern Pennsylvania. Pennsylvania Historical Survey. Harrisburg, 1941.
Wright, John W. *The Development of the Bastioned System of Permanent Fortifications.* 1500-1800. Washington, D. C., 1946.

FOOTNOTES

DECISION AT THE FORKS

[1] Alfred P. James, "Approaches to the Early History of Western Pennsylvania" *Western Pennsylvania Historical Magazine* XIX (1936), 203-11.

[2] See *Documents Relative to the Colonial History of New York* (Albany 1858-87), 15 vols.

[3] Much of the material is in the *Pennsylvania Colonial Records* and the *Pennsylvania Archives*. See Julian Boyd, "Indian Affairs in Pennsylvania, 1736-1762" in *Indian Treaties* printed by Benjamin Franklin (The Historical Society of Pennsylvania, 1938).

[4] See the account of this expedition in the *Journal of Chaussegros de Léry*, Pennsylvania Historical Commission, Harrisburg, 1940.

[5] Adequate illustrative material is found in the *Executive Journals, Council of Colonial Virginia*, V, Willmer L. Hall, editor (Richmond 194?).

[6] Much of this data is found in Maryland manuscript archives at Annapolis and at western Maryland courthouses. It is given attention in *The Ohio Company, Its Inner History . . .* by Alfred P. James (University of Pittsburgh Press, 1958).

[7] An excellent recent history of the company is *The Ohio Company of Virginia*, by Kenneth P. Bailey (Glendale, California, 1939). But much new light on the subject appears in *The George Mercer Papers*, Lois Mulkearn, ed. (Pittsburgh 1954) and *The Ohio Company, Its Inner History*, Alfred P. James (Pittsburgh 1958).

[8] "The First English Speaking Trans-Appalachian Frontier," *The Mississippi Valley Historical Review*, XVII (June 1930), 55-71.

[9] The great source of information is the Washington Papers, in the Library of Congress. Much of the material is printed in editions of writings, such as that of John C. Fitzpatrick, and an edition of letters to Washington by S. M. Hamilton.
On Braddock's expedition and defeat, the best stated and best documented account is in the *Ill-Starred General. Braddock of the Coldstream Guards* by Lee McCardell, University of Pittsburgh Press, 1958.

[10] *Lord Loudoun in North America*, by Stanley Pargellis is indispensable on this topic.

[11] For documentary material consult *The Writings of General John Forbes Relating to his Services in North America*, compiled and edited by Alfred P. James (Pittsburgh, 1938) and also, *The Papers of Henry Bouquet* Volume 11 (Harrisburg, 1951).

[12] James, *Writings of Forbes*, pp. 31-33.

[13] With few exceptions the documents mentioned below are found in the two references cited in footnote 11.

[14] The writer has in manuscript ready for publication, a forty thousand word biography entitled, "George Mercer, Frustrated Virginia Aristocrat."

[15] James, *Writing of Forbes* pp. 94-96.

[16] *Ibid.*, 94-95; 102-04; 115-16.

[17] The basic documents are found in the papers of Bouquet, Forbes and Washington. Most of them are in print.

[18] Conveniently found, chronologically arranged and well edited, in the *Papers of Henry Bouquet*, 11, *The Forbes Expedition*.

[19] Bouquet to Forbes, August 20, 1758. B. M. Add. M.S.S. 21640, f. 147, A.L.S. and in *Papers of Bouquet* 11, (391-95) (in French) and 395-99, in English translation.

[20] The best and most detailed account is that of Major Grant himself. See B. M. Add. MSS, 21652, f. 64, Copy, well printed in *Papers of . . . Bouquet*, 11, 499-505.

[21] Bouquet to Forbes, September 17, 1758, BP. 21640, f. 169 A.L.S., well edited in Papers of Henry Bouquet, 11, 513-17 (in French), 517-22 (translation); Joseph Shippen to Edward Shippen, September 1778, H.S.P. Shippen Military Pa-

pers, Letter Book I, 98.A.Df., in *Papers of Henry Bouquet*, II, 527-28.
[22] Burd to Bouquet, October 12, 1758, B.P., 21643, f.235, A.L.S.; and October 13, 1758, *ibid.*, f. 237, A.G.S.
[23] "Proposals for a Writer Expedition," c. November 5, 1758, B.P. 21643, f. 282 A.Df.
[24] "Council of War," November 11, 1758, *ibid.*, f. 280, A.Df.
[25] *Ibid.*, f. 247, D.S. of Harry Gordon and Richard Dudgeon.
[26] Forbes Orderly Book, in Washington MSS, Library of Congress.
[27] *Ibid.*
[28] The Forbes letters of November 26, 1758 to Abercromby and Amherst, and to Governor Denny, and of November 27, to William Pitt are in James, *Writings of ... Forbes* ... 262-69; the letters of Bouquet to Stanwix, Amherst Papers P.R.O. W.O. 34:44, f.141, A.G.S. and to William Allen, November 25, 1758, H.S.P. Penn Papers IX, 391-95, are, well edited, in *Papers of Henry Bouquet*, II, *The Forbes Expedition*, pp. 609-12.
[29] B.P., 21640, f. 147, A.L.S. (in French), well edited and translated, in *Papers of Henry Bouquet II, the Forbes Expedition*, 139-95 and 395-99.
[30] Bouquet to Anne Willing, November 25, 1758, *Pennsylvania Magazine of History and Biography* III (1879), 135-36.
[31] *Ibid.* On the continuing beauty of Western Pennsylvania, see *Penns Woods West*, by Edwin G. Peterson, with Thomas M. Jarrett, Photographic Editor, University of Pittsburgh Press, 1958.

Defense in the Wilderness

[1] Forbes to Abercromby and Amherst, November 26, 1758, P. R. O. C. O. 5:54 (L.C. trans.) pp. 5-8: P. R. O. W. O. 34:44, f.385, Copy.
[2] A. B. Hulbert, *Historical Highways*, III, 80, quoting Sir Guy Carleton.
[3] Charles M. Stotz, *The Early Architecture of Western Pennsylvania* (William Helburn, Inc., New York, 1936. For the Buhl Foundation, Pittsburgh).
[4] Bouquet to Amherst, July 13, 1763, Bouquet Papers, British Museum Additional Manuscripts (hereinafter cited as BP), 21634, f.321, Copy.
[5] BP, 21643, f.247, D.S. November 16, 1758.
[6] Hulbert, *Historic Highways*. IV, 48-49. Napier to Braddock, November 25, 1754, *Olden Time*, II, 222.
[7] Chatham Papers, P. R. O. 30-8-95.
[8] Instructions to Braddock, November 25, 1754.
[9] Stotz, *The Story of Fort Ligonier*, Fort Ligonier Memorial Foundation, Ligonier, Pa. 1954.
[10] P. R. O. S. P. Domestic Military 38.
[11] B. to F., June 28, 1758, BP, 21652, f.49, A. L. S. In French.
[12] Instructions to Col. James Burd, September 25, 1758, BP, 21643, f.230, Df.
[13] Bouquet to Napier, June 30, 1757, BP, 21631, f.32, Df.
[14] Bouquet to Tulleken, July 16, 1759, BP, 21652, f.119, Copy. Bouquet to Burd, October 13, 1758, H. S. P., Shippen Papers, III, f.211, A. L. S.
[15] B. to G., January 22, 1765, BP, 21653, f.343, A.Note.
[16] B. to P. (In French), December 3, 1758, BP, 21652, f.73, Df.S.
[17] B. to Gov. Henry Ellis, September 17, 1757, BP, 21632, f.5, Df.
[18] B. to A., March 11, 1759, BP, 21634, f.11, Df.
[19] F. to B., September 23, 1758, BP, 21640, f.173, A. L. S.
[20] Burd to B., September 7, 1759, BP, 21644, f.367, A. L. S.
[21] F. to A., July 25, 1758, P. R. O. W. O. 34:44, f.339; and F. to A., August 11, 1758, *ibid.*, f.527, L. S. and P.R.O.W.O. 34:44 f.343, Copy. See James, *Writings of* ... *Forbes*, pp. 159 and 172.
[22] S. to B., August 8, 1758, BP, 21643, f.174, A. L. S.; S. to B., August 10, 1758, *ibid.*, f.176, A. L. S.; *ibid.*, f.269, August 11, 1758, A. L. S.
[23] C. to B., June 2, 1758, BP, 21643, f.98, A. L. S.; B. to Forbes, June 7, 1758, *ibid.*, 21652, f.32, A. L. S.
[24] S. to B., August 1758, BP, 21643, f.268, A. L. S.
[25] Cochrane to Tulleken, July 12, 1759, BP, 21644, f.230, A. L. S.; T. to B., July 21,

1759, BP, 21644, f.245, A. L. S.; T. to B., July 22, 1759, *ibid.*, f.247, A. L. S.
[26] A. to B., September 10, 1759, BP, 21644, f.377, A. L. S.; F. to A., September 21, 1758, AB 709, A. L. S., in James, *Writings of . . . Forbes*, pp. 215-218.
[27] BP, 21644, f.119, A. L. S., March 31, 1758.
[28] B. to P., November 27, 1759, BP, 21652, f.200, Copy.
[29] Burd to William Allen, cited in Lily Lee Nixon, *James Burd*, p. 57.
[30] BP, 21655, f.32, Copy.
[31] December 9, 1761, BP, 21647, f.278, A. L. S.
[32] BP, 21654, f.31, Df., 1759.
[33] *An Historical Account*, pp. 44-45.
[34] B. to A., July 26, 1763, BP, 21634, f.333, Copy; B. to Macdonald, August 28, 1763, BP, 21649, f.316, Df.
[35] B. to Forbes, September 17, 1758, BP, 21640, f.169, A. L. S., in French; B. to Stephen, October 23, 1763, BP, 21653, f.235, C. S.
[36] BP, 21631, f.38, Df., July 15, 1757.
[37] B. to Forbes, May 29, 1758, BP, 21652, f.17, A. L. S.; August 11, 1764, BP, 21653, f.308, A. Df.
[38] S. to B., May 31, 1758, BP, 21643, f.96, A. L. S.
[39] B. to John Harris, July 19, 1764, BP, 21650, f.349, A. L. S.
[40] B. to F., May 25, 1758, BP, 21652, f.12, A. L. S.; B. to F., July 11, 1758, BP, 21652, f.53, A. L. S.; B. to F., June 11, 1758, *ibid.*, f.36, A. L. S.
[41] B. to F., May 25, 1758, BP, 21652, f.12, A. L. S.
[42] c. November 5, 1758, BP, 21643, f.278, A. Df.
[43] B. to F., May 30, 1758, BP, 21652, f.17, A. L. S. in French; Burd Proposal mentioned in Lily Lee Nixon, *James Burd*, p. 41; Forbes Orders as reported, George Stevenson to Bouquet, June 2, 1758, BP, 21643, f.99, A. L. S.
[44] Baillie to Bouquet, August 28, 1762, BP, 21648, f.341, A. D. S.
[45] BP, 21643, f.249, Note.
[46] Blane to Bouquet, September 17, 1763, BP, 21649, f.345, A. L. S.; R. to S., August 6, 1759, *ibid.*, 21644, f.286, A. L. S.
[47] A. to S., May 4, 1759, BP, 21644, f.148, A. L. S.; *Travels in New France* by J. C. B., page 32.; S. to B., December 7, 1762, *ibid.*, 21648, f.468, A. L. S.
[48] B. to P., July 11, 1758, BP, 21652, f.53, A. L. S. in French.
[49] Stewart to Bouquet, November 11, 1763, BP, 21649, f.458, A. L. S.; Ecuyer to B., November 13, 1763, *ibid.*, 21649, f.467, A. L. S. in French.
[50] Ecuyer to Bouquet, April 9, 1763, BP, 21619, f.106, A. L. S. in French; S. to Bouquet, June 30, 1761, *ibid.*, 21646, f.326, A. L. S.
[51] E. to Bouquet, April 23, 1763, BP, 21649, f.117, A. L. S.; Order . . . of December 31, 1760, *ibid.*, 21653, f.46, A. Df.; B. to Cochrane, July 12, 1761, BP, 21653, f.71, A. Df.
[52] Potts to Bouquet, January 8, 1763, BP, 21649, f.9, A. L. S.; E. to Bouquet, January 8, 1763, *ibid.*, f.7, A. L. S. in French.
[53] Lily Lee Nixon, *James Burd*, p. 89.
[54] A List, BP, 21646, f.139, Df.; Ecuyer to Bouquet, March 19, 1763, BP, 21649, f.85, A. L. S. in French.
[55] Prices of Goods, BP, 21646, f.39, c. February 5, 1761.
[56] BP, 21653, f.8, Draft, c. April 1760; Fauquier to Bouquet, January 17, 1762, 21648, f.5, A. L. S.
[57] Bouquet to Francis Fauquier, February 8, 1762, BP, 21648, f.25, A. L. S.; B. to G., December 22, 1764, BP, 21653, f.333, A. Df.
[58] Captain Donald Campbell to B., July 3, 1762, BP, 21648, f.243, A. L. S.
[59] B. to Fauquier, August 25, 1759, BP, 21652, f.155, C.
[60] Bouquet to Croghan, August 10, 1759, BP, 21655, f.78, C.; B. to James Pemberton, September 1, 1759, BP, 21652, f.162, Copy; B. to Croghan, August 10, 1759, BP, 21655, f.78, Copy; Ecuyer to B., April 23, 1763, BP, 21649, f.117, A. L. S. in French.
[61] G. to B., July 5, 1764, BP, 21636, f.445, Copy; T. to S., July 12, 1759, BP, 21644, f.228, A. L. S.
[62] Bouquet to Forbes, June 16, 1758, BP, 21652, f.44, A. L. S.; Memorandum, May 4, 1763, BP, 21634, f.243, A, Note; account against the Crown, August 15,

1763, BP, 21654, f.168, Copy; Bouquet to Amherst, July 13, 1763, BP, 21634, f.321, Copy.
[63] Gage to Bouquet, July 5, 1764, BP, 21636, f.445, Copy. Also in Gage Papers, William L. Clements Library. Gordon to B., BP, 21644, f.1, A. L. S.; M. to B., 21644, f.16, A. L. S.; A. to S., December 18, 1759, BP, 21634, f.27, Copy.
[64] May 29, 1751, *Pa. Col. Recs.*, V, 538, cited in S. J. and E. H. Buck, *Planting of Civilization in Western Pennsylvania*, page 63.
[65] *George Mercer Papers*, pp. 147-149.
[66] Copy in *George Mercer Papers* opp. p. 226.
[67] *Journal of George Washington*. In Harpster, *Pen Pictures of Western Pennsylvania*. See p. 25.
[68] Deposition of Ensign Ward, June 30, 1756, H. S. P. MS, printed in Kenneth Bailey, *Ohio Company Papers*.
[69] *Ibid*.
[70] Of June 30, 1756, *loc. cit.*; of May 7, 1754, William Darlington (ed.), *Journal of Christopher Gist*, pp. 275-278.
[71] *George Mercer Papers*, page 88.
[72] Deposition of May 7, 1754, *loc. cit.*, p. 278.
[73] J. C. B., *Travels in New France*, p. 56.
[74] D. to C., January 27, 1754, *Papiers Contrecoeur*, pp. 92-96. See p. 94.
[75] *George Mercer Papers*, page 88.
[76] D. to C., May 11, 1754, *Papiers Contrecoeur*, p. 125.
[77] Vaudreuil to the Minister, August 8, 1756, Arch. Nat., C" A101, f.88, (*Wilderness Chronicles*, p. 97)
[78] Dahlinger, *The Marquis Duquesne*, p. 238; De Lery, in Quebec Archives, Rapport, 1927-28, p. 418-429.
[79] Vaudreuil to the Minister, July 12, 1957, Arch. Nat., C" A102, f.53, (*Wilderness Chronicles*, p. 103)
[80] *Papiers Contrecoeur*, Planche VII, opp. p. 231.
[81] Stobo, July 28, 1754. *Olden Time*, I, 61.
[82] Darlington, *Christopher Gist's Journals*, 148-51.
[83] John Haslet to Rev. Dr. Allison, November 26, 1758, in Irene Stewart, *Letters of General John Forbes* (Pittsburgh 1927), pp. 71-72. In *Olden Time*, I, 184-85.
[84] Vaudreuil to the Minister, January 20, 1759, *Wilderness Chronicles*, pp. 126-131.
[85] MS Joseph Shippen Orderly Book.
[86] BP, 21644, f.9, Copy Signed.
[87] B. to Mercer, December 26, 1758, BP, 21652, f.74, A. Df.
[88] Amherst to Forbes, December 25, 1758, P. R. O. C. O. 5:54, L. C. tr. p. 67.
[89] P. R. O. W. O. 34:44, f.411, printed in James, *Writings of . . . Forbes*, p. 299.
[90] BP, 21644, f.1, A. L. S.
[91] *Pennsylvania Magazine of History and Biography*, XXXVII (1913), 395-449.
[92] Mercer to B., December 19, 1758, BP, 21643, f.271, A. L. S.; M. to B., December 23, 1758, *ibid*., f.275, A. L. S.
[93] B. to Mercer, December 26, 1758, BP, 21652, f.74, A. Df.
[94] M. to B., BP, 21644, f.9, Copy Signed.
[95] M. to B., *ibid*., f.16, A. L. S.
[96] BP, 21634, f.20, L. S.
[97] Neville Craig (ed.), *Olden Time*, II, 1-5, John Ormsby Narrative, reference to p. 3.
[98] M. to Stanwix, BP, 21655, f.45, A. L. S.
[99] M. to B., April 24, 1759, BP, 21644, f.133, A. L. S.
[100] B. to M., May 8, 1759, BP, 21652, f.90, A. Df. S.
[101] *Western Pennsylvania Historical Magazine*, XXVII (1944), 49-50.
[102] Vaudreuil to the Keeper of the Seals, April 22, 1757, *Documents Relative to the Colonial History of New York*, X, 542.
[103] August 2, 1759, BP, 21655, f.66, A. Df.
[104] B. to G., August 2, 1759, BP, 21644, f.275, Copy.
[105] P. R. O. W. O. 34:45, f.100-1, L. S.
[106] A copy of his report is filed with the Carnegie Library of Pittsburgh.

[107] John Ormsby: Return of Provisions, December 6, 1759, BP, 21654, f.116, A. D. S.
[108] Instructions to Grant, January 19, 1764, BP, 21653, f.250, A. Df.
[109] Stanwix to Amherst, March 17, 1760, P. R. O. 280 W. O. 34/45.
[110] From Pittsburgh, March 21, 1760, *Olden Time*, I, 198.
[111] Gordon to Bouquet, August 12, 1759, BP, 21644, f.304, A. L. S.; Colonel Jehu Eyre's Diary, *P. M. H. B.*, III (1879), 302.
[112] "Present State of Fort Pitt and Posts Depending" (Philadelphia, December 24, 1760), *Wilderness Chronicles*, pp. 201-2.
[113] *W. Pa. Hist. Mag.*, XXVII, (1944), 49-50.
[114] Above—p. 82.
[115] E. to B., March 11, 1763, BP, 21649, f.76, A. L. S.; Amherst to B., April 3, 1763, BP, 21634, f.224, L. S.
[116] Ecuyer to Bouquet, June 2, 1763, BP, 21649, f.138, A. L. S. in French.
[117] Ecuyer to Bouquet, June 16, 1763, BP, 21649, f.170, A. L. S. in French. B. to Amherst, June 13, 1763, BP, 21634, f.321, Copy.
[118] B. to Amherst, August 11, 1758, BP, 21634, f.358, Copy. The original is doughtless in the Amherst Papers, P.R.O.W.O. 34:44.
[119] Captain William Murray to Bouquet, September 23, 1763, BP, 21649, f.349, A. L. S.
[120] Gage Papers, Am. Series II, December 27, 1763, William L. Clements Library, Ann Arbor, Michigan. In BP, 21637.
[121] For the full story of this quaint building, see Charles W. Dahlinger, *Fort Pitt*, Chapter VII, "The Old Redoubt," a reprint from *W.P.H.M.*, V, 108-12.
[122] G. to B., February 24, 1764, f.54, A. L. S.; H. to B., April 10, 1764, BP, 21650, f.126, A. L. S.; H. to B., May 15, 1764, BP, 21650, f.203, A. L. S.; G. to Gage, April 2, 1764, W.H.C.L., Gage Papers, American Series.
[123] William Grant to Bouquet, May 15, 1764, BP, 21650, f.199, A. L. S.; and June 1, 1764, *ibid.*, f.234, A. L. S.
[124] William Grant to B., June 25, 1764, BP, 21650, f.293, A. L. S.; *ibid.*, f.479, A. L. S.
[125] September 17, 1764, BP, 21658, f.102.
[126] Gage Papers, Am. Series. W. L. C. L.; Bouquet to Gage, March 4, 1765, BP, 21637.
[127] *Sir William Johnson Papers*, V. 30; Report to Gage, 1766. Estimate of Expenses of Works at Forts in District of New York (Public Archives of Canada, Gage Papers, Vol. 51).
[128] W. P. H. S. Transcript of P. R. O REF: T. G4/21. 20/34.
[129] Stanwix to Amherst, September 17, 1759, PRO, 280: W.O. 34:45, 100-1, L. S.
[130] Mercer to B., February 7, 1759, BP, 21644, f.43, A. L. S.
[131] B. to M., May 26, 1759, BP, 21652, f.100, Copy.
[132] B. to M., April 13, 1759, BP, 21652, f.84, A. C.
[133] L. to B., March 5, 1761, BP, 21646, f.75, A. L. S.
[134] B. to Walters, April 10, 1762, BP, 21648, f.98, Copy.
[135] Barnsley to B., June 10, 1762, BP, 21648, f.206, A. L. S.
[136] BP, 21655, Orders and Regulations, October 18, 1762, f.195-202, Df.
[137] B. to St. C., December 25, 1761, BP, 21653, f.97, Df. B. to Bentinck, May 2, 1763, BP, 21653, f.119, A. Df.
[138] B. to Amherst, January 11, 1763, BP, 21634, f.184, D. S.; B. to Ecuyer, February 18, 1763, BP, 21653, f.159, A. Df. S.
[139] Burent to B., February 21, 1763, BP, 21649, f.62, A. L. S.
[140] E. to B., March 19, 1763, BP, 21649, f.85, A. L. S.; *ibid.*, f.78, A. L. S., March 11, 1763.
[141] Ecuyer to B., March 19, 1763, BP, 21649, f.85, A. L. S.; E. to B., June 16, 1763, BP, 21649, f.170, A. L. S.; Instructions to Grant, January 19, 1764, BP, 21653, f.250, A. Df.; Grant to B., April 2, 1764, BP, 21650, f.115, A. L. S.; Grant to B., April 13, 1764, BP, 21650, f.137, A. L. S.; Grant to B., April 26, 1764, BP, 21650, f.166, A. L. S.
[142] B. to G., May 3, 1764, BP, 21653, f.284, Copy; G. to B., May 15, 1764, BP, 21650, f.199, A. L. S.; G. to B., June 25, 1764, BP, 21650, f.291, A. L. S.; G. to B., July 9, 1764, BP, 21650, f.328, A. L. S.

[143] R. to B., September 4, 1764, BP, 21650, f.479, A. L. S.; G. to B., September 4, 1764, BP, 21650, f.477, A. L. S.
[144] H. H. Brackenridge, *Gazette Publications*, collected and published 1806. Cited in Neville B. Craig's *Pittsburgh*, p. 176.
[145] Zadok Cramer, *Navigator*, 1808, p. 33.
[146] A. B. Hulbert, *Historic Highways of America*, III, "Washington Road," p. 37.
[147] Wm. G. Johnston, *Life* . . ., p. 25.
[148] K. to C., December 16, 1791, Craig, *History of Pittsburgh*, p. 198; C. to K., December 29, 1791, Wm. G. Johnston, *Life* . . ., p. 25, Craig, *Pittsburgh*, p. 199.
[149] C. to K., *Life* . . . *of Wm. G. Johnston* (Pittsburgh 1901), p. 26.
[150] George Henri Victor Collot, *A Journey in North America*, p. 41.
[151] Mrs. Elvert M. Davis, "Fort Fayette," *W.P.H.M.*, X (1927), 66.
[152] Fortescue Cuming, *Sketches of a Tour to the Western Country*, p. 245.
[153] U. S. Grant 3rd, *The Key to the West*, Fort Ligonier Memorial Foundation, 1954.
[154] Reverend David McClure, *Diary* (New York, 1899); cited in part, Harpster, *Pen Pictures*, p. 121, and in Dahlinger "Fort Pitt," *W.P.H.M.*, V, 29.

INDEX

(Not indexed are commonly familiar names of oceans, continents, and countries; and somewhat antiquarian names of historically insignificant places and unidentified persons,)

Aborigines, 6, *see* Indians
Administration of Colonial Affairs, 9, badly scattered, 9
Abercromby, General James, 38, 40, 41, 42, 47, 70, 91, 94, advances against Ticonderoga, 42, 70; becomes commander-in-chief, 40; defeated, 42, 47; kept informed by Forbes, 91, 94, relieved from command, 41, second in command to Loudon, 40; succeeds Loudon, 38, 40, succeded by Amherst, *D.A.B.*
Aix-la-Chapelle, Treaty of Peace of, 22
Albany, 8, 20, 22, 68, 78, built in 1695 and well fortified, 68; dominant early fur trade center, 8; frontier advances beyond, 20; its fur trade watched by French, 22; masonry construction of defenses, 78
Alexandria, Va., 32, Braddock's troopships sent there
Algonquians, important in American colonial history, 7; *see* Indians
Allegheny River, 4, 16, 18, 30, 89, 99, 110, 112, 136, 141, 155, 159, 178, 180, 188, 189, blockhouse near, 155; called La Belle Riviere and Ohio, 141; early route to the Forks, 4, 89; expedition down, 189; fort relation to, 110,112, 136; French come down, 30; gardens along, 180; houses along, 178; old banks of, 159; Pennsylvania traders of 1725, 18; Wayne camps along, 188
Allen, William, 55, letter to, November 24, 1758, by Bouquet, 55
Amerinds (American Indians) 7, antiquity, 7; background of decision at the Forks, 7; numbers, 7; *see* Indians
Amherst, General Jeffery, 35, 39, 40, 41, 47, 70, 115, 118, 142, 149, 152, 153, 172, advised about Indians by Bouquet, 47; captures Louisbourg, 47; commanded attack upon Louisbourg, 40; commander-in-chief, 35, 41; correspondence about a fort at forks, 149; made suggestion of giving small pox to Indians, 118; one of younger military men of Pitt, 40; sends Eyre to inspect Fort Pitt, 152-153, 172
Ammunition, 104, 105, 141, 142, 149, 172, amount needed, 104, 104; at Fort Pitt, 172; at Pittsburgh secured in 1759 from attacks, 149; removed from the ruins of Fort Duquesne, 141, 142
Anglo-French Rivalry, 7, 9, 10, 12, 15, 18; a world empire the stake, 7; began in New World in early seventeenth century, 18; European background, 10; role of Pennsylvania, 15; very old, 9; wars resulting, 12
Anglo-French Wars, 7, 16, 20, 21, 27, 28; Hundred years War, 1338-1443, 7; War of the Palatinate (King Williams War), 1690-98, 16; War of Spanish Succession (Queen Anne's War), 1701-13, 16; War of Jenkin's Ear, 1739-40; War of the Austrian Succession (King George's War), 1740-44, 20; French and Indian War (Seven Years War), 1756,-63, 21, 27, 28
Annapolis, Md., 26, 28, 29, 32, conference called by Braddock, 32; informed about Ohio Company, 26; about French at Venango, 28; about projected French at the Forks, 32
Appalachian Mountains, 3, 4, 17, 63, 65, densely forested, 63; greatly eroded, 4; significant geological feature, 4; sixty miles across, 65; very old, 4; western limit of early English settlements, 65
Approaches or Routes to the Forks of the Ohio, 6, 46-49, 68, 69, 70, 71, 72, 90, 91, similarly to spokes and hub of a wheel, 6; Champlain route, 68; Hudson-Mohawk Route, 68; Allegheny route, 69; Braddock route, 70; Forbes route, 46-49; 70-72, 90-91
Arms and Equipment, 103, 104, a grave problem, 103; guns dangerous, 103; in Bouquet's Detail for a march, 104; inadequate equipment, 103; many guns unfit, 103; militia use rifles, 104; scarcity of tents, 103
Armstrong, Major George, Pa. Regt., 49, 94; does scouting for Bouquet, 47
Armstrong, Colonel John, senior colonel in the Pennsylvania militia, 44, 106; mentions lack of vegetables and resulting scurvy, 106; his regiment with Bouquet at Lancaster, 44; *D.A.B.*
Artificers (Artisans), 52, 53, 84, 85, 153, 166, 167, 169, at Fort Pitt in 1761, 169; bags rarely used, 84; companies of under Washington, 52, 53; coopers, 84, 167; types of, 84, 85, 166, 167
Artillery, 30, 43, 50, 104, 131, 140, 144, 176, 177, at Fort Duquesne, 131; at Fort Machault, in 1759, 144; at Mercer's Fort, 144; at Fort Pitt, 176, 177; carried off, 140; guns needed, 104;

INDEX 205

late in arriving for Forbes, 43; plays a role at Loyal Hannon, 50; with Contrecoeur, 30
Atkins, Edmund (Southern Indian superintendent), 46, criticised by Forbes, 46
Aubry, Charles Phillipe, (from Illinois), led in attack on Loyal Hannon, October 12, 1758, 53
Ayres Hill (later site of Duquesne University) recommended as site for a fort, 154; mined for coal and limestone, 167; *see* Duquesne Crest

Baker, Lieutenant James, First Va. Regt., makes report on route from Raystown, west, 49
Baltimore, Lord (George Calvert), in 1626 attempts colony on New Foundland, 13
Barnsley, Captain Thomas, 111, 182, had officer's house with three servants, 111; writes on gardens in 1762, 182
Basset, Thomas, Captain, engineer, 88, 173, at Fort Loudoun in 1758, 88; assisted in repair work at Fort Pitt, 88, 173
Bastions, 73, 80, 120, 122, 130, 131, 142, 144, 146, 151, 159, 160, 161, 162, 165, 168, 172, 177, at Fort Duquesne, 130, 131; at Ohio Co. proposed fort, 122; at Mercer's Fort, 142, 144, 146; at Fort William Henry, 80; first used, 73, five named at Fort Pitt, 119, 120, 151, 159, 160, 162, 165, 168, 172, 177, flood damage, 172
Battle of the Monongahela (Name commonly given to Braddock's defeat), account of, 33-34
Bay, Reverend Andrew, in 1758 with Pennsylvania troops, 53
Beale, George, meeting in his large room, 1
Beatty, Reverend Charles Clinton, 51, 151, with Pennsylvania troops, 51; describes burning coal mine, 151
Beaujeu, Daniel Hyacinthe Marie Lienard de, French officer, 34, 136, 156; urges attack, 34; killed at Battle of the Monongahela, 1755, 34, 156; buried in burying ground, now near Trinity Church, 136
Bedford, (Pa.) (Old Raystown), frontier archives at, 26; supplies in 1759 and 1764, 97; *see* Fort Bedford and Loyal Hannon
Beverley, William, 25; at 1744 Lancaster conference, 25; great colonial Virginian Piedmont and transmontane land speculator, 25; rival of Lees and Washingtons, 25
Bibliotheque Nationale; repository of maps, 79, 129
Bicentennial of Pittsburgh's founding, Foreword, ii
Bladen, Thomas, Gov. of Md., 24; land speculator, 24; uses Thomas Cresap as surveyor, 24
Blair-Russell Company, 28; makes survey around Ohio Co. settlement, 28
Blane, Archibald, commandant at Ligonier, complains about lack of supplies, 106
Bliss, Wesley L., 106, 158; made a study of the Point, 158; his report on file at Carnegie Library, footnote 106
Blockhouse, 119, 154, 158, 175, 177, 186; an outlying redoubt, 119, 175; at Fort Fayette, 186; blockhouse policy recommended by Eyre, 154; not a part of fort, 119; oldest authenticated building, 119, 175; once a residence of Isaac Craig, 177; only outward vestige of old forts, 119; origin of the word, 175; reconstruction of Fort Pitt not feasible, 119
Blue Ridge Mountain (Va), 17, 19, 23; crossed by early westward moving pioneers, 19
Board of Trade and Plantations, set up in 1696, 9; its functions largely investigative, advisory and secretarial, 9
Boats, 49, 99, 166, 167, 172; at Point in 1759, 166; boat yard, 167; floated into Fort Pitt, 172; of many kinds, 99; used between Point and Redstone Creek, 167
Boscawen, Edward, Admiral, 34; in command of a large fleet sent with Braddock in 1754-55, 34; *D.A.B.*
Bouquet, Colonel Henry, 34, 42, 44, 45, 46, 47, 48, 49, 50, 51, 52, 53, 55, 70, 85, 86, 89, 90, 92, 93, 94, 95, 96, 97, 99, 101, 102, 103, 105, 106, 107, 108, 109, 110, 114, 115, 116, 117, 118, 141, 144, 146, 148, 149, 150, 152, 153, 155, 157, 164, 166, 173, 174, 175, 177, 178, 180, 181, 182, 183, 184; account of his 1764 expedition, 99-101; advises ropes to pull wagons, 93; advises Mercer on fort construction, 146; advises Gordon on fort plans, 157; astonished at St. Clair proposal to abandon Pa. road, 47; at Fort Loudon in June, 45-46; brigade commander, 52; commander of battalion of Royal Americans, 42; commands advance in Forbes illness, 48; comments on need of horses, 95; concerned about pasturage, 180, condemns white settlement of Indian lands, 116; consents to Grant's expedition, 49; considers another fort site than the Point, 152-153; decides to cross Laurel Ridge, 48; discusses

soldiers doing non-military work, 85; distressed by Grant's defeat, 50; draws up a plan of winter operation, 51; efficient subordinate, 70, 90; endorses voucher for cost of house construction, 178; establishes harmony and gets work done, 48; exercises troops, 71; finds benefit from Grant's experience, 50; gets 1,600 men beyond Allegheny Mountain, 48; goes up the Monongahela, 99; his great patience, 108; his orderly book, 52; incomparable subordinate, 101; in 1757, in S.C., 42; instructions from Forbes, 44; invited to be guest of Adam Hoops, 97; leaned upon heavily by Forbes, 44, 48; letters from mentioned, 48, 50, 53, 55, 85, 86, 89, 92, 94, 96, 99, 101, 102, 103, 106, 107, 114, 115, 116, 117, 118, 144, 146, 149, 155, 157, 164, 174, 175, 177, 180, 181, 182, 183; letters to mentioned, 44, 93, 94, 95, 97, 102, 105, 106, 108, 109, 110, 117, 118, 141, 146, 148, 150, 173, 174, 175, 176, 180, 181, 182, 183, 184; likes farming as a recreation, 182; ordered from S.C. to N.Y., 42; ordered to avoid outlay on fort repair, 173; orders about artificers, 85; orders farmers near forts to grow forage, 180; persuaded not to use Braddock's road, 91; praises work in 1763 of Ecuyer, 175; presents a technique for fighting the Indians, 99-100, 101; reaches Raystown, June 24, 1758, 46; recommends four steps, 45; recommends to Gage conversion of Fort Pitt into a trading post, 177; sends express from Bushy Run, 108; sent ahead by Forbes, 44; trouble with Indian allies, 34; troubled by Indians at Forts, 116-17; uses small pox infection as weapon, 118; warns Amherst, in 1759, of danger, 149; writes Forbes about equipment, 103; wrote in Swiss French, 89; younger military man, advanced by Pitt, 39, D.A.B.

Boyd, Surgeon, brawls and fights with Lieutenant Donellan, 108

Brackenridge, Hugh Henry, describes his recollections of the ruins of Fort Duquesne, 140, D. A. B.

Braddock, General Edward, 32, 33, 34, 35, 40, 45, 54, 60, 63, 70, 71, 76, 78, 89, 90 91, 141, 155, 166; accompanied by a large fleet, 32; advised not to use masonry construction, 78; an able strategist, 33; blunders in keeping troops in column, 34; bones of his soldiers buried three years later, 141; builds no forts enroute, 70, 71; campaign a failure, 54; defeat a shock to the British, 33; defeat less discreditable than that of Abercromby at Ticonderoga, 40; divides his forces in face of the enemy, 33; estimation of him now modified, 33; fought by Indians, 63; Gordon with him, 60, 156; his campaign a matter of great historical interest, 33; instruction about forts, 78; letters to mentioned, 32; maintained Maryland troops, 45; might better have aimed at Niagara through N.Y., 90-91; plan of large fort found among his papers, 76, 155, 156; relations with Indians, 34; route difficult, 70, 89-90; sails from Europe in December, 32; sent to America, 32; straddles alternate plans, 33; triple instructions, 32, D.A.B.

Braddock's Road, 45, 46, 47, 70, 71, 89, 90, 91, 96, 97; began at Fort Cumberland, 90; Bouquet passes criticism of to Forbes, 46; Braddock started a Pennsylvania Road, 46; criticised by Burd, 91; depicted on end paper, 91; favored by Virginians, 45; most difficult route, 79, 89, 90; recommended by St. Clair, 47; re-opened in 1759, 96-97, route in 1755 a mistake

Bradford, David, leads Whiskey Rebels against Pittsburgh, 1794, 188

Bradstreet, Captain John, 39, 40, 42, 49, 70; acts in August 1758, 49; captures Fort Frontenac, 42, 49; got necessary troops, 41; instructions probably drawn by himself, for the attack, 39, 40, 70; plans the attack, 70; rises under Pitt regime, 39; should have a statue in Pittsburgh, 40; D.A.B.

Bridges, 90, 94; at Ligonier, Little Crossing and Wills Creek, 94; none on the Susquehanna nor on Juniata, 94; small ones needed on road, 90

Britain, British Isles, Great Britain, 8, 10, 14, 20, 21, 36; ally of Austria, 20; attention to necessary, 8; cultural contributions, 10; Franco-Austrian alliance moves Britain into alliance with Prussia, 36; makes war on Spanish imperial monopoly, 14; political, financial and military contribution, 10; provided capital for colonization, 10; trans-Appalachian claims of, 21

British America, 3, 6, 9, 10, 11, 12, 14, 17, 18, 19, 20, 30, 31, 35, 36, 40, 50, 166; attention here given to, 8; badly defeated at Ticonderoga, 40; British retire to western forts after 1783, 185; defeated at Forks in 1755 and retire, 30; drab but sorrowful years, 35-36; driven out of Ohio Valley 1755, 35; Elizabethan in culture, 10; establishment in Ohio Valley aided by New

INDEX 207

England, 11-12; final establishment on the Ohio, 166; forces of, 3; frontier advance, 17-20; frontier counties, 18, 19, 20; frontier in danger 1755-58, 35; growth in strength and resources, 17; losses at Loyal Hannon, 50; on the defensive, 1754-55, 31; organization for conflict, 14; policies of in Trans-Appalachian, 6; protected by Mother country, 10; repel desperate assault on Loyal Hannon, 50; repelled at Fort Duquesne, September 1758, 50; triumph and success, 9
British Empire, 7, 9, 11, 12, 21, 36; early royal control of colonies, 9; hardly existent at the time of the discovery of America, 7, 11; important affairs depended upon, 36; origin and development of, 7, 9; role of Cromwell, 12; role of Charles II, 12; trans-Appalachian claims of, 21
British Museum (London), 71, 79, 143; depository of maps and drawings, 71, 79; map of Mercer's Fort, 143
British Treasury, 9, 41, 178-179; costs of Fort Pitt, 178-79; heavy financial drains, 41; high cost of war, 41; participates in colonial matters, 9
British War Office, 9, 32, 84; called upon for tools, 84; controls Independent Companies in America, 32; participates in colonial affairs, 9
Brunot's Island, 154, 157; in Ohio River just below the Point, 154; once known as Chartees Island, 157
Bullit, Captain Thomas, his convoy attacked near Ligonier, 97
Burd, Colonel James, 44, 46, 48, 49, 50, 51, 52, 91, 107, 110; arrives at Loyal Hannon September 3, 49; attacked at Loyal Hannon, 50; commander of a battalion of Pa. militia, 48; condemns Braddock's Road, 91; distressed by Grant's defeat, 50; expected at Carlisle, 44; had five companies of his battalion, 48; in command of troops sent to Loyal Hannon in August, 48; left at Loyal Hannon with 600 troops, 52; overestimated number of attackers, 51; reached Raystown, June 24, 1758, 46; residence in Pittsburgh, 110; suggests law to compel owners of wagons to make one trip, 110; worked on road, 1755, 91; worried about scurvy in army, 107
Burent, Sergeant John, 182, 183; works on gardens and trees, 182-83
Bushy Run, Westmoreland County, Pa. 53, 63; battle of, type of Indian warfare, 63; reached by Forbes army, November 16, 1758, 53
Byng, Admiral John, loses Minorca, 38

Byrd, Colonel William, III, 34, 43, 45, 46, 49; commands Second Virginia Regiment, 43; Indians meet at Winchester, 43; late in collecting his regiment at Winchester, 45; marched from Winchester late in June, 46; regiment lacking equipment and supplies, 49; troubles with Indians under him, 34

Cadillac, Antoine de la Mothe, Sieur, founder of Fort Detroit, 67; *D.A.B.*
Callendar, Robert, (old fur trader), 93, 98; advises use of ropes, 93; contractor for pack horses, 98; his list of horses killed, captured, etc., 98; partner of Barnabas Hughes, 98
Calvert, George, First Lord of Baltimore, attempts Newfoundland colony of Avalon, 11
Camps between Loyal Hannon and Fort Duquesne, November 15, 1758 to November 24, 1758; Camp at Chestnut Ridge; at Bushy Run, Nov. 16; Bullock Camp, Nov. 17; at New Camp, Nov. 18; at Turtle Creek Camp, Nov. 19; at Washington's Camp, Nov. 20; Camp Cross Turtle Creek, Nov. 21; Bouquet's Camp, Nov. 23
Canada, (New France), 8, 14, 15, 16, 20, 21, 27, 65, 68, 70; events in, affect British colonies, 21; government of reorganized, 14, 15; lacked surplus colonists, 70; leadership riddled with graft, 66; linked with Louisiana, 20; little change in government of, 27; numerically and economically weak, 16, 65; part of the picture, 8; prominent figures of, 15; rivalry with British North America, 14; threatened by Oswego, 68; *see* New France
Cape Breton Island, (Fr. Isle Royale), 11, 40, 47, 67; captured by British in 1758, 40, 47, 67; Louisbourg on, 40, 47, 67; New England forces fight there, 11
Carlisle (Pa.), (Fort Lowther), 44, 45, 46, 47, 48, 54, 71, 95; Bouquet reaches it, 44, 45; first important post west of Lancaster, 44; Forbes leaves in mid-August, 48; Forbes makes it his headquarters in early July, 46; laid out in 1755, 44; road from Phila. to, old, 54, 71; wagons wanted at, 95
Carmack, Captain Jacob, retires as commandant at Fort Fayette and becomes tavern keeper, 188
Carolinas, 6, 12, 20, 22, 30, 31, 32; a fill in a gap, 12; cooperation asked by Dinwiddie, 30; frontier advance 20; governments stable, 35; governors consulted by Braddock, 32; Indian trade of, 6; lands troops to aid Virginia, 31

Casualties, 34, 50; at Battle of Loyalhanna, 50; at Braddock's Defeat, 34; at Grant's Defeat, 50
Cataraqui (Fort Frontenac), 15, 39, 40, 49; attack made in August, 1758, 40, 49; attack planned in early 1758, 39, 40; its capture an irreparable damage to French, 40; established by Comte de Frontenac, 15
Catholicism, 17, 102; dominant in New France, 17; introduced by French, 17; Papist mentioned, 102
Cattle, 45, 48, 71, 140, 174, 179, 182; at Raystown, 71; bullocks driven along with Burd in advancing to Loyal Hannon, 48; Bullock Pen at Point, 182; collected in 1763 at the Point, 174; cows break into gardens, 182
Celoron de Blainville, French Canadian, 26, 128, 189; claims the territory for France, 26; his map discussed, 128; his trip 1749, 189; makes a famous expedition 1749, 69; *D.A.B.*
Champlain, Samuel de, 14, 15, 68; becomes leader in New France, 1608, 14; death of, 15; Frontenac, a worthy successor, 15; route along lake, 68; *D.A.B.*
Charles II, 9, 12; continues Cromwellian economics, 9; "fills in gaps," 12; motives in seizing New Netherland, 12; rounds out British Empire, 12
Charleston (S.C.), 20, 42, 102; Bouquet called from to New York, 42; envied by French, 20; fur trade center, 20; its trade reaching to the Mississippi; recruiting at, 102
Chartiers Creek, 122, 151, 152, 153, 154; bordered by McKee's Rocks, site near often advocated for a fort, 122, 151, 152, 153, 154
Chautauqua Lake, (N.Y.), 27, 69; route abandoned by M. Marin, 27; vital part of first French route down the Allegheny, 27, 69
Cherokee Indians, aid asked by Forbes, 44
Chestnut Ridge, 52, 53, 54; westermost high ridge of the Appalachian System in Pennsylvania, 52, 53; reached November 14, 1758, roads over laid out, 54
Claims to ownership of the upper Ohio Valley, 21, 55, 66, 68, 69; possession vital to the French, 55, 66, 68, 69; problems of, arises 1730-40, 21
Clapham, Captain William, had an officer's house with three servants, 111
Clayton, Captain Asher, Pa. Reg't., reports on scouting trip westward from Raystown, 49
Clergymen with the military forces, 51, 61; Beatty, Bay and Steele, 51; follow traders, 61
Clothing and Equipment, 41, 104, 105, 106; Bouquet, Burd and Forbes mention shoes; 104; Highlanders in rags, 106; weight of carried by a Grenadier, 105
Coal, 84, 151; coal mine on fire, 151; Kenny mentions coal mine, 151; Mercer discovers coal across the Monongahela, 151; mine on Saw Mill Run, 151; outcroppings, 84
Cochrane, Captain Gavin, 93; comments on bad roads, 93
Coehorn, Menno (1641-1704) Baron, 76; Dutch inventor of the mortar, 76; legendary genius, 76
Colbert, Jean Baptiste, Marquis de Seignelay, great minister of Louis XIV; reorganizes New France, 17
Collot, Victor, 187; cited, 187; disparages Fort Fayette, 1796, 187
Colonial governments, 9, 10, 11, 12, 13, 14, 35; colonial development, 10-14; communication with Crown, 9; not upset by defeat of Braddock, 35
Commandant's House, 111, 130, 131, 169, 176; at Fort Duquesne, 130, 131; at Fort Pitt, 173, 176; General's House, Fort Pitt, 111; "Governor's House," 169
Commander-in-Chief of His Majesty's Forces in North America, 35, 37, 41; Abercromby succeeds Loudoun, 35; Amherst replaces Abercromby, 41; Braddock the first one, 37; changes after Braddock's death, 35; Loudoun succeeds Shirley, 37; most important position, 35, 37; Shirley takes over, 35
Conemaugh River (Pa.), 24, 51; Bouquet proposes to use it, 51; eyed by both Pennsylvanians and Virginians, 24
Conewango Creek (Pa.), 27, 69; outlet of Lake Chautauqua into French Creek and the Allegheny, 27, 69
Connecticut Colony, 8, 11; chartered corporate, 8; on territory of former Council for New England, 11
Conocockeague, Maryland, town on creek of same name, 49; agreement made there for Virginia and Maryland troops to use Braddock's Road, 49; Bouquet and Washington confer at June 12, 1758, 49
Contrecoeur, Claude Pierre Pecaudy, Sieur de, 27, 31, 125, 126, 127, 128, 131; arrives at the Forks, 125; commandant at Fort Duquesne, 1754-56, 31, 125, 126, 127, 128; comments on his artillery, 131; his papers recently published, 27; leads French to the

INDEX 209

Forks, 31; lodged within the fort, 131; prepares in 1755 to abandon fort, 128; receives surrender of Ward, 125; second in command in 1753, 27

Contrecoeur Papers; lately printed as *Papiers Contrecoeur*, 27, 127, 130, 134; cite cost of Fort Duquesne, 134; Fort Duquesne, 130; furnish little information about, 27; reveal French shrewdness, 127

Contributions to British American Success, 43; of the colonies; of the mother country, 43; naval, military, financial, 43

Council of Virginia, 23, 25; controlled land grants, 25; petition to it made by the Ohio Company in October, 1747, 25; petitions to it, 25; Thomas Lee a member, 25; with the governor, the executive and upper house of the legislature, 23, 25

Craig, Major Isaac; builds a stone powder magazine, 177; correspondence about fort, 1791, 188; Craig writes about new fort, 186; engages Turnbull and Marmie to make cannon balls, 186; resided later in Blockhouse, 177

Cresap, Thomas, 19, 22, 24, 25, 28, 122; alleged instigator of Ohio Company, 25; and the western boundary of Maryland, 22; authorized to start fort, 1753, 122; land surveys and speculation, 24; of Old Town, Maryland, 19; Ohio Company member, 25; on Monongahela in early 1753, 28; surveyor, 22, *D.A.B.*

Crisis, ultimatum, and rejection, 28, 29

Cromwell, Oliver; credited with establishment of British Empire, 12; his economic imperialism retained, 9; navigation ordinances under Cromwell continued for a century, 9; stabilized British imperialism, 9, *D.N.B.*

Crown Point, 12, 40, 68, 161; built by British, 1759, 68; constructed of limestone, 161; French stronghold in 1758, 40; New Englanders in attacks upon it, 12

Croghan, George, 24, 29, 97, 98, 109, 111, 114, 115, 117, 179; afraid of Indian attack on roads, 97, 98; condemned for excessive gifts to Indians, 117; dispenses liquor, 109; does flourishing trade, 114, 115; fur trader, 24; has house in Lower Town, 111; his old fields used for cattle pasturage, 179; his scale of prices, 114; in Fort Pitt social life, 109; pays Samuel Young for building house, 178; probably visited by Washington in 1753, 29; respected by Indians, 114, 115; western Pennsylvania land speculator, 24, *D.A.B.*

Cumberland, William Augustus, Duke of, 32, 36, 37, 42, 78; abandons military career, 37; commands in Hanover but defeated, 37; friend of Forbes, 42; his instructions to Braddock about forts, 78; imperial military chief, 32; son of George II, 32, *D.N.B.*

Cumberland, (Md.), 46, 49, 54; later name of early settlement on Wills Creek, 19; on Braddock's Road, 46; roads to projected from Shippensburg, Fort Frederick (Md.), and Raystown, 54; sometimes in need of equipment and supplies, 49; Virginians urge its use by Forbes, 46 *see* Fort Cumberland and Wills Creek

Cumberland County (Pa.), 1750, 19, 21, 26; early frontier county, 19, 21; valuable archives, 26

Cuming, Fortescue, English traveller, 188; praises the site of Fort Fayette, 188

Curtains of fort, 162, 165, 168, 172, 174

Dahlinger, Charles W., *Fort Pitt*, describes last days of Fort Pitt, 178

Davis, Mrs. Elvert M., 187; article on Fort Fayette, 187; describes Fort Fayette, 187

DeLancey, James, Gov. of N. Y., not unseated by military failures of 1755, 37; *D.A.B.*

Delaware (Lower Counties), 13, 14, 16, 24, 90; a grant of James Duke of York, 13; commonly called the Lower Counties 1781-1776, 14; contributions to colonial wars, 14; furnished troops to Forbes, 90; had an assembly 1701-1776, 14; once part of New Netherland, 13; and later of New York, 13; once part of Virginia, 22

Delaware River and Valley, 7, 13, 14, 18, 23; as related to Pennsylvania boundaries, 14, 18; frontier advance from, 18; in relation to eastern and western boundaries of Pennsylvania, 23; once under Dutch or Swedes, 7, 13

Denny, William, Governor of Pa., letter from Forbes asked for aid to Forbes in campaign, 42

Desertion and deserters, 107; at Venango, 107; Bouquet, 1759, writes Forbes about, 107; explicable, 107

Detroit, 4, 26, 63, 67, 116; a rude earth and log fort, 63; Campbell at, 116; important site along Great Lakes water route both to the east and the west, 4, 67; its inhabitants aware of British activities in the Ohio Valley, 26

Dinwiddie, Robert, Lt. Gov. of Va., 1751-

1758, 27, 28, 29, 30, 32, 90; gets bad news about French, 28; has continental outlook, 30; has lively correspondence, 30; influential in determining Braddock's route, 90; makes frantic appeal for imperial aid, 32; member of Ohio Company, 29; not unseated by military defeats of 1754-1755; reports regularly to London, 28; sends messenger to the French, 28, 29; *D.A.B.*

Divine service at the Forks, November 26, 1758, 55

Dobbs, Arthur, Gov. of N. C., 12, 26, 31, 35, 42, 45, 52; colonies, 12, 31, 42, 45, 52; consulted by Forbes, 42; early member of Ohio Campany of Virginia; not displaced as a result of imperial disasters, 35; in control in 1753, 26; *D.A.B.*, *D.N.B.*

Dudgeon, Robert (erroneous for Richard), engineer and draughtsman, 49, 88, 120; at Loyalhanning in 1758, 49, 88; drawing of Fort Pitt, 88; his survey of Pittsburgh in 1759, 120

Donellan, Lieut. John Ormsby, 108; quarrels and fights with Doctor Boyd, 108

Dulany, David (Md.), 24; used Thomas Cresap as surveyor, 24; western Maryland land speculation, 24; *D.A.B.*

Dumas, Jean Captain, 36, 155; signs old Fort plan, July 10, 1755, 155; succeded Beaujeu on the battlefield, 36, 155

Dunbar, Thomas Colonel, 33, 35; in command of one of Braddock's regiments, 33; left behind on the mountains, 35; retreats to seacoast, 35

Du Plessis, Ensign Victor, engineer, 87; favorite of Bouquet, 87; killed at Venango, 1760, 87

Duquesne, Marquis de, Sieur de Menneville; glowing prophecies all in vain, 190; instructs Contrecoeur, 127; plan defeated by low water, 98; plans fort at Forks, 126; sends out expedition of 1763 under M. Marin, 29, 124, 125; tries to avoid war, 125

Duquesne University Crest (old Ayres Hill), 154; once known as Ayres Hill for Colonel William Eyre, who recommended it as a site for the main fort, 154; *see* Ayres Hill

Dutch, 5, 6; fur trade, 6; fur trade with French Canadians; information from about Indians, 5; settlement, 6

Ecuyer, Captain Simeon (Simon), 63, 108, 109, 117, 165, 173, 174, 183; commandant at Fort Pitt, 1763, 165; condemns Indian gifts by Croghan,
117; criticism by Bouquet, of extensive forts, 63; describes Indian activity around fort, 183; measures of defense, 1763, 174; reports an insubordination at Bedford, 108; reports on sodding at fort, 173; work done at Fort Pitt, 1763, 165

Edmonstone, Captain Charles, later major, 178; makes minor repairs at Fort Pitt, 178

Engineering and engineers, 49, 52, 85, 86, 87, 88; engineering accounts, 86; engineers advise Forbes, Nov. 16, 1758, 52; engineers and draughtsmen, 86, 87, 88; English engineers bad before 1757 no military rank, 85; first as military designers, 85; Gordon, a highly valued engineer, 86; scarcity of engineers, 86; started by Vauban in his "Corps de Genie" 1690, 85; used on roads and bridges as well as upon forts, 86; with Burd at Loyal Hannon, 49

English, or (better still) British, 5, 6. 7, 8, 10, 32, 63-72, 76-79; build frontier forts, 63-72, 76-79; government and policy, 8; history of, 8; more prosperous than French colonials, 65; original American capital was English, 10; overseas support by, 32; rulers and dynasties

Erie Bay, 27, 28; discovered in 1753, 27; French at, 28; *see* Presque Isle

"Expresses" or messengers; important activity, 108; killed by Indians, 109; not often mentioned by name, 109

Eyre, Colonel William, 60, 87, 94, 153, 154, 172, 173; at Ticonderoga with Abercromby, 87; chief engineer, 60, 87; constructed Fort William Henry, 87; criticised mountain roads without diagonal drainage, 94; defended Fort William Henry, 87, 153; succeeded by Harry Gordon, 60, 87; recommends old Ohio Co. site for Fort Pitt, 154; recommends use of site on hill later known as Ayres Hill (site of Duquesne University), 154; visited and reported on Fort Pitt, 94, 172; was with Braddock, 87

Factors in the background of triumph at the Forks in 1758, 3, 5, 6, 7, 36

Fallen Timbers, Battle of, 63; Indians fought and defeated in their own style of fighting, 63

Filling in gaps in colonization, 12, 13

First English-speaking trans-Appalachian frontier, 30; located on lower Youghiogheny, 30

First Virginia Regiment, 30, 35, 43, 45, 47, 49, 52; Colonel Joshua Fry the first commander, 30; established in

INDEX 211

January 1754, 30; hurriedly raised, 30; lacked equipment and supplies, 30, 49; moved in 1758 to Forbes Road, 47; reached Fort Cumberland late in June, 45; reached Winchester in early June, 1758, 45; six companies of work on Forbes Road in June 1758
Five forts at the Forks, 59, 60, 119, 189; base of operations and symbols of intent, 189; involved military establishment for two generations, 189; varied military construction
Floods, 149, 152, 159, 169, 172, 173, 181; discussed by Eyre, 172; feared in 1759, 149, 152; in 1757, in 1762 and 1763, 159, 169, 182; in 1936, 159, 173; probably carried away gardens, 181; "siege of water," 169,f.
Florida, 12, 81; under Spanish, 12; gap, between Florida and Virginia, filled, 12; Lake and Coasts of West Florida explored by Gordon, 81
Forage, 44, 48, 96, 99; a problem, 44, 48, 96; bothers Forbes in August, needed for a march, 99
Forbes, General John, 33, 36, 38, 40, 41, 42, 43, 44, 45, 46, 47, 48, 49, 50, 51, 52, 53, 54, 55, 57, 60, 70, 71, 89, 90, 91, 94, 141; after a month in N.Y. moves to Phila., 42; arrives at Halifax in July 1757, 38; asks colonial governors for aid, 42; assembles about 6,000 men, 90; assumes responsibility for maintenance of Maryland, 45; at Halifax and N.Y. with Loudoun, 38; builds forts enroute, 70, 71; called Iron Horse by Indians, 57; campaign a distinct success, 54; decides on route across Laurel Ridge, 48; defends the cutting of a new road, 91; divides his forces into three brigades, 52; drab years preceding his campaign, 36; establishes relations with Abercromby, 42; follows the plan of advance with power, 33; friend of Loudoun, Cumberland, Ligonier and others, 42; gets 1600 men beyond Allegheny mountain, 48; gets some colonial support, 43; great aid to Loudoun, 38; had great aid from Bouquet, 40, 44; had Gordon with him, 60; halted a month at Shippensburg, 48, 49; his reputation based on his campaign, 41; his work made easier by capture of Fort Frontenac, 40; informs Abercromby about roads, 91; informed by Amherst that a blockhouse at the Point would suffice, 141; instructions to Bouquet, 45; leaves Phila. in early July, 46; letters from mentioned, 42, 43, 44; letters to mentioned, 91, 94; like Caesar he had to do all things at once, 42; made brigadier general in command of expedition, 36; moves over bad terrain, 70; news late in reaching him, 47; orderly book, 49; orders regulars and Pa. militia to Juniata Crossing, 46; pushes forward men and supplies, 43; reaches Carlisle and sends troops ahead, 46; reaches Fort Loudoun, 49; reaches Loyal Hannon, 51; reaches Raystown, 50; receives his appointment, 38, 42; records of campaign in Bouquet papers, 89; relationship with Bouquet, 54; remains at Carlisle until mid August, 48; renames Raystown, 71; retarded by Grant's defeat, 50; successful Indian diplomacy, 55; takes possession of ruins of Fort Duquesne, 53; testimony to his march, 55
Forbes Road, west from Bedford, 46, 47, 48, 49, 71; an immortal accomplishment, 54; astounded at St. Clair's proposal to abandon his route, 47; built in August and September 1758, 46, 48; decision to cross Pa. mountains, from Phila. west, 71; Forbes troops follow it, 49; map of on end paper, 71; projected in mid June 1758, 46
Forbes, Thomas, 130, 133-135; left an account, 130, 133-135; prisoner of French, 1754, 129-130
Forks of the Ohio (the Point); continuously guarded by forts, 1754-1815, 189; death of French civilization at, 141; Forbes occupied in 1758, 59, 67; fort begun February 1753, 29; goal of routes, 4, 70; like an arrow pointing at the heart of French power mentioned as terminus, 71; not entirely approved as site for fort, 151; occupied by French for four years, 70; Ohio Company fort started at, 29, 30, 69, 71; peaceful condition at, 1758-1763, 110; re-occupation by British Americans in 1758, 3, 40; site of five successive forts, 119; under obligation to Bradstreet
Fort Augusta (Pa.), site of later Sunbury, 86; built by Gordon, 86
Fort Bedford (Pa.), 46, 48, 54, 71, 91, 169; article begins with, 71; earlier Raystown, 71; of the simplest construction, palisade and ditch construction, 71; on Forbes route, 91; power at, damaged, 169; renamed in 1758, 54; temporary western base of advance of Forbes, 46, 48, 71
Fort Burd (Redstone Creek) (later Brownsville), 70, 97, 99, 124; a fortified depot for goods, 124; built in 1759, 70, 97; supplies at 1759 and 1764, 97; revisited by Bouquet, 99
Fort Carillon (British Ticonderoga), 68,

70; built to guard entrance to Lake Champlain, 68; captured in 1759 and renamed; drive against, 70; Lake Champlain, 68; Ticonderoga, 68

Fort Crown Point, 68, 161; built by Amherst 1759, 161; built near site of Fort Frederic, 68, 161; impressive ruins, 161; its circumference and size, 161

Fort Cumberland (Md.); garrisoned by Md. troops, 47; on Wills Creek and Potomac, 70, 94; rendezvous of Va. regiments, 47, 48; road begun to Raystown, 48; St. Clair proposes to march on its route, 49; supplies for in 1759 and 1764, 97; Va. proposes use of it by Forbes as a route, 48, 91

Fort Duquesne, 13, 20, 30, 31, 33, 35, 39, 46, 49, 50, 51, 52, 53, 60, 67, 69, 70, 80, 89, 91, 103, 119, 126, 127, 129, 135, 136, 137, 140, 141, 159, 161, 189; abandoned without defense, 129; a British objective, 39; a nest of robbers, 30, 35; an objective of Braddock, 33; a poor small fort, 128; approached by Braddock, 33; background of its fall, 13; begun in April 1754, 127; Braddock expected to march from against Niagara, 91; British made little use of the ruins, 141; buildings around, 135; built in 1754, 69; built on low level along Allegheny, 159; capture of, 7, 11, 31, 89; captured by Forbes, 69; cost of construction, 134; described, 128 following; deserted by Indians, 50; desperate situation at revealed, 151; destroyed and abandoned, 140; difficult to supply with building materials, 128, 189; diverted French power needed elsewhere, 128, 189; drawings of, 129; flooded in 1757, 134; Forbes advances upon, 51, 52; French troops depart, 51, 140; hurriedly constructed in 1754, 30, 127; Indian allies depart, 35; in territory claimed as of Augusta Co., Va., 20; its last days described by Vaudreuil, 137; last vestige of in 1786, 140; mentioned, 103; not a star fort, 161; objective of Forbes, 70; nearly reached by Grant, 49; palisaded wall, 80, 119; partly protected by mountains east of, 65; planned in 1753, 126; raids from against frontiers, 35; reported as burning, 53, 140; route to it disputed, 46; scouted by British Americans, 47; second fort at, 60, 136; supplied by water transportation, 89; supplied from Quebec and Illinois, 67; timber and earth fort, 119; under Contrecoeur in 1754-1755, 31; scouts go from 1755, 33; water attack upon projected by Bouquet, 51

Fort Fayette, 60, 119, 184, 186, 187, 188, 189, 191; a bastioned stockade with blockhouses, 119; an expression of fear, 191; construction ordered 1792; headquarters for supplies for Perry in 1812, 188; described in a newspaper, 186; demand for protection, 1785-92, 184; epilogue limit, 189; few extant drawings, 137, its location, 186; of little historical or architectural importance, 60; work on started 1791, 186

Fort Frontenac (Indian Cataraqui); American attack (1758), 39; Canadian life line at, cut in 1758, 165; capture aided Forbes, 67; captured Aug. 1758, 47; important objective of British; its capture elates Forbes, 50; strengthened foothold of New France, 20

Fort LeBoeuf, (present Waterford, Pa.), 27, 28, 70, 93, 123; abandoned after the battle of Niagara, 70; camp and fort of French on route from Presque Isle to Venango, 27; Indians carry information about French at, 28; road to corduroyed, 93; Washington at, 31, 123

Fort Ligonier (earlier Loyal Hannon), 51, 63, 71, 76, 77, 78, 80, 106; articles found in reconstruction, 120; attacked by French and Indians, 63; bad conditions at, 106; begun, 71; conference at, 76; fascines at, 80; last advanced post of Forbes, 51; "post of passage," 71; reconstruction of by Stotz, 79; rude fortification, 63; site of changed at last moment, 76-78; typical palisade wall at, 80

Fort Loudoun, Pa. (variously spelled), 44, 45, 46, 49, 71, 97, 102, 117; Bouquet reaches it in June, 45; Forbes reaches it late in August, 49; important post on eastern side of Tuscarora Mountain, 71; Indian conference at, 117; recruits to muster at in 1764, 102; supplies to be delivered at in 1764, 97

Fort Machault (Pa.), 69, 70, 125, 144, 149; abandoned after battle of Niagara, 70; basis for projected attack on Pittsburgh, 144; built by French in 1753; French assemble at 1759, 149; on site of modern Franklin, 69; springboard for advance to Forks, 125

Fort Necessity, (Fayette Co., Pa.), 31, 70, 129; captured by de Villiers, July 4, 1754, 31; hurriedly built by Washington in 1754, 70; Stobo captured at, 129

Fort Niagara; built in 1726 at old post of 1679, 67, 82, 107, 149, 150; be-

INDEX

213

sieged in 1759, 67, 82; fascine construction at, 82; fell to English, 67; Fort Little Niagara, 67; French concentration for its defense, 67; probably saved attack on Pittsburgh, 149; scurvy at, 107; the necessity of its defense in 1759, 150

Fort Oswego, (N. Y.), 37, 47, 68, 69, 161; a star fort, 161; attacked and captured by Montcalm, 1756, 69; built in 1722, 68; on Lake Ontario at mouth of Oswego, 68; protected by Iroquois, 68; rebuilt by the English in 1759, 69

Fort Pitt, 8, 59, 60, 76, 78, 82, 83, 86, 94, 96, 97, 106, 110, 119, 152, 153, 155, 156, 157, 158, 159, 161, 165, 169, 173, 174, 175, 178, 179, 191; a good and sufficient fort, 59, 76; a most elaborate work, 60, 78, 161, 179, 191; a part of Forbes program, 59; a plan of construction was necessary in 1759, 155; activities at, 169; and the Gentlemen Adventures, 8; an exception, 76; bad conditions in 1759, 106; begun September 3, 1759, 165; besieged by Indians 1763, 174; Bouquet asked Mercer to seek a better site, 152; Bouquet, in 1763, orders three redoubts, 175; buildings decay, 175; built by Harry Gordon, 60, 86, 156-157; built only partly of masonary, 83, 119; census of 1760, 110; change in 1763 urged by Amherst, 173; complete reconstruction inadvisable, 158; earthworks sodded, 82; excavation showed fort corresponding to early drawings, 121; heyday passed in late 1763, 175; inspected by Eyre, 94; its cost, highly conjectural, 178-179; largely a dirt fort, 158, 161; Mercer and Robertson examine and recommend McKees Rocks, 152; Mercer depicts defects of the Point as a site, 152; motley colony at, 110; name of fort not on recently found map, 155; not a star fort, 161; not on site of Mercer's fort, 152; on higher ground than Fort Duquesne, 159; one redoubt became "Blockhouse," 176; only restoration will be two bastions, 119; packhorses used to reach it in 1763, 96; so-named November 1759 by Stanwix, 165; pentagonal shape well adopted to Point, 159; Ratzer not the planner, 155; site condemned by engineers in 1762, 153; Stanwix rejects plan to use another site, 153; Stotz finds the plan, probably of 1755, 155, 156; supplies to be delivered at 1759 and 1764, 97; three wells within, 83

Fort Prince George (possibly St. George), 30, 59, 69, 119, 121, 122, 123, 124, 125, 126; a military post, 126; a stockade, 125-126; a storehouse of squared logs, 119; a tiny fortified storehouse, 156; captured, 69; early proposal of Ohio Co., 125; epilogue, boundary, 189; first of five forts at the Point, 59; named supposedly for prince who became George III, 124; more than merely an Ohio Co. trading post, 121-126; taken and destroyed, 30; Trent started construction in February 1754, 124

Fort William Henry (N. Y.), 68, 70, 80; built in 1756 at southern end of Lake George, 68; captured by the French, 70; destroyed by Montcalm in 1757, 68; replaced by Fort George, 1759, 68; typical log and dirt wall, 80; walls impervious to artillery, 80

Forts (other, French and English), 29, 44, 45, 46, 54, 66, 67, 68, 69, 70, 71, 87, 130, 136, 137, 144, 161, 165; Beau Sejour, on Bay of Fundy, 66, 67; Brewerton, a star fort, 161; Chambli, on Richelieu River, 68; Chartres in Illinois, 67, 87; Cumberland, on Bay of Fundy; Detroit, 67; Edward (N. Y.), built by Gordon in 1756 at headwaters of Hudson River, 68, 86, 144; Frederick (N. Y.), at southern end of Lake Champlain, 68, 70; Frederick (Md.), garrisoned by Mr. troops, 45; George, near site of Fort William Henry, 68; Herkimer, built in 1756, 68; Lawrence, (N.S.), 67; La Gallette, on St. Lawrence, 67; Littleton, on Forbes Route, 44, 46, 54; Lowther (Carlisle, Pa.), 71; McHenry, bastion of stone, 165; Ontario on Oswego River, large but inferior to Fort Pitt, 69, 130, 161; Presque Isle, built in 1753 and abandoned by French 1759, 29, 70; Quebec, first fort 1541, 67; St. Jean, upper Lake Champlain, 68; second French fort at Forks, 136, 137; Stanwix, (1758), 68; Vincennes (on Wabash), 67

Fraser, John (Pa.), 24, 28, 29; according to his commission, looks after his private business, 125; cabin in Turtle Creek, visited and revisited by Washington in winter of 1753-7, 54, 29; fur trader and gunsmith, located at Venango, as early as 1742, 28; his place taken by the French in 1753, 28; land speculator, 24; on Turtle Creek in late 1753, 30, 125; second in command at Point in 1754

Frederick, (Md.), 19, 32; early frontier town, 19; on route followed by Braddock, 32; settlers from Pennsylvania,

19
Frederick County (Md.), 19, 21; early frontier county, 19, 21
Frederick County, (Va.), 19, 21; erected, 1748, 19; one of the two early Shenandoah Valley Virginia counties, 21
Frederick II (the great) of Prussia, 39; his brilliant campaign of 1757 saves the situation, 39
Fortification and fort construction, 44, 46, 49, 59, 71, 73, 79, 83, 101, 152; at Forks asked by Indians, 121; at Juniata Crossings, 46; at Loyal Hannon, 49, 71; at Raystown, 44, 46, 71; description of frontier fort as type, 79; five forts at the forks, 152; fortified castles and towns in Europe, 73; the usual frontier fort of earthwork and timbers, 59
Forts, as frontier defense, 37, 63, 79, 89, 119; built in haste, 79; built in 1758, 89; exceptional one at Forks, 78; erected against French rather than against Indians, 63
Fox, Henry, Sec. of War, under George II, 34, 38; uprooted 1756, 38
France, 7, 8, 11, 14, 20, 21, 69, 73; allies (1740–45), 20; disorganized and weak, but rich, 14; early nationalism, 7; has little doubt of success, 69; its imperialism begins in 16th cent., 14; leads in military science, 73; makes inroads on Spanish claims, 14; New England opposition to, 11; Old France and New France, 8, 14; trans-Appalachian claims, 21
Franklin (Pa.), 29, 30; French site of old Venango and Fort Machault, 29, 30
French, 5, 6, 12, 15, 16, 20, 26, 28, 29, 30, 31, 37, 40, 50, 51, 54, 62, 69, 114, 126, 156, 190; abandon Fort Duquesne, 53; alert in 1754, 156; at Fort Duquesne, 29; at Niagara, Erie, Fort Le Boeuf and Venango, 30; attacked by New Englanders, 15; break up British trade in 1753, 114; capture Fort Prince George, 126; capture Oswego, 37; claims to upper Ohio Valley, 16; come down the Allegheny River, 30; communications damaged by British navy, 37; defeat attack of Abercromby, 40; dispirited by result of battle of the Loyalhanna, 51, expedition in response to Ohio Col., 26-28; French civilization at Forks, 69; furnish information about Indians, 5; get ready to seize the Forks, 28; good relations with Indians, 62; have many forts, 66-69; in Louisiana, 12; lose Indian allies, 50; losses at Loyal Hannon, 50; move early in 1754, 124; offer no opposition at Fort Duquesne, 54; overreached themselves south of Great Lakes, 190; political confusion and weakness, 14; political consolidation, 1589, 14; posts eventually all lost, 40; reject ultimatum of British, 29; repel attack upon Fort Duquesne, 50; reported weak at Fort Duquesne, 51; rival of Dutch in fur trade, 6; scout Braddock's advance, 33; sent force against Loyal Hannon, 50; settlement, 14, 65; suffer fatal loss at Cataraqui, 40; take counter measures, 20; trappers, traders, military personnel and priests, their expulsion did not restore Indian trade, 44; under Contrecoeur at Fort Duquesne, 31
French Creek (Pa.), 98, low water on defeats plan of 1753, 98
French and Indian War, 1751-1763, 10, 13, 28, 34, 49, 61, 70; a picturesque episode, 61; Braddock attacked, 34; formal declaration of war, 1756, 10; known in Europe as the Seven Years War, 10; Pa. contrib., 13; repel Grant's attack on Fort Duquesne, 49; said to have begun at Venango, 28
French Kings, 16
Frontenac, the Camte de, 15, 26, 27; build Fort Frontenac and navy on Lake Ontario, 15; governor of Canada, 1672-81, 15; great figure of New France, 15; Lake Ontario, 15; long trip from, to Niagara, 27; Ohio Co. matters known, 26
Frontier advance, 17, 18, 19, 31, 35, 128; advance, 1700-1750, 17; coastal and tide-water, 17; frontier forts, 1756-1758, 35; frontiersmen on the defensive, 1754-55, 31; in New England, 18; significant in Pa., Mr., Va., 18, southwest from Pa. into Md., Va., N. C., 18; trans-Piedmontese Virginia advance, 19; Virginia transmountain advance diverts French strength from the northeast, 128; wide open to attack 1755-58, 35
Fry, Colonel Joshua, 30, 31; dies on the frontier, 31; first commander of the First Virginia Regiment, 30; succeeded by Col. George Washington, 31
Fur trade and traders, 6, 12, 14, 15, 20, 61, 69, 113, 117, 119; actors in the drama, 6, 61; a great activity, 114; antedates soldiers, 61; Carolina trade, 12; French Canadian, 15; French dislike growth of rival trade, 20, 69; integrity in fur trade, 117; in the Carolinas, 13, 113; made the Indian economically dependent, 61; monopoly

INDEX 215

in New France, 14; on Hudson River, 6; on St. Lawrence River, 6; once lively, 117; Pa. Commissioners establish stores at forts, 114; reorganized by Colbert, 15; some wampum manufactured commercially, 113; the fall buck, the standard of fur values, 113; variety of goods handled, 119; wampum used as currency, 113

Gage, Lieutenant Colonel Thomas, 34, 120, 157, 177; advised by Johnson to abandon frontier forts, 177; complains of costs of forts, 120; decides to retain Fort Pitt, 177; his squad thrown into confusion, 34; informed of decay at Fort Pitt, 177; led advance of Braddock on the day of defeat, 34, 157, *D.A.B.*

Galissoniere, Comte de, 27; sent out Celoron, 1749, 27; succeeded by the Marquis de Jonquiere, 27

Gardens and Gardening, 112, 135, 136, 140, 143, 167, 179, 180, 181, 182; at Fort Duquesne, 140; at Fort Pitt, 167; at Point, 179; at Mercer's Fort, 143; Bouquet orders Mercer to large gardens, 180; flourish in 1762, 182; for food and forage, 179; food and forage brought in, 180; gardens near Fort Pitt, 180-81; H. H. Brackenridge in 1786 recalled orchards and gardens of earlier origin, 185; Kings Garden, 112; little information about garrison gardening after 1764, no mention of flowers, 179; renewed in 1764, 183; threatened by locusts and grasshoppers, 184; vegetable gardens, 180; Zodok Cramer in 1808 recalled orchards, 184

George, the Second, King, His Majesty, etc., 32, 36, 59

Georgia, 6. 12, 18, 20; at first proprietary, later royal colony, 12; Indian trade, 6; role in filling in a gap, 12; southern frontier advance, 18, 20

Gist Christopher, 26, 29, 31, 122; authorized to start fort, 122; explorer, 26; his place visited by Washington, on trip of 1753-54, 29, 31, 122; messenger to Indians, 26; *D.A.B.*

Glen, James, Gov. of S. C., 26, 35; in control, 1753, 26; not upset by Braddock's defeat, 35

Gooch, William, Gov. of Va., 25, 29; in office until 1749, 29; refers Ohio Company petition to the government in London, 25; *D.A.B.*

Gordon, Captain Harry, 49, 60, 86, 87, 99, 117, 120, 144, 148, 153, 156, 157, 162, 166, 167, 168, 177, 178; advises Mercer to use axes to cut frozen ground, 144, 148; after inspection 1766, suggests repairs, 178; agreed with Stanwix that dirt forts were preferable, 162; chief engineer at Pittsburgh 1759, 60, 153, 157; comments on lurking Indians, 117, 120; commissioned engineer, 1756, 156; conference at Loyal Hannon, 60; dedication to, 60; designed four forts, 86; discusses batteaux, 99; explored coasts of West Florida and Hudson River route, 87; his extensive voyages and journeys, 87; his financial accounts, 178; his inadequate reward, 87; makes full report, 168; makes progress on fort, 166; makes trips east for men and supplies, 167; mentions surveys of Pittsburgh, 120; orders stoppage of further work on Fort Pitt, 177; praised by Bouquet, Burd and others, 86; probably designed place of fort as found in Braddock's papers, 156, 157; ranks in importance with Forbes and Bouquet, 60; surveyed courses of the Ohio and of the upper Mississippi, 87; thought well of old Ohio Co. site on Chartiers Creek, 153; was with Braddock, 60, 156; worked on fort at Loyal Hannon, 49

Governors of Canada, *see* Duquesne, Galissoniere and Vaudreuil

Grant, Major James, 48, 49, 141; his men killed in September, buried in November, 141; reports of French weakness at Fort Duquesne induce him to advocate a surprise attack in mid September, 49; sent to Loyal Hannon with Col. James Burd, 48

Grant, Captain William, 175, 176, 184; complimented by Bouquet on his work at Fort Pitt, on fort and gardens, 183; reports extensive crops in 1764, 184; reports on redoubts at Fort Pitt, 175-176; writes Bouquet about gardening, 184

Grant's Defeat, September 14, 1758, 49, 50, 63; attack on Fort Duquesne repelled, 49, 50; injured others, 50; Indians in, 63

Grant's Hill, 112, 155, 181; blockhouse for advocated, 155; gardens extend to, 181; houses on its slope as early as 1763, 112; site of the defeat of Major Grant in September 1758, 112

Great Lakes; the Upper, 4, 16, 17, 21, 64, 87, 89; affairs on, affect English colonies, 21; area claimed by the Iroquois, 17; British-Americans south of, 16; Canadian shores described by Gordon, 87; center from which came various overland routes to the Forks of the Ohio, 4; on French are, 64; used

as water route, 89
Great Meadows, (Fayette Co., Pa.), 32; hit upon as a military base by Washington, 32
Griswold, Ralph, landscape architect, 158; makes study for a park at the Point, 1945, 158

Hagerstown (Md.), 18, 24; early frontier town, 18, 24; settlers from Pennsylvania, 18
Half King (Tanacharison Seneca Indian), 124, 125, 126; at the Point, February 1754, 124, 125, 126
Halifax, Lord, 90, 91; insists on Braddock effort against Niagara by way of New York, 90-91
Hamilton, James, gov. of Pa., 13, 28, 35, 43; has trouble with his legislature, 13; in office, 1753, 28; not unseated by military trouble, 35; throws his support to imperial troops, 43, *D.A.B.*
Hampton, Va., 34; Braddock arrives there in 1755, 34; troops not landed but sent north, 34
Harmar, General Josiah, 185; defeated by Indians 1790, 185, *D.A.B.*
Harris Ferry (Pa.) (modern Harrisburg), 71; road from Philadelphia to Carlisle built before 1758, 71
Haslet, John, 137; describes ruins at Point, November, 1759, 137
Highlanders, 37, 41, 44, 46, 52, 90, 101, 106, 148; five companies sent to Loyal Hannon, 46; in bad condition at Fort Pitt, 1759, 106; in Montgomery's brigade, 52; lose themselves in the woods, 101; Montgomery's Battalion arrives in June, 44; Scottish regiments under Pitt, 37; sent from Carlisle to Juniata Crossings; the bravest men, 101; to be marched to Carlisle, 44; under Forbes, 90; under Montgomery, thirteen companies, 41, 44, 46
Historiography, regional and local; often an element of national history and sometimes of universal history, 3
Hogan, John, 131; prisoner, left a description of Fort Duquesne, prisoner in 1757, 130, 131
Hogg's Pond, (on site of Kaufmann's Store), 135; drained by stream to Monongahela, 135
Hoops, Adam, 96, 97, 103; brought supplies from Virginia by Braddock's Road, 96, 97; invites Bouquet to be his guest, 97; principal contracts for conveying food and supplies, 96, 103
Horses, 45, 71, 91, 93, 94, 95, 97, 98, 118, 136, 179, 180
Hospitals, 46, 111, 134; at Fort Duquesne, 134; at Fort Pitt, 1761, 111;

"General Hospital" at Bedford, 46
Houses, 110, 111, 112, 130, 131, 143, 161, 167, 169, 172, 178
Howe, Lord, George Augustus, third Viscount, 39, 40; killed at Ticonderoga in 1758, 40; young commander promoted by Pitt, 39, *D.A.B.*
Hudson River, 4, 6, 13, 18, 35, 38, 40, 68, 87; Dunbar marches back to, 35; frontier advances to its sources, 18; fur trade along, 6; *Half-Moon* built at junction, 68; Hudson-Mohawk Route, 68; important in frontier war, 38; large military forces, upon, 40; natural route to the St. Lawrence and by the Mohawk River, west and northwest to the Great Lakes, 4, 13, 64; Route of Abercromby in 1758; Surveyed by Gordon, 87
Hughes, Barnabas, 98; partner of Robert Callender as contractor for horses, 98; puts out list of horses killed or taken, 98
Hundred Associates, 15; French Canadian fur monopoly, 1627, 15
Huntington Library, San Marino, California, 155, 156, 157; maps and drawings, 155; valuable anonymous map. 155, 157
Hutchins, Lieutenant Thomas, 87, 88, 143, 149, 175, 176; describes redoubts at Fort Pitt, 175, 176; drawing of Bushy Run, 88; drew plan of old Fort Machault; his papers in H.S.F., 143; illustrator, 87; left map of Mercer's Fort, 143; map maker, 88; prepared a drawing of Fort Pitt, 87, *D.A.B.*

Illinois, 20, 50, 64, 67, 89, 136; French forces at, strengthened, 20; guarded by lake forts, 67; inadequate population; 20; in French arc, 64; sends supplies to Fort Duquesne, 89, 136; the "breadbasket" of New France, 20; under French, 20
Independent Companies, 30, 32, 35; follow Dunbar in retreat, 35; late in reaching frontier, 32; occupy key positions, 30; regular troops, colonially recruited, and stationed at key positions in colonies, 32; their aid sought by Va., 30
Indian Relations; Bouquet formulated a policy for Amherst, 115; Communications attacked, 117; Forbes successfully negotiated with Delawares, 55; great expenses involved, 115-116; Indian type of warfare, 101; smallpox inoculation, 118; white intrusion on unceded lands, 115, 116; Whites began to hate them, 118
Indians, a sinister legend, 99, 115, 116; an additional hazard, 99; beautiful

INDEX

names, 118; Bouquet's recommendation on Indian policy, 115; claim to lands, 6; conference at Fort Loudoun, 46; did not trouble building of Forbes Road, 93; disliked both French and English, 99, 115; first Americans, 4; fur trade credit structure, 112,; idle Indians at Fort Pitt, 1759, 167; idle Indians consume Trent's supplies, 125; Indian fighting described by Bouquet, 100; Indian trade often on free enterprise basis, 112; Iroquois Indians important in American history, 5, 64; Neutrality, 1701-1709, 19; Ohio Valley Indians, 21, 28, 31; on warpath in Ohio, 103; raids on frontier after 1755, 35; scout in Appalachians, 117, siege of Fort Pitt, 1763, by Indians, 174; smuggling, 112; storehouses and conference houses constructed at the Forks, 113, 148; their numbers, 5; trading carried on at forts and posts, 113; trans-Appalachian claims, 21; with French at the Point, 1754, 30, 31

Indian siege, 1763; attack cattle, 183; interrupt gardening, 183

Insubordination, 107, 108; a common problem, 107; on road from Bedford, 108

Irvine, General William, repairs roofs, etc., at Fort Pitt, 178, *D.A.B.*

James (Stuart), Duke of York, later King James II, given claim to New Netherland, 12; grants other colonies, 13

Johnson, Sir William, 34, 35, 37, 44; able to use Indians successfully, 34; criticised by Forbes, 44; his success in 1755 no offset for Braddock's defeat, 35; unfriendly relations with Shirley, 37; *D.A.B.*

'Jonquiere, Marquis de, gov. of New France 1749-52, predecessor of Duquesne, 27

Jumonville, Joseph Coulon de, 31, 61; escape of one of his men, 31; French military figure killed by Indians and Virginians in 1754 at Jumonville's Glen, 31; episode, 61

Juniata Crossings, 46, 94; a stockade, raft and fording, 94; fort begun by Captain Harry Gordon, 46; military post east of Loyal Hannon; reached by Bouquet before June 22, 46

Kenny, James, 114, 143, 150, 151, 160, 165, 169; comments on building, 165; comments on coal mine, 151; comments on panic of June 1759, 150; had store in 1759, 143; his journal mentioned, 143, 160, 161, 162; kept a store at Fort Pitt, 114; mentions activity at Fort Pitt, 169

Keppel, Augustus, Admiral, 1st Viscount, convoys troopships of Braddock, 32

Kiskiminetas River, Bouquet proposes its use as route, 51

Kittanning (Pa.), county seat of Armstrong Co., expedition against it, 1756, 35

Knox, Henry, Secretary of War, 185, 186; a blockhouse for 100 men, 185; advises Mifflin about the new fort, 185; issues order to Major Isaac Craig to build palisades; ordered by Washington to build a new fort at the Forks, 185; writes Craig to select site, 185, 186, *D.A.B.*

La Belle Riviere, name applied by the French to the Allegheny and its continuation the Ohio as far as the Wabash, 140

Lake Champlain, 13, 20, 37, 40, 64, 68; attack on forts there, 1758, 40; French strengthens footholds, 20; objective, in 1756 of troops under Loudoun, 37; on French water route, 64, 68; on strategic communication, 13

Lake Chautauqua (N.Y.), part of old French route down the Allegheny, *see* Chautauqua

Lake Erie, 21, 27, 67, 69; on Quebec-Illinois route, 69; post, 67; 250 feet higher than Lake Ontario, 27; vital link in navigation and trade route, 21

Lake George (French Lake Sacrament), 13, 37, 40, 41, 64, 68, 80; an objective in 1756 of troops under Loudoun, 37; attack on French forts 1758, 40; entrance defended by Carillon, 68; Fort William Henry, 80; on strategic communication, 13

Lake Le Boeuf (modern Waterford), road to, 69; *see* Fort Le Boeuf

Lake Ontario, 27, 49, 68; Fort Frontenac captured in August, 1758, 40, 49; Fort Oswego built upon, 68; on French route westward from Montreal, 27

L'Allee la Vierge (later Virgin Way) (Oliver Avenue), first street named in Western Pennsylvania, 136

Lancaster County (Pa.), 1750, 19, 24, 54; early frontier county, 19; its archives, 24; road from Philadelphia to, an early one, 54

Lancaster (Pa.), Treaty of 1744, 23, 44; early post of Bouquet, 44; the land cession clause, 23

Land, 23, 24, 115; companies, 23, 24; Indian claims to, 115; purchases, 23; speculation, 23; titles, 23

Langdale, John; regent for the Pennsyl-

vania store, writes about gordens at Fort Pitt, 1761, 181
LaSalle, Robert Cavelier, Sieur, 15, 16, 67; claim of discovery of La Belle Riviere in 1669, discredited, 16; his alleged discovery lay at root of territorial dispute in 1679, founds post at Niagara, 67; made amazing voyages, 15; promoted establishment of La., 16; *D.A.B.*
Laurel Ridge, next ridge of importance to the west of Allegheny Mountains, 47, 49, 54, 70
Lee, family, interested in frontier and transmontane lands, 25; rivals of Beverly and Patton, 25
Lee, Thomas, 23, 25, 27, 48; president of Va. Council 1749, 27, 48; probable instigator of the Ohio Company of Va., 25; Virginia representative at the Treaty of Lancaster, 1744, 23
Le Mercier, Francois Chevalier, engineer, 129; probably built Fort Duquesne, 129
Lewis, Andrew, Captain, 31; commander of Augusta Co. Va. troops in Spring of 1754, 31; sent to cut road to mouth of Redstone Creek, 31; *D.A.B.*
Léry, Joseph Gaspard, Chaussegros de, 128, 129, 130, 134, 135; comments on houses at Fort Duquesne, 123; comments on defense of fort, 135; engineer, 128; left a poor map, 129; Mount Washington, 134, 135; on vulnerability, 134; not an engineer, 130; reported in 1755 on Fort Duquesne, 128; reports unfavorably on needs of Fort Duquesne, 128, 130, 131; *D.A.B.*
Ligneris, (Deligneris), Francois Le Marchand, Sieur de, commandant at Fort Duquesne, 51, 129; 137, 140; abandons the fort, 140; gives numbers of men sent against Loyal Hannon, 51; last French commandant at Fort Duquesne, 140; makes repairs at Fort Duquesne, 139; prepares to retreat, 137
Ligonier, (Loyal Hannon), name given by Forbes to Loyal Hannon, first named Pittsburgh, 71, 97, 144, 169; Indians attack his convoy, 97; powder at, damaged, 169; supplies to be delivered in 1759 and 1764, 97; surrounded by retrenchments, 71; threatened by French, 1759, 144
Logstown (Pa.) (French Chiningue), 29, 121; treaty of 1751, 121; *see* Chiningue; visited by George Washington on his trip to Fort Le Boeuf, 29
Lougueil, Jaques Charles Lemoine Baron de; expedition of 1739, 20, 69

Lords of Trade, largely a committee of the Privy Council, 11; reorganized as the Board of Trade and Plantations, 1696, 11
Loudoun, John Campbell, Fourth Earl of, 35, 36, 37, 38; appointed gov. of Va. February 17, 1750; succeeds William Shirley as commander in chief, 35, 37; arrives in New York, 37; expedition against Quebec falls short, recalled, 37-38; finds conditions chaotic, 36; Forbes winds up his affairs, 44; had assured maintenance of Md. troops, 47; friend of Forbes, 44; furnished a place for attack upon Fort Frontenac; gets into difficulties with fellow commanders of troops, 37; plans attack on Louisbourg and Quebec, 38; replaced by Abercromby, 35, 38
Louisbourg (Louisburg), great French stronghold; attack planned against, 1757, 38; attacked under Amherst, 70; captured by New Englanders, 21; its capture furnishes a base for British attack on Quebec, 47; objective of campaign of 1758, 40; of masonry type, 78; on Isle Royal (Cape Breton Island), outer defense of Quebec and Montreal, returned to France, 21
Louisiana, 20, 21, 39; French power at strengthened, 21; route linking it with Quebec, 20; southern end of global conflict, 39
Lower Town, along the Allegheny, 159, 172; demolished in 1763, 174; gardens in, 184
Loyalhanna Creek, 51, 84, 94; Bouquet proposes to follow it, 51; bridge over, 94; dammed for water power, 84
Loyalhanna, the Battle of, 50, 51; a final desperate French effort, 50; an inglorious battle, 50, 51; description of, 51; in the nature of a counter attack, October 12, 1758, 50; possibly the climax of the struggle, 50
Loyal Hannon (variously spelled), 47, 48, 49, 50, 51, 52, 53, 94; attacked, 52; safe after battle, 51; bridge at, 94; Burd arrives, September 3, 49; colonial troops march through, 47; Forbes and Bouquet decide to cross mountains to, 47; Forbes reaches, 53; Grant marches from, 49; Grant's stragglers return to, 50; its occupation projected in late August, 48
Loyal Land Company, of Virginia, important in annals of southwest Va., later W. Va. and Kentucky, 24

McClure, Reverend David, in his diary discusses abandonment of Fort Pitt,

INDEX

1772, 191
McGowen, Philip, 98; driver, killed near Stoney Creek, 98
McKees Rocks, 29, 123, 151; described by George Washington, 123; described on George Mercer's map, 122; inspected by Mercer and Robertson, 151; inspected in 1753 by Washington, 29, 123; on Chartiers Creek, 123; once an Indian fort, 122; selected as early site for fort, 122
McKinney. John, 129, 130, 131, 133, 134, 136; comments on Fort Duquesne, 130, 131, 133, 134, 136; comments on Mount Washington, 135; comments on source of supplies, 136; left a description of Fort Duquesne published in *Papiers Contrecoeur*, 139; prisoner of French, 129
McNeil, Donald J., traffic engineer, makes study for Regional Planning Association 1945, 158
Maine, 10, 11, 17, 18; began as propriety colony, 8; northern frontier adcance, 17-18; once territory of Council for New England, 11
Mal Enguelee, French name and spelling of Monongahela, 140; *see* Monongahela River
Marin, Pierre Paul, 27, 69; difficult trip in 1753, 27; discovers a better route, by way of Erie Bay, 69; French commander of expedition of 1753 against British Americans of Ohio Valley, 27
Marinism, on sea, similar to militarism on land, 7, 8; began under Henry VII, 7; under Elizabeth I, 8
Maryland, 6, 8, 11, 12, 19, 21, 22, 23, 24, 30, 31, 32, 35, 36, 44, 45, 46, 47, 52, 55, 90; a propriety colony, 8; along Potomac, 11; boundary claims, 21; Braddock moves through, 32; chartered as proprietory colony 1632, 11; does not maintain her troops, 46; frontier threatened, 35; furnishes little support to Forbes, 44; gap between and New England, 12; government in, 21; her cooperation asked in 1754, 30; in G. W.'s brigade, 52; its militia in bad shape, 45; Indian trade, 6; its charter, 11; land speculation parallels that in Va., 24; frontier on the defensive, 31; model for later land acquisition, 23; settlement and trade, 6; settlers from Pa., 19
Massachusetts Bay, 6, 8, 11; chartered corporate, 8; old part of empire, 8; Pilgrims settle and trade, 6; strongest New England colony a model, 11; territory from Council for New England, 11
Mercer, George, 31, 43, 45, 122; aids in road cutting, June, 1754, 31; made Ohio Co. map, 122; regiment not ready until June, 45; remarks on the map, 122; second in command of Second Virginia Regiment, 43; with Washington in 1754, 31
Mercer, Doctor Hugh, colonel in Pennsylvania militia, 120, 141, 144, 146, 150, 151, 180; advised by Bouquet, 144, 146; correspondence with Bouquet, 141; feared French attack, 144; food and supplies low, 144; hurries construction, 144; Indians use his supplies, 144; lacked forage and pasturage, 180; left in command at Pittsburgh in December 1758, 141; mentions Plan of Pittsburgh, 120; explores natural resources, 151; reports on situation in July 1759, 150; searches for a better fort site, 151, 152; *D.A.B.*
Mercer's Fort, 1758-59, 60, 67, 86, 119, 140, 141, 142, 143, 146, 150, 151, 152, 166, 190; built quickly, 144; description of, 142; desined by Gordon, 86; designated on map, 142; four drawings survive, 143; fortunately escaped French attack, 152; historical account, 140; in danger in June 1759, 150; mainly log houses, 119; merely improvised shelter, 190; no formal name, but so designated on map, 142; of great historical importance, 151; site of along Monongahela, a thousand feet west of Point, 142; temporary, 60, 67, 142; used to house workers on Fort Pitt, 166; work on it stopped in July, 151
Meyer, Elias, 88, 115, 135, 157, 159, 181; engineer, surveying for a drawing of Fort Pitt, by William Twiss and for the environs, 88, 115, 135, 157; excavations indicated his accuracy, 159; depicts gardens, 181
Michilimacinac, only a post, 67
Military enterprises, 1758, 39, 49; a fourth enterprise, 39; advance against Ticonderoga, 40; attack on Louisbourg, 40; Captain Bradstreet's expedition, 39, 40; three main enterprises, 39
Military forces, 42, 43; First Battalion of Royal American Regiment, 43; Maryland contribution small, 42, 43; Montgomery's Highland Regiment, 43; Pennsylvania provincial troops, 43; Virginia regiments, 43
Military operations, much more difficult in North America than in Europe, 89, 99; under incessant threat of Indian ambush, 99
Military terminology, *see* Fortification Terms

Mississippi River and Valley, 5, 8, 15, 17, 21, 39, 67, 87; affairs along, affect British colonies, 21; an approach to Pittsburgh, 5; explored under Frontenac regime, 15; forts protecting, 67; Spanish influence beyond, 5; upper river surveyed by Gordon, 87; valley reached by British Americans before 1750, 17

Missouri, 20; foothold strengthened, 20; under French, 20

Mohawk River, 6, 18, 40, 68; advancing frontier moves up it, 18; fur trade route, 6; large forces under Abercromby along it in 1758, 40; military route, 64; part of Hudson-Mohawk route, 68

Monongahela River, The: branch of the Ohio, 4, 24, 26, 28, 30, 33, 70, 99, 123; area in dispute between Va. and Pa., 24; beautiful Indian name, 118; Bouquet goes up, 99; low water, 99; crossed and recrossed by forces of Braddock, 33; deep and good for water carriage, 123; its bank once extended 150 feet further north, 159; linked up with the Potomac route to the West, 4; objective of Braddock, 70; Ohio Co. settlers there in early 1753, 28; road to from Gist's place, 30; settlers get news of French on the Allegheny, 28; western objective of Ohio Co. Road, 26

Montcalm, Marquis de, great military figure of New France, 16; a worthy follower of early Frontenac, 15

Montgomery, Colonel Archibald, 43, 52; commanded Highlanders (77th regiment), 43; put in command of a brigade, 52

Montreal, 6, 15, 26, 27, 39, 40, 47, 67; British objective in 1758-59, 39; Celoron starts out from, 26; endangered by capture of Louisbourg, 47; fur trade center, 6; knows of Ohio Company activities in the Ohio Valley, 26; M. Marin starts out from, 27; protected by Louisbourg, 40; settlement begun by Champlain, 15; taken in 1760, 67; threatened from New York, 1758, 40

Monts, Sieur de, heads Canadian trading monopoly, 16

Morgan, Captain Jacob, Pa. Regt., his convoy of supplies for Fort Pitt, attacked at Turtle Creek, May 23, 97

Mount Washington, 134, 135, 151, 167; comment on by McKinney, 135; commented on by Kenny, 161; excavated for coal and limestone, 167; site of coal deposit, 151, 167

Nationalism, 7, 8, 10; Britain merely a national state in 1600, 8; dominant feature of modern times, 7

Navigable waters and navigation, 65, 89, 98; related to strategic routes, 65, 89, 98; less difficult than land for travel and transportation, 88

Neville, John, house attacked by "whiskey boys," 188, *D.A.B.*

Newcastle, Thomas Pelham-Holles, Duke of, 17, 32, 36; head of ministry 1754, 32; prime minister until 1756, 36; resigns late 1756, 36; secretary of state under Walpole, 17

New England, 6, 10, 11, 12, 16, 17, 18, 21; acts with vigor in Anglo-French wars, 11; discontinuation of capital causes disaster, 10; early attacks by, on New France, 16; early trouble with French, 16; frontier expansion, 18; gap between and Maryland, 12; important features of, 11; its militia regiments serve under Abercromby in 1758, 40; New Englanders in 1754 capture Louisbourg, 21; organized attack on French, 16; populous and wealthy, 11; six colonies in one generation, 11; settlement and early fur trade, 6

New Hampshire, 8, 11, 18; began as proprietory colony, 8; once territory of Council for New England, 11; westward advance across, 18

New Jersey, 13, 22; becomes a royal colony, 13; formerly part of New Netherland, 13; later a part of New York, 1664, 166; granted by James, Duke of York, 13; once a part of Va., 22

New Netherland, 6, 12, 13; a lively fur trade, 6; early trouble with French, 16; established by the Dutch, 6; included present day New York, New Jersey, Pennsylvania, and Delaware, 13; seized and renamed New York, 12

New Store of the Ohio Company, 28, 29; personnel gets news of French, at Venango, 28; point of departure of Washington, 1753, 29

New York, city and state, 6, 7, 12, 13, 16, 17, 18, 22, 26, 31; attack on French in King Williams War, 16; had Dutch cultural deposits, 7; former, New Netherland, 12; frontier advance up the Hudson, up the Mohawk and to Lake Ontario, 18; fur trade trouble with French, 16; interested in activities of the Ohio Company in the Ohio Valley, 26; interested in fur trade, 6; illiberal proprietary colony, 1664-1684, 12; in 1664, included N. J., Pa., and Del., 13;

INDEX

neutrality of Iroquois and peace, 1701-09, 17; on famous route, 13; once part of Virginia, 22; troops from awaited by Washington, 31
Niagara, a British objective, 1758-59, 39, 70, 90-91; abandoned by French 1759, 70; battle of, 165; difficult portage, 27; French defeat, 1759; eases tension at Fort Pitt, 165; French foothold at, strengthened, 20; French there in 1753; important aim of British American campaigns, 6; on important water route, 27; success at, 117
North Carolina, 12, 43, 45, 90; contribution to the Forbes expedition 90; democratic, 12; earlier known as Northern Carolina, 12; furnished men for Forbes, 43; its companies in bad shape, 45; royal colony eventually, 12; troops sent toward Fort Duquesne, Nov. 20, 1758
Nova Scotia (old Acadia), 13, 19, 32; ceded to Britain in 1713, 19; governor of, addressed by General Braddock, 32; New Englanders fight there, 13, 19

Ohio Company of Virginia, 23, 24, 25, 26, 27, 28, 29, 30, 36, 69, 122, 123, 152, 156; abandons proposal for fort at McKees Rocks, 124; as a land company, 24; appeals to the Crown, 25; becomes quiescent, 1755-58, 36; begins settlement in Ohio Valley in winter of 1752-1753, 30; buys property near Wills Creek, 26; constructs storehouse on Redstone Creek, 29; distressed about Ohio Indians, 28; Fairfax example, 22; fort at Chartiers Creek planned, 122, 123, 156; French counter measures, 25; fundamental fact in backround of 1758, 24; gets permission to build forts, 28; holds Indian conference at Winchester, 28; Indian treaty of 1744, 27; influenced by 1744 Indian treaty, 23; influences back of it, 25; in June, 1752, got permission to build forts, 122; its activities precipitated warfare, 25; its early conferences and discussion not recorded, 25; its genesis not documented, 25; its map, 122; its origins, 25; knows French will attack in 1754, 28-29; meets opposition in Va. Council and delay by Gov. Gooch, 25; orders and sells cargoes of goods, 28; original proposal mentioned, 152; petition to Va. made October 24, 1747, 25; plans fort at Forks, 29, 69; preliminary executive committee and articles of agreement, 25; rumors about it in Paris and Quebec, 25; sends out Gist as explorer, 26, 122; several recent books on its history, 26
Ohio Company Road, The, 26, 29, 33, 122, 129
Ohio River and Valley, 4, 6, 12, 15, 17, 20, 24, 31, 51, 59, 68, 87, 89, 99, 118, 122; beautiful Indian name, 118; British American establishment in, 12; Carolina troops in, 12; control taken by Forbes, 59; controlled by French, 31; course surveyed by Gordon, 87; French retreat down, 1758, 51; French turn to it, 68; itself one of the great approaches up-river to the Forks of the Ohio, 4; fur trade in, 6; military campaigns in, 24; not explored by La Salle, (1669-70), 16; part of route from Quebec to La., 20; reached by British Americans, 17; route discovered under Frontenac regime, 15; seasonal low water, 99; strong spots on upper Ohio, 122; traversed upstream by French, 89
Old Town (Md.), 19, 24, 28; Cresap gets news of French at Venango, 28; early far western Maryland settlement, 19; home site of Thomas Cresap, 19
Oneida, 45, 68, 69; carrying place on Mohawk route to Great Lakes, 45, 68, 69; Fort Stanwix built at, 68; General Stanwix sent there to construct a fort, 45
Orderly books, *see* Bibliography
Ormsby, John, his journal in *Olden Time*, see footnote 97; reports on panic of June 1759, 150
Oswego, 12, 18, 37, 68, 70; captured by French under Montcalm, 37; lost to French, 70; military and settlement outpost, 18; New Englanders in expedition to re-capture it, 12; on route of Bradstreet, 1758, 47

Papiers Contrecoeur, recent publication of valuable papers. *See* Bibliography
Parker, Hugh, old Pennsylvania and Maryland fur trader, factor of the Ohio Company 1750-1751, 29; succeeded by William Trent, 29
Patton, James, 23, 25; active colonial Virginia transmontane land speculator, 23; rival of Lees and Washington, 25
Pearis, Captain Richard, (Va.), 94; reports on Divisions of Bridge, to be made over Wills Creek, Md., 94; ordered to repair bridge at Little Crossing, 1759, 94
Penn, William and his heirs, 13, 14, 22, 23; boundary trouble, 22, 23; gets land grant, 13, proprietors of Delaware territory, 14; provides liberal

government and laws, 13, *D.A.B.*
Pennsylvania, 6, 13, 17, 18, 20, 21, 22, 24, 30, 31, 35, 36, 42, 43, 45, 46, 52, 90, 91, 121, 141; a land grant of James, Duke of York, 13; boundary trouble with Md., N. Y., and Virginia, 22; central government in, 21; chartered 1781, 13; fails in crisis, 1751, 121; frontier on the defensive, 31, 35; furnishes troops to Forbes, 43, 90; had supplies, 45; her cooperation in 1754, against French, asked, 3; important Dutch and Swedish cultural deposits, 7; internal political strife, 13; merchants and traders, 6. 18; militia left at Pittsburgh, 1858, 141; once a part of Virginia, 22; party strife, 42; Pa. fur traders become land speculators, 24; Pa. militia march toward Juniata Crossings, June 14, 46; Pa. Reg't. ordered to Raystown, 46; populous and rich, 13; rivalry with France, 6; sad and drab years, 36; significant frontier advance, 18, 20; the granary of America, 91; three battalions of in Bouquet's division, 52; trans-Appalachian claims, 21; trade with Indians, 6, 18

Pennsylvania G e r m a n s (Deutsch, "Dutch"), 18, 19; move west and southwest across Pa. boundary into Md., Va., N. C., etc., 18, 19

Peters, Richard, Pennsylvania clergyman, politician, and land speculator, 24, *D.A.B.*

Pfister, Francis, Draughtsman of realistic plan of Fort Ontario, 161

Philadelphia (Pa.), 18, 20, 26, 28, 29, 35, 42, 44, 56; artillery arrives at, 44; Dunbar retreats to, 35; expects French attack in 1754, 29; French rivalry with, 20; gets information about French at Venango, 28; merchants engage in frontier and Indian trade, 18; Ohio Company of Virginia, commented upon in Phila., 26; reached by Forbes in April 1758, 42; road to Lancaster and on to Shippensburg an old one, 56

Pitt, William, the Elder, 10, 15, 36, 38, 39, 40, 41, 57, 70, 152, 179; as secretary of State, 1757, 36; disliked by royal family, 38; dismissed, 36; enlistment of Highlanders, 36, 38; explains success, 10. 15; financed Britain's European allies, 38; four objectives of, 70; higher taxes, 38; his system, 40; hydra-headed attack on French Empire, 39; Pittsburgh properly named, 37, 57; popular with the people, 38; promises financial aid to colonies, 39; restored to power, 1757,

36; uses naval power, 39; wants fort to hold Ohio Valley, 152, 179; younger commanders, 41

Pittsburgh, 8, 20, 31, 38, 53, 57, 59, 71, 96, 110, 111, 112, 142, 148, 150, 155, 166, 167; Bicentennial mentioned, 38; census of April 1761, 110, 111; civilian occupations, 166, 167; formally named December 1, 1758, 71, 59; fort buildings at 110, 111, 148, 150, 167; four districts in, 1761, 110; good news of French departure from Venango, 150; frontier advance in background, 17; Gentlemen Adventurers in background

Pittsburgh, houses needlessly pulled down in 1759, 150; in area, once claimed by Augusta Co. Va., 20; increase in population, military and civil, 110, 112; mentioned as end of Braddock route, 96; name used 1758-1759, 142; formerly concerned with its records, Foreword, I; not mentioned on old fort plan, 155; properly named, 31, 57; site visited and revisited by Washington on first famous trip, 29; the beauty of its site and region, 53, 57; the village of, 112

Pittsburgh Foundation, makes a generous gift to the Society, ii

Pleydell, J. C., 49, 71, 88; probably engineer, architect and map maker, 49, 71, 88; in Forbes expedition, 49; left behind drawings of Fort Bedford, Fort Duquesne and Fort Ligonier, 71; plan by, 71

Plymouth Colony, (1620-1691), 8, 11; established on territory of Council for New Eng., 11; old part of British Empire, 8

Plymouth Company (1606), 11; later reorganized as the Council for New England, 11; once owned all New England, 11

"Point" (or Forks of the Ohio), 155, 156; on site of proposed fort, 156; only a blockhouse on, recommended by Eyre, 155; *see* Forks of the Ohio

Point Park Commission, 1942-1943, 158; project abandoned, 158; set up, 158; study made by Bliss, 158

Point State Park, will contain restorations of two bastions of Fort Pitt, 119, 158

Pontiac, Pontiac's War, 13, 103, 172; featured by trickery, 63; his uprising, 103, 172

Population, 5, 6, 110; five hundred thousand Indians, two hundred thousand in the East, 5-6; population count at Pittsburgh June 1760, 110; population return April 15, 110

Portland, William Henry Bentinck,

INDEX   223

Duke of, 89
Port Royale, older name of Annapolis Royal in Nova Scotia, 166
Post, Christian Frederick, 55; his trips to Indians a feature, 55
Potomac River, The, 4, 11, 12, 19, 22, 24, 25, 32, 70; provided a low level route into the mountains, 6, 4; boundary of Md., 22; Carolina troops along, 12; early settlement on North Fork, 19; Fort Cumberland, on, 70; gentlemen along from Ohio Co., 25; land speculation along, 24; Maryland located along, 11; migration from lower Potomac, 19; on South Branch, 19; anxiety along upper Potomac, 32
Potts, Lieutenant William, 109; comments on social life at Fort Pitt, 109
Presque Isle (Erie Bay), 27, 69, 93, 107; road to Le Boeuf, corduroyed, 93; scurvy, at, 107; utilized by French in 1753
Privy Council, 9; sits with the King, 9; an institution of great antiquity, 9
Prussia, 20, 36, 39; ally of France in war of Austrian Succession, 20; supported by William Pitt, 1757-1761, 36, 39
Public Record Office (London), 79, 86; library of maps and drawings, 79; Gordon's accounts at, 86

Quebec, 6, 12, 14, 17, 20, 26, 33, 38, 39, 40, 43, 67, 70, 78, 89; abandoned in 1759, 70; an objective in 1758, of British, 39; attack planned by Loudoun fails, 38; aware of British American ground, 20; endangered by capture of Louisbourg, 47; first fort built at, 1541, strengthened in 1749, captured in 1759, of masonary construction, 40, 78; fur trade center, 6; men and supplies, 1755, from, 33; New Englanders in attack on it, 12, 17; planned by Champlain, 14; site of first fort in 1541, 67; supplies Fort Duquesne by water route, 89; threatened from New York, 1758, 40

Ratzer, Lieutenant Bernard, 88, 155, 159, 181; drew excellent 1761 plan of late Fort Pitt and a plan of New York, 88; Fort Pitt was found to be as on his plan, 159; was not the original designer, 155; depicts gardens, 181
Raystown (variously spelled), 22, 44, 45, 46, 49, 54; early settlement on the upper Juniata, main advanced post of Forbes expedition, 45, 71, 91; objective in Forbes advance, 44; plan of, 71; road begun, to Fort Cumberland, 46; roads projected from Fort Loudoun, from Fort Cumberland and to west, 54; reached by Bouquet, June, 22; Va. and Md. troops moved to, 49
Records of Indian and of fur trade, enormous in amount, 6-7
Recruitment, 102, 103; advertisements for recruits, 102; for Forbes' campaign, 102; French deserters not welcomed, 102; in 1764 Bouquet is despondent 103; Pennsylvania reaction poor, 102; requirements set up by Bouquet, 102
Redoubts at Fort Pitt, 175; described by Hutchins, 176; ordered 1763 by Bouquet, 175
Redstone Creek, 29, 31, 70; objective of Washington May 1754, 31; possible route for Braddock, 70; storehouse intended as supply base for main fort at the Forks, 31; Trent builds storehouse January 1754, 29
Regional Planning Association, 158; authorizes a study of the Point, 158
Reid, Colonel John, 91, 109, 110, 176, 184; carries a new supply to Fort Pitt, 110; comments on road, 91; mentions "expresses," 109; praises work of Captain Grant, 176; reports on crops raised, 184
Reports or accounts of scouts, spies, viewers and others, 47; many turned in in June, July, and August 1758, 47; valuable for local history, 47
Rhode Island, 8, 11; chartered corporate colony, 8; on territory of olr Council for New England, 11
Rhor, Ensign Charles, engineer, 47, 49, 51, 88, 93; directed Burd in building of Fort Ligonier, 51; went to scout enemy, 47; with Bouquet in 1758, 88, 93
Richelieu River, Canada, 64; connects Lake Champlain and the St. Lawrence, 64; vital link of the Lake Champlain route, 64
Roads, 27, 44, 46, 48, 51, 54, 89, 91, 92, 99; additional roads projected, 54; built between Raystown and Wills Creek, 46, 91; famous quarrel about, 46; follow old Indian paths, 54; Forbes Road projected in mid-June 1758, 44; French build corduroy road to Lake Le Boeuf, 27, 92; merely cleared, not constructed, 89, 99; opened through woods, 91, 92, 99; road to Allegheny Ridge laid out in 1755, 54; unlike roads in Europe, 99; work of Forbes expedition, 54; work on west of Loyal Hannon, 51, 92; work on west from Raystown in August, 48
Robertson, Captain James, 88, 106, 148,

151, 152; arrives at Pittsburgh in 1759, 148; assisted as engineer at Bedford, Ligonier and at Forks, 88; complains about conditions of troops, 1759, 106; searches for a better site for Fort Pitt, 151, 152

Robinson, Thomas, sec. of state under Geo. II, 32

Rogers Rangers, takers of Fort Detroit in 1760, 67

Royal Americans, 43, 44, 52, 90, 148; arrived at Pittsburgh, 1759, in bad shape, 148; composed of four battalions, first Battalion under Forbes, commended by Bouquet, 43; in Bouquet's brigade, 52; to be moved to Carlisle, 44; under Forbes, 90

Rum (Liquor), 104, 110, 166; used at posts, 110; amount needed, 104; for workers, 166

Ryswick, Treaty of 1697; re-established the status quo, 18; really a truce, 18

St. Clair, Major General Arthur, defeated by Indians 1791, 185

St. Clair, Sir John, Quartermaster General, 47, 90; a vacillating incompetent, 90; recommends use of Braddock's Road, 47

St. Lawrence River, 4, 6, 14, 16, 21, 64, 67, 87, 129; affairs along affect English colonies, 21; dangerous route from Montreal to Lake Ontario, 129; French posts along, 67; in fur trade, 6; location of early French colonial effort, 14; on French boundary arc, 64; part of a wide approach to the Forks of the Ohio, 4; surveyed by Gordon, 87; the British Americans south of it richer and more numerous, 16

Saw Mill Run, lime kiln and coal mine on, 151

Saw Mills, 84, 167; at Fort Ligonier, 84; on Monongahela, 167; on Saw Mill Run, 84, 167; use of water power, 84

Schenectady, 18, 68; attack upon by French, 18; established in 1695; 68

Schenley, Mrs. Mary Elizabeth, in 1894 gives the blockhouse to D.A.R., 119

Schlosser, Captain John, reports falling barracks at Fort Niagara in 1760, 111

Scotch-Irish, 20, 21; westward moving, 20, 21

Second Virginia Regiment, 43, 46, 49, 52; commanded by William Byrd III, 43; in Montgomery's brigade, 52, Lieutenant Colonel George Mercer second in command, 43; lacks equipment and provisions, 49; moved to Raystown and Forbes Road, 49; moves from Winchester to Fort Cumberland late in June, 46; raised in 1758, 43;

Settlers and settlements, 61, 70, 103, 116; backward in defense, 103; British American colonies have surplus settlers, 70; condemned by Bouquet, 116; disliked by the Indians, 61; forbidden, 1762, to settle in Ohio Valley, 116; New France lacks settlers, 70; the important factor, 61

Sharpe, Horatio, gov. of Md., 26, 32, 35, 42; in control in Md. 1753, 26; in high military command, 1754-55, 32; not displaced by imperial disasters, 35; not upset by military defeat of 1755; letter to from to Forbes, 42

Shenandoah Valley, 19, 20, 23; region of frontier migration and settlement, 19; widely settled by 1750, 20, 23

Shippen, Edward, Pennsylvania merchant, politician and frontier land speculator, 24

Shippen, Joseph, Major, 50, 52; comments on revenge for Grant's defeat, 50; leaves behind an orderly book, 52

Shippenburg, Pa., 45, 46, 48, 54; Bouquet advances to, 45; Forbes arrives and is halted for a month by illness, 48; important settlement and military post west of Carlisle, 45, 46; key point on route, 46; new roads from, 1758, 54; road to from east before 1758, 54

Shirley, William, gov. of Mass., 34, 35, 37; commander-in-chief on death of Braddock, 37; efforts do not offset defeat on the Monongahela, 35; his campaign against Niagara fails, 37; his strategic ideas, 37; in difficulties with fellow commanders, 39; meets popularity in New England, but antagonism elsewhere, 37; not immediately upset by Braddock's defeat, 35

Shoes, soldiers carried three pairs

Sickness, 47, 106, 107, 111, 149; among French at Presquile, 107; causes of, 106; contagious diseases, 47, 111, 149; J. C. B., Stevenson, and Burd, 107; lime juice used only after 1795, 107; mentioned by Colonel Armstrong, 106-107; scurvy the most pernicious 106, 180

Sideling Mountain and highway hill; Tulleken deplores it, 93

Significances in Forbes campaign, 54, 55; colonial and imperial cooperation, 54; laying out of roads, 54; successful Indian diplomacy in his mastery of the Forks, 55; glory assigned to Forbes, 55; importance of General Forbes, 55; unusual cooperation of Forbes and Bouquet, 54-55

Smith, Russell, makes a water color sketch c. 1830 and a painting of the Blockhouse, 177

INDEX

Smith, William, Pennsylvania educator, politician, land speculator and author, 26
Society, low and high, at the Forks, 109; clubs, balls, 109; dram shops, 109; Grand Assembly, 109; restriction on liquor sales, 109; scum of nature, 109; theft, 109; white hangers-on, 109
"Sodding," used at Fort Pitt, 82
Soldiers and their equipment, 61, 89, 99, 101; Europeans unfamiliar with wilderness conditions, 61, 89, 99, 101
South Branch of the Potomac, 19, 22; its sources further west than those of the North Branch, 22; place of early settlement, 19
South Carolina, a fill in the gap, 14; earlier known as Southern Carolina, 14
Spain, 7, 12, 14, 20; early nationalism, 7; Spanish in Florida, 12; intrusions on Spanish Empire, 7; accounts of Indians, 5; defeated in 1558, 7; dominant imperially, 14; operated mainly below 35, 14; ally of France (1740-45), 20
Stanwix, Brig. General John, 47, 106, 117, 120, 121, 153, 157, 159, 166; approves of plan of Fort Pitt, 159; comments on construction of Fort Pitt, 157; disapproves of McKees Rocks as site for great fort, 153; first successor of Forbes, letter from Tulleken, 117; reports to Amherst, 157, 166; complaint of troops at Fort Pitt, 106; sent up Mohawk to build a fort, 49; thanked by Amherst for plan of Pgh., 120-21
Star Forts, not true of Fort Duquesne and Fort Pitt, 161
Steele, Reverend John, in 1758 with Pennsylvania troops, 53
Stephen, Adam, Lieut. Col. Va. Regt., 48, 93; accompanies Burd to Loyal Hannon, 48; has six companies of Virginians worked on roads, 93
Stevenson, George, criticises equipment of Pa. militia, 102
Stevenson, Doctor James, 107, 108; mentions scurvy, 107; complains of want of society at Fort Niagara, 108
Stewart, Captain Robert, (Va.), reports insubordination, 108
Stobo, Captain Robert, 129, 131, 132; imprisoned in Fort Duquesne, 129; his sketch, 129; tried in Canada, 129; comments on Fort Duquesne, 131; his drawing shows artillery, 132
Stony Creek, Pa., 92, 98; a lead swamp at, 92; horses lost at, 98; road corduroyed, 92; site of post in Forbes campaign

Storehouses, 46, 48, 51, 94, 147; at Forks of the Ohio, 147; at Juniata Crossings, 46, 94; at Loyal Hannon, 51; at Pittsburgh in 1759, 147, 172; at Ravstown, 48; at Redstone Creek, 124; at Wills Creek, 28
Swauger, James J.; makes excavations on site of Fort Pitt, 1953
Suke's Run; once partly encircled hill where Duquesne University is located, 154
Susquehanna River, 6, 20, 34, 71; anxiety along, 1754-55, 34; its western branches approaches to the Forks of the Ohio, 6; on Forbes route, 71; Pa. frontier advances to and beyond, 20

Ticonderoga, French stronghold, Carillon, 14, 42, 83; attacked unsuccessfully by Abercromby, 42; defeat worse than that of Braddock, 42; New Englanders in attack upon, 14; stone revetment, 83
Tools, 83, 84, 93, 96, 104, 106, 147, 148; camp necessities, 106; cross cut saws needed for petrified trees, 93; for pack horses, 96; grindstones, vital, 83; iron, steel and lead brought from east, 83; local blacksmith, 83; saws and sawing, 84; tools needed for a march, 104; sent to Mercer, 147; sent to Pittsburgh, 1759, 148; some from England, 84; intrenching tools, 83
Transportation, 85, 99, 167; by water, 99; low water on French Creek, 85; used on Monongahela, 167; water transportation used wherever possible, 99
Trent, 30, 97, 122, 125; authorized by Ohio Co. to start fort, 122; built a storehouse at Redstone Creek, 97; compelled to return to Wills Creek for supplies and recruits, 125; goes to Wills Creek for supplies and troops, 30
Trinity Church; Beaujeau buried there, 136; its graveyard the site of French burying ground, 136
Tulleken, Major, 93, 117; comments on lurking Indians, 117; criticises the bad roads, 93
Turnbull and Marmie Furnace; engaged by Craig to make cannon balls, 186
Turtle Creek Valley (Pa. Allegheny County), 33, 53, 91, 97; avoided by Braddock, 33; avoided by Forbes and Bouquet, 91; Captain Morgan attacked, 1759, 97; considered a dangerous gorge, 33; Forbes Troops encamped there November 24, 1758, 53
Twiss, William, draughtsman; prepared

the drawing of Fort Pitt by Meyer, 88

Upper Town; at Fort Pitt, 172; burned in 1763, 174

Utrecht, Treaty of, 1713, 17; establishment of British protectorate over Iroquois, 17; recession of New France, 17; two important features, 17

Vauban, Sebastien le Prestre de, (1633-1707); conducted fifty or more sieges, 76; constructed more than one hundred structures, 76; greatest authority on fortifications, 76

Vaudreuil, Phillippe de Rigaud, Marquis de, 128, 129; boasts of French threat to frontiers, 128; deplores weakness of Fort Duquesne, 129; letter, 129

Venango (Later Franklin), Pa., 27, 28, 29, 67, 69, 107, 150, 185; desertion at, 107; fort built at, 69; fort projected at, 28; French in 1759, assembled at, 67; information about French there spread by Indians, 28; its seizure believed an act of war, 27; news from 1759, alarms Pittsburgh, 150; reached by French in 1753, 27; reached by Washington in 1753, 29; threatened in 1791, 185

Vermont, part of New England frontier, 20

Vetri, M. de, wrongly believed to have led the French against Loyal Hannon, 51

Villiers, Louis Coulon, Sieur de; forces capitulation of Washington at Great Meadows or Fort Necessity, 31; leads march against Washington, June 1754, 31

Virginia, 6, 8, 10, 12, 15, 18, 21, 22, 23, 31, 35, 36, 43, 45, 47, 70, 90, 91, 121, 141; at first a chartered corporate colony, 8, 10; based her later land claims on old charters, 22; became first royal colony, 8, 10; boundary trouble with Pa., 22; central government in, 21; contemporary with empire, 8; dozens of Western land companies, 23; early attack by Va., on New France, 15; favors Braddock Road, 45, 91; frontier on the defensive, 31, 35; furnishes troops for Forbes, 90; gap between Va. and Florida filled, 12; her cattle wanted by Forbes, 45; its boundaries, 22, 23; its charters, 22; in 1758, her regiments in unfavorable condition, 45; in 1783 in possession of present Va., W. Va., and Ky., 22; lays claim to Old Northwest, 22; little fur trade, 6; militia companies move west from Fort Loudoun, 46; militia left at Pittsburgn in 1758, 141; old colony drained by Ohio River, 70; promises Forbes two regiments, 43; settlement, little, 6; significant frontier advance, 18; sad and drab years, 36; some militia kept on Braddock's Road, 47; takes the initiative in 1750, 121; trans-Appalachian claims, 21; troops reach Raystown, June 24, 1758, 46

Wagons, 44, 91, 92, 93, 95; advertised for, 95; a problem, 44, 93, 95; Braddock has poor ones, 91; commented on by Burd, 95

Walpole, Sir Robert, political supremacy of, 19

Ward, Ensign Edward, 30, 47, 124, 156; at the Forks of the Ohio in latewinter of 1753-54, 30; carries bad news to Williamsburg, 30; depositions mentioned, 124; his garrison overwhelmed, 156; with Forbes expedition, scouted enemy, 47

Washington, Colonel George, 29, 30, 31, 32, 33, 34, 35, 43, 45, 48, 49, 51, 52, 54, 61, 63, 70, 123, 125, 153, 185, 188; at Gist's place, 31; attacked by French Indian allies, 63; at Wills Creek, 30; authorized in August 1758 to move by Braddock's Road, 48; busy about frontier forts, 35; Colonel in the First Va. Regiment, 31, 35, 54; built Fort Necessity, 1754, 70; capitulates, 31; chooses Wayne as commander in 1792, 188; disapproves advance from Ligonier by water, 51; heroic role at Braddock's defeat, 34; his troops assemble at Winchester, June 1758, 45; Hobson's choice, 1758, 48-51; in 1754 follows plan of speed with a mobile force, 33; inspects the Point and McKees Rocks, 123; Jumonville episode, 61; lacks equipment and supplies, 30; late starting in 1754, 125; preserved a Forbes orderly book, 52, put in command of a brigade in 1758, 52; makes an advance in early 1754, 31; messenger to the French, 29; none too successful relations with Indians, 34; objects to superior rank of British regular officers, 32; ordered to raise a militia company and join Trent, 29-30; orders Knox to build the fifth fort at the Forks, 185; recommends in 1754 a fort at the Forks, 153; resigns and retires to private life, 32; succeeds Colonel Fry in command, 31; unsuccessful campaign of 1754, 54

Washington, Lawrence; possible instiga-

INDEX

tor of the Ohio Company, of Virginia, 25
Wayne, General Anthony, 188; assembles his troops in Pittsburgh, 188; moves to Legionville, 188
Western Pennsylvania; effected by ice ages, 4
Western Pennsylvania history; truly of world importance, 1740-1787, 3
Westmoreland County, Pa.; its archives, 24
Whiskey Insurrection; threatened Fort Fayette, 188
Williamsburg, (Va.), capitol of colonial Virginia, 28, 29; expects French attack in 1754, 29; gets news of French expedition of 1753, 28; Washington reports in January 1754, 29
Wills Creek, 19, 24, 26, 28, 30, 31, 35, 70, 94; area of early settlement, 24; area of land speculation, 24; Braddock reaches it, about May 10, 1755, 32; bridge over, 94; Dunbar retreats to (1755), 35; eastern end of Ohio Company Road, 26; Fort Cumberland on, 70; near headwaters of Youghiogheny, 70; settlers get news of French at Venango, 28; Trent and Washington at in April 1754, 30; Washington retreats to, 31
Winchester (Va.), Braddock's assembly at, 91; early rendezvous of Va. forces, 1758, 45; frequently lacked needed military equipment and provisions, 45, 49; Indian conference at, 1753, 28; on Braddock's route, 33; Virginia regiments assemble at in June, 1758, 45
Windsor Castle, 71, 19; maps, plans and other data, 71, 79; revealed to public in recent years, 71
Wolfe, James, Brig. Gen., 39, 40; gives great aid to attack on Fort Louisbourg, 1758, 40; young commander rapidly advanced by Pitt, 39
Wright, George, draughtsman, 88, 157; drawing of Fort Pitt, 88, 157
Wright, Robert, with Hugh Mercer inspects Chartier's Hill, 152

Xerxes, surfaced bridge floor at Hellespont, 94

York County (Pa.), 19, 21, 24, 54; 1729, early frontier county, 19, 21; its archives, 24; old road to from east, 54
Youghiogheny River, The, branch of the Monongahela; bridge over, 94; drains old Virginia, 70; not navigable, 70; not navigable through the mountains, 70; Ohio Co. settlers in area, 1753, early, 28; related to Potomac route to the west, 4; rivalry along, of Va. and Pa., 24; Washington crosses, 31
Young, Samuel; erects a trading house, 1762, 178

This book is printed in Linotype Old Style on Saturn Wove Book Paper by The Mayer Press, Pittsburgh, and bound in Holliston Waverly by the Penn State Bookbinding Co., Pittsburgh. The illustrations, including portraits, drawings and maps were engraved by the Superior Photoengravers, Inc., Pittsburgh. The cover of the book, and its jacket, are the work of T. Ward Hunter, Pittsburgh artist, who also drew his interpretation of the Forbes Medal. Lawrence Irwin, formerly of the University of Pittsburgh Press, served as consultant on the format of the book.

www.ingramcontent.com/pod-product-compliance
Lightning Source LLC
Chambersburg PA
CBHW031239290426

44109CB00012B/355